CONSUMING FIRE

Other Books by Terry Fritts

BIO-TERROR SERIES

TAKA
KONA SNOW
KAPU 'ĀINA
(Forbidden land)

The Kevin Bridges Spiritual Warfare Series

BROTHERHOOD OF THE DIVINE
SEVEN OF THE CROSS

CONSUMING FIRE

A KEVIN BRIDGES SPIRITUAL WARFARE NOVEL

BY

TERRY FRITTS

THRILLOGY
PRESS

The **Kevin Bridges Spiritual Warfare Series** came as a surprise. I had just returned from Russia with an idea of writing a spiritual warfare novel about archangels and End Times. As I began writing, I had several bizarre vivid dreams. I remembered them all in detail which guided the direction of the first book **Brotherhood of the Divine**. The book took on a life of its own with characters and historical events arriving at the right time. Kevin Bridges became a wonderful character that needed to be explored so I wrote a prequel, **Seven of the Cross**. It deals with fallen angels and it too spurred some characters I hope to explore in later books. It also inspired me to write another prequel featuring Keven Bridges, **Consuming Fire**. **Consuming Fire** is a very intense look at evil and the power of prayer and the Holy Spirit. In this new Thrillogy Press edition of the series, all three books have been edited and slightly modified from the originals to allow continuity of character and story.

This book is a work of fiction. Any similarity between characters in the book and real people is coincidental. The prologue is a fictitious follow-up interview to the 1967 documentary by Peter Adair entitled *Holy Ghost People*. The documentary is available on-line. As I wrote this novel I did so hearing an accompanying soundtrack to many of the chapters. In fact, some songs became integral parts of the story. Several songs are mentioned throughout the novel and listening to them may heighten your reading experience. Foremost, the song *In A Gadda Da Vida* by Iron Butterfly plays a major part in this story and it would be a shame if you failed to listen to it at the appropriate times. Enjoy.

Thrillogy Press Edition 2019
ISBN:978-1-950376-04-9
Epub:978-1-950376-05-9
First published by ECHO PARK PRESS LLC 2010
ISBN-13: 978-0-9845889-0-9
Copyright © 2010 by Terry Fritts, All rights reserved.
Library of Congress Control Number: 2010930098

All rights reserved under International Copyright Conventions, including the right to reproduce this book or portions thereof in any form.

Title page photo by Kyna

Manufactured in the United States of America

ACKNOWLEDGEMENTS

Consuming Fire for now, is book one in the Kevin Bridges Spiritual Warfare series but it was the third I wrote in the series. I want to thank Berch Papikyan for his Armenian transliteration and Spencer Fang for his Chinese transliteration. I also want to thank Brandon Beirne for his editing input. I'm grateful to have such encouraging friends to bounce ideas off of and a network of experts willing to answer any and all of my questions. Mostly I would like to thank my family for their continuing support especially my wonderful wife Pauline who has become such a great editor and still thinks of me as a hunk. (editor's note, should be chunk)

CONSUMING FIRE

CONSUMING FIRE

"And these signs will follow those who believe: In My name they will cast out demons; they will speak with new tongues; they will take up serpents; and if they drink anything deadly, it will by no means hurt them; they will lay hands on the sick, and they will recover."
Mark 16:17-20

PROLOGUE

1968 Scrabble Creek follow-up testimonials

Cameraman: "We're rolling."

Commentator: "Tell us about your family and how you became a 'Holy Ghost Person'."

Emily Sue: "Can't rightfully say I is a 'Holy Ghost Person' anymore."

Commentator: "That's all right; but you are the one who was playing the tambourine in the movie aren't you?"

Emily Sue: "Neva' seen the movie, but Momma did let me play the tambourine night you's there."

Commentator: "Then just tell us about your family and how things have gone this past year."

Emily Sue: "Well, you know my daddy died in the mines. Momma say he died of the lung but he work in the mines 'til his heart just stop beatin' one day.

I loved my daddy.

I miss him a lot.

I love Momma, too.

Daddy was a man of God, least 'til he got so sick. You'd think being so sick'd make him closer to God, 'stead he seem to blame God for's pain and suffer'n. Momma tried to tell 'im wasn't so, but Daddy din't believe 'er. 'Fore Daddy got sick we used to go to the Baptist Church over in Pond Gap. Momma was a Sunday school teacher and Daddy was a deacon. When Daddy stopped goin' to church I think Momma was too embarrassed to go 'ithout 'im. After while Momma started goin' to a Holy Ghost Church down in Scrabble Creek. I din't like it much, but Momma seem to believe that's where God was calling her and they'd be able to help Daddy get well, so that's where me and Momma went. Couple times a week preacher man and two 'r three others'd come by the house and lay hands on Daddy pray'n for the Holy Spirit to heal 'im. They'd be shout'n and a holler'n and speak'n tongues; Daddy din't like it much but knew it made Momma happy so he put up wit' it. He might notta been so accomadatin' if'n he seen what all went on down at dat church.

Like I said, I din't much care for it first neither, wit' dem snakes and all that holler'n and jump'n round. They drank some kinda poison and was hold'n dem burn'n rags in their hands, but I sure 'nuf liked the music. All dem guitars and the sing'n and the tambourines. I love it when the preacher man would play his guitar and sing or some of dem other boys be play'n guitars and girls be sing'n along wit' dem. I weren't much of a singer but Momma let me play the tambourine. What I din' like was how friendly Momma was with that preacher man and how he got Momma to handlin dem rattlen' snakes the way he did. I told Momma that Daddy wouldn't want her a doin' that. She told me to mind my business. Momma never talk like that to me 'fore. Some boys was a say'n Momma do'n more than justa pray'n with the preacher man afta church but I didn't believe 'em. Momma wouldn't do that to my daddy. Momma was just filled with the Holy Spirit and so was the preacher and together the miracles of God flowed."

Commentator: "How do you explain the preacher being bitten that night by the snake? Was God testing his faithfulness?"

Emily Sue: "Daddy laughed when I told him the preacher man got bit. Then he gots mad when he saw Momma been cryin'. I din't know if'n God was a testin' him but I do know God musta healed 'im 'cause he din't die. Momma and Daddy had a long talk that night and Daddy tol' me he was movin' over to the boardin' house ova' by the mine cause his hacking had got so bad and was keepin' Momma 'wake all night. He was a cough'n all night, but I know that's not why he moved. What dem boys at church been say'n had been true. Momma got bit two days later by the same rattlen' snake. Ev'body was a lay'n hands on 'er, yell'n and a shout'n to the Lord to heal 'er. I was so scared! I wanted to run to my daddy but he was too far away so I laid my hands on Momma's head and started calling for the Lord to heal Momma and save 'er from the evil that had entered 'er body. Before I knew it strange sounds were pour'n from my mouth, words I'd never heard before, sounds that minutes before were a jumbo of nonsense were prayers that made perfect sense. What I'd thought to be gibberish coming from some of them Holy Ghost people around me now was comin' outta my own mouth and I knew Momma be get'n better. And she did get better but they found out that the preacher and Momma been living in sin so they ran 'em both out of Scrabble Creek. Daddy moved back into the house but died a couple of weeks later. I've been living with my Aunt Sarah up in Charleston but plan on going to nurs'n school down in Jacksonville, Alabama. Momma and the preacher man livin' down that away, too. Momma says preacher man got a new Holiness Church with lots of sing'n, shout'n, and a holler'n, and 'course he still gots dem snakes."

Commentator: "Do you still speak in tongues?"

Emily Sue: "Oh yes suh, I'm filled with the Holy Spirit. I'm an Apostle of our Lord Jesus Christ."

Commentator: "Anything else you'd like to add?"

Emily Sue: "No suh, I reck'n I said just 'bout all I gots to say."

CHAPTER ONE

Simon tried to wipe the sweat from his already stinging dull eyes.

"Help me," he pleaded, flailing his arms wildly until grabbing what he thought was the sleeve of a man's jacket.

"Back-off freak," a voice yelled from several feet above him. The man pulled away and then slammed his stilted pant leg into Simon's rib cage, knocking Simon into the gutter.

"Damn drunk almost pulled me over," the man on stilts said to his similarly dressed partner as they hurried along the parade route.

The voice coming from above added to Simon's confusion. Blurred images swirled around Simon as if he was caught in the eye of a tornado. Surreal images of freaks and clowns melding and transmogrifying into horrifying visions suitably only for a nightmare. A nightmare that now enveloped all his senses.

"God help me," he whimpered in his hallucinating state, but only a raucous dissonance of voices filled his now ringing ears.

"It won't be much longer now," a voice whispered in his left ear.

"Who's there?" Simon screamed. "You must help me."

"Only your faith can save you now," another voice seemed to say somewhere in the distance.

"Here, have another," a man slurred, yanking Simon to his feet and forcing a bottle of cheap wine into his mouth as he pulled Simon into the heavily inebriated pack of revelers.

The flood of alcohol into his dry mouth caused Simon to gag and the wine spewed from his lips.

"You ungrateful wretch," the man shouted, pulling the bottle away and shoving Simon back to the ground.

Simon was unfazed by the encounter. To him it was just part of the hallucination that was growing dimmer and dimmer. He lay there staring into the vastness with empty eyes, life slowly ebbing from his poisoned body.

"There you are," a voice said softly. "You had me worried. I was afraid I'd lost you."

Simon's head fell towards the direction of the voice more by accident than in response.

A hand reached down and touched the two fang marks on Simon's neck. "You did get a nasty little bite." The man closed his eyes and began to pray, pressing hard on the two puncture wounds. The redness slowly faded and the wounds sealed.

Simon tried to raise his arms, but was too weak to lift them more than a few inches off the pavement.

"Had you sought Jesus first, this never would have happened," the man lectured the near comatose Simon. "Obviously, you are not right with God and for that you must pay."

The man grabbed Simon's shirt front and quickly jerked him off the ground placing him over his shoulder jarring a small assemblage of consciousness from the quickly fading Simon.

"Help me," a tearful Simon begged. "Please God, help me."

"It is you who has forsaken God by turning your back on Jesus' Apostolic teachings. You are nothing more than a liar and a sorcerer. Soon brother," the man replied. "Soon you will be free from your misery."

Simon's heart was racing and sweat continued to flow from his pores. Breathing was becoming labored as with each step the man took, precious air was forced from Simon's depleted lungs. His neck swelling had begun to subside but his body began to spasm in preparation to wretch. Simon lurched as his stomach heaved but no vomit remained. Only a hacking dryness escaped his parched throat.

CHAPTER TWO

"Maybe our informant got something right for a change," Supervisor Akers exclaimed. "Looks like Imelda and the kids have visitors."

"All units stand-by," Agent Samuelson alerted. "This could be Vasquez."

"There's no way Vasquez will come here. He knows we're always watching his family. If he's really in the U.S.A., which I seriously doubt, he's going to have the children brought to him," Campos declared.

"It's not him," Samuelson announced over the radio. "It's just the usual bodyguards."

"It looks like the kids are going someplace," Akers exclaimed.

"Probably the mall again," Campos guessed.

"Saddle-up boys, looks like we're skipping school today," Akers ordered.

"Mobile One," Samuelson called, "Let's find out where they're going."

"Roger that," a voice replied over the radio.

Several blocks away a second Grand Marquis sat idling outside a neighborhood *panderia*.

"I think we might be hurting their business parking here," one of the agents laughed.

"Not with all the sweet breads you've been buying and eating," his partner replied.

"They all think were '*la amigra*' here to ship them back to Mexico," the first agent said. "You think by now these '*pendejos*' would know the difference between FBI and ICE agents."

As they were talking a young pre-teen in a hoodie covering his shaved head walked out of the bakery and flashed a gang sign at the two agents.

"That's the kind of jerk that needs to be shipped back to Mexico," the first agent replied, flipping off the kid.

During the exchange the two agents failed to notice two other teens on bicycles ride up from behind them.

"He's probably third generation gangbanger born and raised in Los Angeles," the partner explained. "The parents raise these kids to…"

Before he could finish his sentence, the left side of his face and most of his brains exploded onto the inside of the windshield and onto the first agent's shirt as one of the bike riders fired a 357 magnum revolver loaded with hollow point bullets pointblank into the agent's ear. The horrific visual was the last thing his partner's brain processed as a millisecond later; a shotgun blast removed most of his head from his torso.

The two boys got back on their bikes and rode away smiling while the young pre-teen turned and continued walking down the sidewalk chewing on his sweet bread.

Three small children exited the house flanked by two bodyguards and climbed into the SUV. The black Chevy Tahoe pulled away from the house, passing the alley where the FBI's white Grand Marquis waited to follow. The kids waved at the two FBI agents as they passed, for it had become a game to them.

"You think they know we're here?" the driver joked as they let the Tahoe get about a half block ahead before they pulled onto the street.

"Yeah, right, like they're going…" his partner was cut off in mid-sentence as the airbag exploded into his face, saving his life but doing nothing to stop the compacting front end from crushing both his legs.

"Call 911," Akers yelled as he watched the dump truck swerve and smash head-on into the Grand Marquis. Then he dialed 911.

"Do you think that was intentional?" Campos asked, as he Samuelson raced out from the surveillance house to see what help they could provide.

"Normally no, but since we got that tip, I've got to think it had to be," Samuelson replied.

"Where's Mobile Two?" Campos asked.

"Mobile Two, come in," Samuelson called, but there was no reply.

"Mobile Two, do you read me?" Nothing but static could be heard.

"I don't like this," Samuelson said. "Something's wrong. They should've answered."

Sirens could already be heard approaching as Campos tried to comfort the two agents trapped in the crumpled car. He didn't know that the driver was already dead and the passenger was still unconscious.

"Call Akers," Campos ordered, "Tell him Mobile One and Mobile Two have been taken out. We need air support now."

"We don't know that for sure," Samuelson replied.

"Tell him!" Campos screamed.

Kevin Bridges and his partner Carlo Caressa had been assigned to air support on today's operation. A wise decision since both were relatively new to the Los Angeles area. Having a driver, in this case a pilot, made surveillance a much simpler task. They didn't like what they were hearing over the radio.

"Maybe we should have a look at Mobile Two," Kevin told the pilot.

From two hundred yards away it was obvious both men were dead.

"I'll call it in," Carlo said.

"Agent Akers, this is Air Support One, Mobile Two is down. Send back-up and paramedics. What is the last position you have on the black Chevy Tahoe? Over."

"Westbound on Manchester headed for the 110 Freeway," Akers responded.

The helicopter banked sharply accelerating towards South Central Los Angeles.

"Attention all units, this is a multi-task force emergency. You are authorized to stop all black Chevy Tahoes in the East, Southeast, and South Los Angeles Areas. The FBI is looking for Juan Diego Vasquez. He is believed to be with his children and is responsible for the deaths of three agents this morning."

"Dispatch, this must be some kind of a joke. I can see three black Tahoes in traffic around me right now," a 77th Street Division patrol officer called in.

"It's no joke, just do what you can do," came the reply.

When the helicopter reached the Manchester/110 Freeway connecter, five black Tahoes were speeding in a line.

"One of those has to be him," Carlo said.

Like fourth of July fireworks the five Tahoes veered off simultaneously each heading in a different direction.

"I've lost two of them," the pilot shouted.

"I only see one of them," Carlo replied.

"If you see it it's not the one we want," Kevin answered. "Juan Diego is too smart for that."

"Look, a 'black and white' is pulling him over now," the pilot said hovering overhead.

"Use extreme caution and wait for backup," Kevin radioed down.

"This is a waste of time my friend," Carlo said to Kevin. "Señor Vasquez was well informed of our stake-out today."

"And very well prepared," Kevin added.

"Any ideas?" Carlo asked.

"Yea, one, but it's a long shot," Kevin replied. "And Akers isn't going to like it."

"Then you can count me in," the pilot piped in, "that Akers is a pain-in-the-you-know-where to work with."

"Can you buy us a couple of hours' time away from the manhunt?" Kevin asked.

"No problem," the pilot replied. "Any certain area we need to head towards?"

"Glendora," Kevin quipped.

"Glendora?" Carlo replied. "Where the hell is Glendora?"

Kevin pointed in an easterly direction concentrating on what the pilot was saying.

"This is Air Support One, calling base, over."

"This is base, go ahead One, over."

"I'm getting an intermittent warning light from my rotor synchronization readout. I just had this thing fixed out in Pomona so I need to go have it checked out," the pilot explained.

"Not a good time, but do what you have to do, your safety comes first, over."

"Roger that, I'll let you know when we're back."

"I've never heard of a rotor synchronization readout," Carlo said.

"I'm sure Akers hasn't either. It's a code I use with dispatch to let them know something important is up and I have to break off my assignment," the pilot replied.

"You won't get in trouble for this?" Carlo said.

"Not if Agent Bridges is as smart as everyone says he is."

The helicopter was already racing towards the San Gabriel Mountains.

Several nervous patrons sat quietly in their booths praying their lives would be spared. In each booth a well-mannered but armed man had collected their cell phones and now sat next to them while they finished their breakfasts. Most were too scared to do so.

"Please don't kill me," a young woman with three children begged.

"I promise I won't if you promise to stop crying. Just enjoy your breakfast. It will all be over soon," the man replied.

In the kitchen, one of the cooks was not as lucky and tried to make a break for the back door. No sooner had he opened it did a rifle butt smash into his face launching him back inside while crushing his jaw and knocking out several teeth.

Juan Diego Vasquez had been waiting in the restaurant when the black Tahoe quickly dropped off his kids and then continued on with a contingent of four other black Tahoes, each containing children of similar ages to his own. He and his children would enjoy the day together but would continue their journey in his armored Mercedes.

When the kids had finished eating, Vasquez and his children were moved to the Mercedes with the precision that the President would expect to receive from the secret service. Five minutes later everyone's breakfast was paid for at the Mariscolandi Restaurant and a pile of cell phones and batteries were left on the counter.

"I don't have the phone number to let them know we are dropping by so we can expect a somewhat hostile welcoming committee," Kevin warned.

"That's just great." Carlo moaned.

"Are you sure this is all right?" the pilot was also starting to get nervous.

"Did you ever hear the joke that if I told you or showed you I'd have to kill you? Here it's not a joke."

Both Carlo and the pilot turned white.

"Just kidding." Kevin laughed.

"We're approaching Glendora," the pilot informed the others.

"Take her higher and up the canyon slowly. It's been a while since I was here," Kevin explained.

"You've been here before?" Carlo asked.

"I was part of some specialized research on application of brain power for military uses," Kevin replied coldly.

"I don't think I'm going to like this place," Carlo said.

"There's some cutting edge research going on all back in through these mountains," Kevin explained.

"I've lived here all my life and never heard anything about this," the pilot said.

"It's a well-kept secret. It's called the San Dimas Experimental Forest. It's fairly well fenced off but try walking through here and the hidden cameras and sensors will have a patrol on you within five minutes to escort you out. Look up at the top of that hill by the water tanks. See all those high tech antennas mixed among the trees?"

"If you hadn't of said anything I never would have known they were there," the pilot replied.

"You're going to set her down in that big open field below that large building to our right. I'm sure the greeting party is on its way," Kevin assured them. "But don't worry, the FBI logo will make them ask before they shoot."

The pilot tried to smile but all Carlo could do was moan.

The blades were still spinning when a Hummer loaded with heavily armed marines skidded to a stop less than fifty feet away. The FBI logo did keep the Marines from training their automatic weapons on the three men but they did fan out in preparation for an attack, just in case.

Once the Marines were in position, a dapperly dressed man in an Armani suit stepped out of the passenger seat of the Hummer.

"Dr. Bridges, what a surprise to see you again so soon."

"Don't say that. You had to know it was me five minutes before we landed Jonathon" Kevin replied.

The man smiled. "I did. And I also knew your good friend Carlo Caressa and Agent Chambers were accompanying you."

"I had hoped as much," Kevin replied. "That's what brings me to see you."

Traffic in Los Angeles had turned into a parking lot filled with a cacophony of blaring horns, piercing sirens, and screaming voices. The Los Angeles Police Department, the Los Angeles Sheriff's Department, the California Highway Patrol, the Los Angeles Unified School District Police, and a host of several dozen local law enforcement agencies were trying to pull over every black Chevy Tahoe they encountered. Each stop required them to wait for a back-up unit to arrive and assist. Every stop took upwards of thirty minutes and some of the black Tahoes had been pulled over as many as four times. It had become complete insanity.

"Call it off," Samuelson said to Akers.

"Call it off? Are you freak'n crazy? That SOB killed three of my agents. Three of my friends."

"He's making us look stupid. We need to call off these traffic stops and come up with a new plan," Samuelson explained. "No agency in Los Angeles is going to want to help us if we keep this up."

"You're right, shut it down," Akers finally conceded.

The silver Mercedes finally reached its destination, the Santa Monica Pier. Juan Diego had arranged for a day of fun for him and his children at the amusement park on the pier. He had gone to great expense to do so and had taken many precautions to ensure his safety while his family enjoyed the short time they would spend together.

A second Hummer had arrived and the three men were packed into the back seat surrounded by marines. It was a short trip to the center just above the open field. The Hummers pulled into a garage area attached to the center making them unobservable to passing aircraft.

The marines disappeared through a back door while Jonathon led Kevin, Carlo, and the pilot out to the front entrance.

"Such a fabulous view," Jonathon remarked, "I so rarely get to see it." He continued to gaze transfixed at the vista before him.

"If you don't mind, Jonathon, we don't have a lot of time," Kevin said.

"Sorry, I'm sure you remember the routine. First we need a full hand screening of both hands."

Each man took his turn as the scanner read their hand prints.

"I would have thought they'd scan your eye," Carlo remarked. "Isn't that supposed to be more accurate?"

"It's not for what you think," Kevin replied. "I'll explain later.

"So where's Herr Müeller this morning? I would've expected him to head the greeting party," Kevin asked.

"Director Müeller is in Washington trying to keep the flow of money running freely," Jonathon replied.

"Successfully I hope," Kevin replied.

"Is there any doubt?" Jonathon giggled.

Next they entered a reception area, where two more armed marines waited.

"You need to leave your weapons with these gentlemen," Jonathon explained.

Only Carlo and Kevin were carrying weapons.

"Now we can head down to the forest," Jonathon laughed.

He walked over to slide his ID card in a slot next to the elevator when the door suddenly opened, startling him and causing him to stumble backwards.

"Ch-Ch-Charlotte," Jonathon stuttered. "What are you doing here?"

"Hello Charlotte," Kevin said, "Wonderful to see you again."

"Wonderful to see you too Kevin, I've missed you very much," Charlotte replied, kissing Kevin sweetly on the cheek.

"This is my good friend Carlo Caressa," Kevin said making the introduction.

"And this is our pilot Agent Chambers."

"A pleasure to meet the both of you," Charlotte replied, but her eyes were fixed on Agent Chambers.

"You'll have to excuse us but we must hurry down to the forest," Jonathon said, obviously uncomfortable being around Charlotte.

"Actually, I was wondering if I could speak with Agent Chambers for a few moments?" Charlotte asked in a voice that was almost hypnotic.

Jonathon turned white and was at a loss for words.

"I'm sure that would be fine. He can join us when you two are finished. You'll show him the way, of course," Kevin said.

"Of course," Charlotte replied sweetly.

Charlotte guided agent Chambers into what looked like a living room that overlooked most of the Los Angeles basin and sat with him on the couch.

"What's that all about?" Carlo asked.

"Charlotte's a counselor here at the center," Kevin replied

"A grief counselor," Jonathon piped in, "Your own grief."

"What's he talking about?" Carlo said.

"Remember those palm scanners when we entered? They weren't for security but are part of an ongoing study that Charlotte is in charge of. She's a palm reader and psychic," Kevin explained.

"Psycho not psychic if you ask me," Jonathon interrupted.

"A very, very good psychic and counselor," Kevin continued. "As a psychiatrist the bureau had me here to run some tests on her and analyze her abilities. She's quite amazing. In fact, almost unbelievable."

"Just what all happens here?" Carlo asked.

"Nobody really knows. There are so many levels and entrances to this place. There are probably ten thousand different laboratories buried somewhere underground in this mountain range. Look at the elevator panel, forty-five sub levels and I can only access five of them. I know some of the stuff they are working on and I've heard rumors about some of the other projects, but some of the stories I've heard are so bizarre they couldn't possibly be true. Five stinking levels and I'm temporarily in charge. Go figure." Jonathon lamented.

"You've had my guys in stitches laughing at that order to stop every black Chevy Tahoe in Los Angeles. What was that Akers guy thinking?" Jonathon asked.

"Akers is a good man, I think losing three of his agents clouded his judgment on this one," Kevin replied, as the elevator door opened onto a room filled with dozens of video screens.

"Well I got bad news for you. We looked everywhere for a previous scan of this Juan Diego Vasquez you're looking for and one just doesn't exist. In fact we can't even come up with a photograph of the guy. Then we looked for his top henchman,...what was his name?"

"Jorge 'Meathook' Cisneros," someone called out from the darkened room.

"Yeah, that's it. *El gancho de carniceria'*. I think 'Meathook' has a better ring to it, don't you?' Jonathon giggled.

"This guy wouldn't go anywhere without an army of muscle. He has to be taking his kids someplace fun like a mall, the beach, or an amusement park. I know you have to have scans of some of his bad guys," Kevin implored. "And I know you have plenty of cameras hidden everywhere by now."

"I thought facial scanning was a waste of time," Carlo piped in. "At least that's what they said at the academy. The Brits tried it and had all sorts of problems.

We tried it in airports and got sued more times than we pulled a match."

"I guess our disinformation campaign is working better than expected," Jonathon said. "We catch the bad guys but they don't know how they are getting caught and we want it to stay that way."

"How can it be so accurate?" Carlo asked.

"Not only do we use an advanced form of three-dimensional facial recognition but we've enhanced it with a skin texture analysis system that can recognize blemishes, skin tone, and even can tell if you are wearing make-up," Jonathon explained.

"Dr. Bridges, I think we might have a possible location from your suggestion," one of the analysts called out. "So far we've got a positive on at least seven members known to be associated with Vasquez' Cartel. Wait, make that ten. This must be the place."

"Put it on the big screen," Jonathon ordered.

Instantly, in high definition covering the entire wall in front of them was the amusement park on Santa Monica Pier.

"Would you look at that," Carlo said. "There are a whole lot of bad guys guarding that pier."

"Jonathon thanks for your help. I promise to tell no one where I got my information," Kevin said.

"I know. It was great seeing you again. Drop by more often, we don't get many visitors," Jonathon replied as they boarded the elevator. "And Carlo it was a pleasure meeting you."

As the door to the lobby opened Charlotte and the pilot were just coming out of the living room.

Jonathon immediately headed back down the elevator.

"I can't thank you enough for what you have done for me," Agent Chambers said to Charlotte and gave her a big hug.

"It's not what I have done, it's what you have done by taking Jesus Christ as your Lord and Savior," Charlotte said.

"We need to go," Kevin told the pilot. "Go prepare the helicopter. Carlo, would you go with him?"

They both could see that the pilot had been crying and from the gist of the conversation they had just heard it sounded like Charlotte had converted him to Christianity.

Kevin walked over to one of the marines who was holding their weapons.

"Could you please have my pilot and partner taken down to the helicopter to prepare it for takeoff then come back for me. I need to speak with Charlotte for a moment," Kevin asked.

"Yes sir, Dr. Bridges."

Now it was Kevin's turn to join Charlotte on the living room couch.

"Why was it so important to lead him to Christ?" Kevin asked.

"He doesn't have long to live," Charlotte replied.

"Does he know?"

"No, he doesn't need to know."

"How long, does he have?" Kevin asked.

"That is my burden to carry and I do not wish to share it," Charlotte replied.

"You are an angel," Kevin said as he got up to leave.

Charlotte softly touched his arm. "God has glorious plans for you Kevin. Stay true to your beliefs. Satan grows strong and his followers are many. You will face great perils but faith in our Lord Jesus Christ will always bring you through the darkest times."

One of the elevator doors opened and two very bewildered looking men stepped into the living room.

"I must attend to my new visitors," Charlotte whispered.

She again gently kissed Kevin on the cheek, but this time he thought he saw a tear in her eye as she turned away.

CHAPTER THREE

When Kevin reached the lower field the helicopter was warmed up and ready to go. Kevin was still trying to process his conversation with Charlotte. Agent Chambers waited patiently with an enlightened grin on his face. Kevin didn't know what to say to him.

"So what's the plan?" Carlo finally asked, snapping Kevin out of his daze.

"We know where we have to go," Kevin said, "the problem is how to go about it."

"So we have to let Akers know Vasquez is probably at the Santa Monica pier without letting Akers know the truth of how we found out," Carlo said, as the helicopter headed towards Santa Monica.

Kevin's phone began to vibrate letting him know he had just received a text. He never received texts so it had to have come from someone who knew he was in the helicopter and couldn't answer the phone.

"Jonathon says he thinks we now have a scan of Juan Diego Vasquez and Meathook. They both just arrived in a silver Mercedes with some kids. He said pictures to follow," Kevin shared with the other two agents.

"Are you sure about this Kevin? I mean what if we're wrong about this? What if it's not Vasquez?" Carlo asked.

"There were ten hit-men from the cartel there and it sure looked like they were setting up a perimeter to protect something or somebody," Kevin replied.

"Okay, I'm in, but what's the plan?" Carlo asked.

"Well we can't go flying in with FBI written all over our helicopter, that's for sure," Kevin said.

Agent Chambers nodded his head in agreement.

"You and I will somehow have to sneak onto the pier and let Akers know what the situation is," Kevin began.

"Oh yeah, we'll blend right in. Two clean-cut white guys in FBI jump suits," Carlo replied, "They won't know what hit 'em. And what about Akers, what are we going to tell him?"

"Tell him we received an anonymous tip from a disgruntled girlfriend. That always works," Agent Chambers chimed in.

"Sounds good to me, I'll leave that part up to you. How close can you get us to the pier without being seen?" Kevin asked.

"If I come in low I can probably drop you on one of the fields at Santa Monica High School. It's about a fifteen minute walk from the ramp leading onto the pier."

"Is that the only way on and off?" Carlo asked.

"Not a chance. There's parking on the pier, below it on both sides, it's accessible by boat. There's a boardwalk that runs up and down the coast that goes right underneath it big enough for two trucks to drive down. There are several staircases from the beach to the pier. Practically impossible to seal off," Chamber explained.

"After you drop us off wait until you hear from me before you call Akers. It will give us a chance to figure out how we're going to get in. Then take off and get high enough not to be suspected but still able to see what's going on. Remember to warn Akers about all the muscle

Vasquez has, we don't want a blood bath," Kevin reminded Chambers.

"Sorry, come back in an hour, all the rides are closed for a private party," the man said shoving the group of teenagers back onto the main part of the pier.

"That's a bunch of crap man. We got just as much right as anyone else," one of the shaved-headed tattooed members of the group said as he muscled his way towards the front.

Two of Vasquez' men were about to do some serious damage to the young man when Meathook intervened.

"Amigo," Meathook said, pushing up his sleeve. "Do you know what this 'tat' means?"

"That's the Vasquez Cartel symbol," the wannabe replied smugly.

"Smart boy," Meathook replied. "How about this one?"

The young man turned pale and started to back away but Meathook grabbed him by the throat. "I asked you a question smart boy."

"It means you've personally killed many men *señor*."

"How many?"

The boy struggled to look down at Meathook's wrist as his friends slowly backed away.

"Eighty-seven *señor*."

"Let's not make it eighty-eight today, shall we?"

"*Si señor*," the boy replied as Meathook eased the pressure on the boys neck.

"Now like my friend said it will only be an hour, so why don't you and your friends take a walk down the pier and enjoy yourselves." He reached into his pocket and pulled out a wad of hundred dollar bills. He peeled off two of them and stuffed them in the boy's mouth. "Adios."

It only took Carlo and Kevin ten minutes to jog from the high school field to Colorado Avenue and 2nd Street.

"I think Chambers is right. Vasquez probably has a man stationed at the entrance to the pier on Ocean Boulevard. We'll have to figure out a way in from back here," Carlo said. "So what happened between Chambers and Charlotte back at the center?"

"Charlotte saw his future and it wasn't good," Kevin said.

"That's bad," Carlo replied.

"Very bad," Kevin repeated. "Stop that truck."

Carlo pulled out his badge and stepped in front of a Bimbo bread and pastries truck. "FBI, are you boys headed for the pier?"

"Yes sir, we're making our deliveries there next." The driver replied.

Carlo gave Kevin a thumbs-up and Kevin immediately called Chambers.

"Tell Akers that Carlo and I will be dressed as Bimbo delivery drivers. Tell him to get the radios back on so we can coordinate the take down," Kevin explained, "And stay safe."

"Will do," Chambers assured him.

"No go," Carlo yelled, "No way we can fit these uniforms."

"Damn, I've already called Chambers," Kevin replied.

"Call him back," Carlo suggested.

"I've got a better idea," Kevin said, eyeing the trash truck in the alley across the street. Carlo looked over and immediately sprinted over blocking the truck from turning.

"FBI," he said holding up his badge. "Do you guys pick up on the pier?"

"No that's County, we're city," the driver replied.

"Well today's your lucky day," Carlo said and explained what he and Kevin needed from the men. Just before the truck pulled out of the alley Kevin saw the FBI helicopter ascend low towards the east and begin to rise and circle back and hover to the north no more than a needle prick in the sky.

Suddenly, the radios in Kevin's and Carlo's ears burst to life.

"Bridges, Caressa, just what the hell is going on?" It was Akers. "And where the hell have you two been?"

"Sir, Air Support One had some mechanical problems that required an emergency landing at some facility in Pomona or Corona… where was that airport Carlo," Kevin asked

"El Monte maybe…"

"Never mind, Agent Chambers explained it to me," Akers said cutting Carlo off as the trash truck rumbled towards the pier.

"I want you two to sit tight we are on our way. If this is a good tip you boys are in way over your heads," Akers warned.

"Sorry to interrupt, but something's going on here," Agent Chambers said. "I'm taking her a little lower."

"Oh, Jesus Christ, get out of the truck, Kevin, Carlo, get out of the bread truck," Chambers screamed.

The trash truck screeched to a stop as several men with automatic weapons diced the two bread deliverymen in the Bimbo truck with dozens of bullets.

"Oh Christ," Chambers said, "They're putting the kids back into the silver Mercedes and it's headed up the pier. I see a group of men surrounding someone heading for what looks like a boat loading area."

"Chambers, it's Kevin."

"Kevin! It's a miracle. How did you survive?"

"Carlo and I are in the garbage truck stopped on the pier. We're heading for the boat area."

"Then who was in the Bimbo truck?"

"Two very unlucky delivery men," Carlo replied.

"Be careful, there are bad guys everywhere, it's real chaos down on the pier," Chambers said.

"This is Akers, which way did the Mercedes go?"

"Looks like it's heading for the 10 Freeway Eastbound."

Kevin and Carlo were working their way towards the boat landing but fighting the crowd the entire way.

"I feel like a fish swimming upstream," Carlo said.

Suddenly the pier started to rumble and several people began to scream fearing it was an earthquake.

"Those are two mighty powerful engines," Kevin said.

No sooner were the words out of his mouth did a Cigarette 39 Top Fish rocket away from the pier.

"What was that?" Carlo asked.

"Probably the fastest boat you'll ever see in your life," Kevin replied.

"Is Vasquez getting away?" Akers asked over the radio.

"If he's on that boat he is," Kevin replied.

"He can't outrun me," Chambers said, as he turned his helicopter in pursuit of the fast moving boat.

"I wouldn't be so sure of that," Kevin said. "Somebody better contact the Coast Guard."

"We did before we left. They should be there momentarily," Akers assured Kevin.

The Cigarette boat wasn't even a mile off shore when someone on board fired a shoulder-launched missile at Air Support One. Agent Chambers had no time to avoid his inevitable fate. The fate Charlotte knew was coming.

"Oh my God," Carlo said. "They took out Chambers."

Seconds later there was a high pitched buzz followed by the explosion of the Cigarette boat as a Coast Guard drug enforcement helicopter equipped with a chain gun shredded the engines and gas tanks before the men aboard could launch a second missile.

Akers arrived with a contingent of several dozen FBI agents and numerous local police agencies

"Any chance he's still on the pier?" Akers asked.

"My money says Vasquez is in pieces at the bottom of Santa Monica Bay." Agent Campos said.

"Highway patrol reports that only the kids are in the Mercedes," Samuelson reported.

"We're doing our best to contain the crowd, but people keep slipping out. We just don't have enough men," Campos complained.

"Did we get any of his men?" Akers asked.

"We've collected about twenty possible candidates but we're going to get hit hard by the ACLU for profiling. We're hoping to find traces of gun powder residue that will tie them to the Bimbo massacre. We've collected about a dozen machine pistols from trash cans around the pier and with any luck we'll find our killers," Campos explained.

"Speaking of which," Campos said, turning to Kevin and Carlo, "Chambers told us you two were supposed to be in the Bimbo truck. It's a damn good thing your plans changed."

"Who all did you tell that we were going to be in the bread truck?" Kevin asked Akers.

"I know what you're getting at and I've already made a list," Akers replied.

"And checking it twice I hope," Carlo added, "because if you don't, I will."

"Calm down, Agent Caressa. We will find out who leaked the information to Vasquez and he will suffer the consequences for his actions. Campos, I think you're right. Vasquez is feeding the local fish population. Let's get these bad guys out of here and let these good citizens go home," Akers announced.

Before the police tape could come down allowing the crowd to disperse Kevin's phone vibrated to let him know he had received a text. When he opened his phone it was a picture of two clowns. Underneath was written the text 'I told you we can even see them through the make-up'.

"Carlo, let's take a walk," Kevin called to his friend.

Kevin's tone told Carlo something was up. "What 'cha got?" Carlo asked.

"Jonathon just sent me a picture. Vasquez and Meathook are still here. We need to find them before they get away," Kevin said quietly, as he scanned the crowd.

"Aren't you going to tell Akers?"

"Bad idea, considering what happened last time we told Akers something."

"Good point. So who are we looking for?" Carlo asked.

"A couple of clowns," Kevin replied.

"These guys are cold blooded assassins, they ain't no clowns."

"No seriously, we're looking for a couple of clowns. They should be easy to spot, they're each holding a bunch of balloons," Kevin said.

"You're kidding right?" Carlo said.

"I'm dead serious."

"Towards the back of the pier, near the boat ramp, I see some balloons."

"Let's have a look," Kevin said, as the tension began to build.

"You know if this guy is as careful as he seems to be he must have more men around here watching his back," Carlo said, growing noticeably more nervous.

"I think most have already been weeded out. I got a feeling it's just the two of them."

"Which one's Vasquez?"

"It's got to be the smaller man. They both look to be in really good shape but the bigger guy keeps checking on the smaller one like he's responsible for him. The big guy must be Meathook," Kevin surmised.

"You think they're armed?" Carlo asked.

"You can count on it."

"I think our best chance is to knock them out and sort things out later," Kevin suggested. "They're not likely to surrender and a lot of people could get hurt if we screw up."

"Any ideas how you plan to get close enough to do it? They're on opposite sides of the pier, covering each other's back and are surrounded by little kids trying to buy balloons." Carlo observed.

Kevin grabbed one of the fifty-five gallon drum trash cans sitting on the pier.

"I think one of these might do the trick," he said as he poured out the contents and hoisted it onto his shoulder. "We are dressed for the part."

Carlo smiled and did the same with the can on the opposite side of the pier, raising the ire of several tourists as the trash was strewn across the wooden beams.

"Sorry," Carlo said.

"We have to time this perfectly," Kevin instructed, setting down his can and joining Carlo on his side of the pier. "It has to look like we're replacing the full cans with empty ones just as they're passing by the other cans."

"Holding this above our heads leaves us vulnerable," Carlo asserted, "so don't screw up."

"Right before they get here we'll go back on the radio and let Akers know what's happening. It will also let us communicate. Let's get the barrels up so they get use to the sight," Kevin suggested.

The good guys and the bad guys slowly moved towards each other.

"Akers, this is Bridges."

"Bridges, where the hell did you go this time? We're trying to clean this mess up and get out of here. You and Caressa need…."

"Excuse me for interrupting sir, but Carlo and I have spotted Vasquez and Meathook and are about to take them down. We could sure use some back-up here," Kevin said calmly.

"Don't play games with me Bridges. Vasquez is dead and besides, no one has ever seen Vasquez before so how could you have spotted him?" Akers reasoned.

"Yikes," Kevin thought to himself. "Sir, Carlo and I did see him playing with his children when we first arrived and Meathook was standing guard right behind him," Kevin lied. "Like you, we thought he perished on the boat but then we spotted him in the crowd."

"Sounds like a bunch of crap to me," Akers replied, "but tell us where you are and what you need."

"Carlo and I are on opposite sides of the pier, as are Meathook and Vasquez. We're sure they're heavily armed. Meathook is protecting Vasquez but we wouldn't be surprised if there aren't other bad guys in the area. There are a lot of little kids around so our plan is to try to knock them out and worry about the consequences later."

"What consequences?" Akers asked.

"The slim chance that I may be wrong about this, but believe me, I'm not," Kevin tried to assure him.

"Oh, that's just freak'n great!" Akers whined. "Okay I see Carlo up ahead to the left."

"I'm a foot taller than the rest of the crowd and I'm carrying a bright orange fifty-five gallon drum. I would hope you could see me," Carlo said.

"Don't be a wise guy," Akers shot back. "That other trash can on the left must be you Kevin."

"I'm under here somewhere," Kevin replied. "Okay we're getting close. Get ready Carlo."

"Who are the targets?" Akers asked

"The clowns," Kevin replied.

"The CLOWNS!" Akers shouted.

Then all hell broke loose.

"*Gancho!*" Vasquez yelled as he saw Carlo about to hammer the trash can on Meathook's head.

It was just enough warning to allow Meathook to soften the blow with his forearm. Although he was still knocked to the pier and dazed he wasn't out.

Carlo was quickly on him tossing Meathook's guns aside while struggling to keep the man pinned until help arrived.

As Vasquez screamed his warning, he was also reaching for his own machine pistol. Kevin allowed his barrel to topple onto the railing as he grabbed Vasquez's wrist and upper arm just as his finger reached the trigger. A splay of bullets ripped through the upper deck of the Mariasol Restaurant. Dozens of people still on the pier started screaming and running knocking into Akers and the other agents coming to assist. Unable to gain control of Vasquez Kevin did the only thing he could think of that would keep as many people as safe as possible. He continued to hold tightly to Vazquez's arm and with all his strength threw his center of gravity over the top rail of the pier pulling Vasquez with him. The shock of freefall loosed the gun from Vasquez's hand and they hit the water hard.

When the crowd ducked at the sound of Vasquez's machine pistol, the young thug who had challenged Meathook earlier that day now found his hand on Meathook's pistol that Carlo had knocked away in the struggle.

"Amigo," Meathook yelled, "grab my gun and shoot the *pendejo*. I'll pay you well."

"I wouldn't do it son," Carlo said, still struggling with Meathook.

"Do it, do it now!" Meathook screamed.

"I ain't that stupid, man," the kid replied. "Look at you, you ain't nothing but a stupid *payaso*."

On the other side of the pier a crowd had gathered to watch the struggle in the water below and began to applaud reassuring both Carlo and the rest of the FBI team. In reality, it wasn't so much a struggle as it was a rescue. Kevin had used his momentum to turn Vasquez beneath him on the plunge towards the water so when they hit Vasquez took the brunt of the impact, which not only knocked him out but cracked two of his ribs and gave him a bad case of whiplash.

"Campos, take some men down there and help out Bridges," Akers ordered.

"Supervisor Akers let me introduce you to Meathook. The Vasquez Cartel's number one enforcer," Carlo said shoving up the clown's sleeve to reveal the tattoos on Meathook's arm.

"You're a dead man," Meathook snarled. You're all dead men.

"Get this clown out of here," Akers said with a smile passing the handcuffed killer to Agent Samuelson. "I've always wanted to say that and mean it."

"How's Kevin?" Carlo asked.

"Let's go find out," Akers said, as they headed towards the beach.

"A little help here," Kevin yelled to the group of FBI agents gathered on the beach waiting for him to drag Vasquez ashore.

Finally, a couple of county life guards ran into the water and assisted in bringing Vasquez onto the beach.

"We didn't want to get our suits wet," one of the agents said when Kevin gave them the snake eye.

"One of you could at least cuff him," Kevin complained.

At once they all realized what jerks they had been and took over cuffing and reading Vazquez his rights. They also called the paramedics over to check out Kevin and Vasquez.

"Nice work, Bridges," Akers said, as he approached, "but I still don't believe how you did it."

"I told you Carlo and I saw them when we first arrived and my instincts told me the clowns were the bad guys," Kevin said.

"What do mean clowns are the bad guys? Clowns are the funny guys," Akers replied.

"Not to me. When I was growing up I'd visit my grandmother and I'd sleep in this bedroom that had these pictures of clowns all over the walls," Kevin explained. "I never slept because it scared me. I've been afraid of clowns ever since."

"I'll give anybody ten million dollars to get me out of here," Vasquez yelled. "Ten million!"

"We better get him out of here before there's trouble," Akers said. "I want a convoy of three vehicles. Campos you and I will be the lead vehicle. Samuelson, I want you and Team Two in the Suburban with the prisoners and Jackson you follow with Team Three. I want Air Support Three overhead the entire time."

"Boss the Coast Guard called, no bodies in the water, just parts," one of the agents reported.

"What about Chambers?" Akers asked.

"They got nothing. Divers should be here in about an hour."

"Keep me informed," Akers replied. "Bridges, you and Caressa finish up here then get cleaned up and meet us back at headquarters."

"We don't have a car," Carlo replied.

"Take mine, I'm riding with Campos," Akers replied and tossed his keys to Carlo.

"Fifteen million to anyone who gets me out of here," Vasquez continued to yell.

"Get that chump in the car," Samuelson said to his partner. "I'll drive."

"Let's move out," Akers ordered and the cars raced out of the lower parking lot leaving a soaking wet Kevin and a battered Carlo standing alone on the sidewalk.

"I sure as hell hope I can find my suit," Carlo said.

"Forgetaboutit," Kevin replied in his best Mafioso accent. "Those garbage men are long gone by now."

"What about you? Your uniform is soaking wet," Carlo said.

"I always wanted one of those Venice Beach muscle shirts," Kevin said.

"Yeah, that should look real cute on you. You'll be a hit with all the boys," Carlo laughed.

"Maybe not," Kevin rethought.

"Just what are we supposed to finish up here?" Carlo said.

"I don't know. Take a walk on the pier maybe so I can dry out and we can say our goodbyes to Chambers," Kevin suggested.

"Was Chambers married?" Carlo asked.

"I think Charlotte would have mentioned it to me if he was."

"So just what was that place we visited? You told me who Charlotte was but what about that Jonathon character? He seemed a little, ...how should I say it, ...affected." Carlo stated.

"Jonathon's a little quirky. Actually, just about everybody at the Experimental Forest except the marines are a little different. They're into a lot of cutting edge research projects that are a bit out of the mainstream," Kevin explained.

"The facial recognition system seems pretty straight forward," Carlo replied.

"You think so. Take a look at the pictures Jonathon sent me on my phone." He passed the phone to Carlo and gave him a moment to scan through several pictures.

"Yeah so what? A lot of different angles of Vasquez and Meathook. What's the big deal?" Carlo asked.

"The big deal is all the angles. Look again. There are shots from below the faces, from the right, left, above, from off the pier, from the beach, from at least ten different cameras wouldn't you say? And just how many security cameras did you see up there? Three, maybe four, if that," Kevin asked.

"Doesn't add up does it?" Carlo said.

"Far from it," Kevin replied.

"So how does he do it?" Carlo asked.

"Some kind of mind astral projections was how it was explained to me," Kevin began. "Remember when we got our first assignments right out of the academy? We were both hoping for D.C."

"Yeah, you got D.C and I got. Kansas City." Carlo complained.

"Well D.C. turned out to be the worst assignment ever for me. Having a medical background got me stuck in a lab all day processing forensic evidence and writing reports. I was so bored I started sticking my nose into cases where I didn't belong. I thought I was helping out but apparently my supervisors didn't think so. After getting my ass chewed out one too many times I got shipped off to the Experimental Forest. It also had to do with me being a psychiatrist. There was a big re-evaluation of the Experimental Forest project going on with Congress and the FBI wanted one of their own involved in the evaluation process but none of the higher ups wanted anything to do with it because of its reputation."

"That's just plain freaky," Carlo replied.

"You have no idea, and sorry, I can't tell you any more about it or I'll have to kill you," Kevin said smiling.

"Fine by me, I'd rather sleep at night in my ignorance," Carlo replied. "Are you dry enough to leave? These clothes are starting to stink."

"I think we're done here," Kevin replied.

The convoy had just passed Fairfax Ave and was struggling to maintain sixty miles per hour in the car pool lane even with their emergency lights on and sirens blaring.

Samuelson's cell phone began to ring.

"Well it's about god damn time," Vasquez muttered in the back seat.

"What'd you say," The agent in the passenger's seat said turning around towards the two prisoners in the back as the convoy raced past the La Brea interchange.

"He said it's about god damn time," Meathook repeated, but the agent never heard the reply. Samuelson shot him pointblank in the forehead.

"Hold tight," Samuelson warned as he cut the wheel sharply to the right in front of a black Chevy Tahoe which swerved directly into the path of the trailing Suburban carrying the four agents of Team Three pinning it against the median barricades. Samuelson bounced off two smaller Toyotas before making the Crenshaw off ramp.

"What in the hell is going on back there? Quick, turn around, Samuelson's taking the off ramp," Akers demanded.

Campos did as ordered, although he thought Akers was crazy. Cars were strewn all over the freeway; there was no way they could get back to the off ramp.

"Air Three, do you see the vehicle?" Akers radioed.

"Roger that, the Suburban is turning left on Crenshaw heading north. Looks like it has some damage," the pilot reported.

"Don't lose it," Akers begged.

"We're on it. Go east about one hundred yards and take the onramp the wrong way back to Crenshaw and rejoin the chase," the pilot said.

Campos was halfway there before the pilot finished speaking.

No sooner had the Suburban gone under the freeway when Samuelson stopped and freed Vasquez and Meathook. The three of them jumped into a waiting catering truck and a couple of young punks took off in the Suburban. By the time the LAPD pulled over the two punks who claimed they had simply taken a joyride in a car they just found idling empty under the freeway, Vasquez and Meathook were safely on their way back to Mexico, swearing vengeance on the two FBI agents who revealed what clowns they really were to the entire world.

CHAPTER FOUR

July 4, 1975 Jacksonville, Alabama

Doug Ingle, the deep voice lead singer of the 60's psychedelic rock band Iron Butterfly, growled as the seemingly endless droning of the continuous ostinato bass line of their hit, *In A Gadda Da Vida* pounded through the stereo speakers shaking the small cabin.

"Please, please. I promise to tell no one. Just let me go," she begged.

"It's too late *glorybedaGoda* for that. Emily Sue, you *alleluia* must die *shamnada* for the Holy Spirit *glorybedaGoda* speaks through me *alleluia glorybedaGoda*."

"You're sick, you can't control your body, and you're having spasms. I can help you, I'm a nurse," she tried to reason.

"Shut up! Shut up! I'm not sick. I'm filled with the holy spirit," the lunatic raged. "The god damned Holy *shamnada hydakom* freak'n *glorybedaGoda alleluia* Spirit. Do you hear me? Do you hear *glorybedaGoda* me?"

His Tourette's diseased body jerked uncontrollably as he continued to babble. He grabbed a small wooden box sitting on a shelf next to the table and carefully opened it.

He had met her in a bar, drugged her drink and had taken her to a remote cabin in the hills east of the city. He had strapped her to a steel coroner's table on which he had bolted an extra collar that held the neck tightly against the table, almost to the point of choking. He had cut a four inch strip out of the table exactly where the neck clamp came to rest, exposing the neck of the person unlucky enough to be strapped to the table. Tonight it was the one he called Emily Sue. She wasn't the first. There had been others, but she was the one that would finally free him, the one that would give him power. The one who the voices had told him about.

"No, get it away from me," she screamed. "Get it away, you're mad."

He began to dance around the steel table constantly babbling, convulsing to the music with interspersed spasmodic jerks that rocked his entire body. In his hand hissed a timber rattlesnake swaying menacingly to the rhythmic thumping of what was now an extended drum solo.

He lowered the snake to her naked stomach and it sank its fangs deep into her abdominal muscles just below her halter top.

"Ahhhhhh," she screamed. "Stop, help me!"

"God promises no *alleluia* protection to the *shamnada hydakom* un-anointed. You lack faith. You need *glorybedaGoda alleluia glorybedaGoda alleluia* anointing by the Holy Spirit. That's *alleluia shamnada* what I'm about to *glorybedaGoda* give you."

"Ahhhh..." her scream was shortened when she slipped into unconsciousness as the snake, this time, sank its fangs into her thigh, just below her cut-offs and very near her femoral artery.

He placed the snake back in the box and set it on the shelf. He dimmed the cabin lights but adjusted the spot light that highlighted Emily Sue's head and neck that rested in the strange collar. Directly above the table was a mirror that would allow her to see all that was about to take place as soon as she regained consciousness.

From the shelf he removed a cloth roll and laid it on the table next to Emily Sue. He untied the cloth bindings and unrolled the bundle revealing a set of surgical tools. He then rolled a modified car dolly, the kind used for working underneath cars, from below the steel table, which allowed him to lie on his back and work through the opening he had cut in the steel table. He had also placed a modified oil pan beneath this opening to collect the blood that was sure to accumulate.

"Water, I need water," she moaned in a weak voice. "What, what, is happening?"

She was completely disoriented from the snake venom pulsating through her body. She had been imbued with enough poison to eventually kill her, but her death would come not from the poison, but from a combination of fright from what she was about to see and the stoppage of the blood flow between her heart and her brain.

With the music pulsating through his head he began to ever-so-slowly drag the razor-sharp scalpel across the epidermis layer of skin being careful not to go through the dermis layer and puncture the fatty layer of subcutaneous tissue.

"St-st-stop," she moaned as the glint of the scalpel blade reflected off the mirror above her head and into her glazed eyes.

"Enjoy the high," he replied. "You're one the chosen few." He lay on his dolly and continued his cutting of the back of her neck. All traces of the Tourette-like jerking and sudden outbursts in tongues had ceased as he meticulously worked with the skill of a seasoned surgeon.

Now the task slowed as with each cut he had to cauterize blood vessels delaying the loss of blood. He moved deliberately but quickly knowing Emily Sue could only last so long. She faded in and out of consciousness. He occasionally would allow a bit of anti-venom mixed with adrenalin to drip into her veins but at this point her blood circulation wasn't functioning very well.

"Just about finished," he tried to reassure her to keep her awake for his grand finale.

He rolled out from under the table and adjusted the lighting in the room.

"Fin-finished?" she moaned hopefully.

"Just about," he replied as he inserted another IV, this one in her head.

"Now watch the mirror above you," he ordered.

Only Satan himself could drive a person to such a sick sadistic desire, but at that precise moment he injected Emily Sue's head with a shot of adrenaline just as he hit a spring loaded blade mechanism that not only severed the spine that still held Emily Sue's head to her torso, but also sharply pulling the head away from the body. The rush of adrenaline into her brain allowed the last visual to be processed in her brain to be that of Emily Sue watching her own head severed from her torso and screaming at herself.

"Noooooooooo!" Then all went black.

CHAPTER FIVE

Kevin's hands were damp and he could feel the sweat dripping down the small of his back.

"Last time I felt this nervous I was in junior high and had been sent to the principal's office. I remember sitting on that bench in the hallway, just like this, waiting for him to finish questioning my best friend," Kevin said to the man sitting across from him.

"What did you do to earn a trip there?" Campos asked.

"Started a rumor about seeing the woodshop teacher kissing another teacher in the supply room," Kevin replied.

"Were they?" Campos asked.

"They were doing more than kissing," Kevin replied with a smile.

"So what happened?"

"We both got five swats and I was kicked out of woodshop and put in chemistry," Kevin replied.

"That must've hurt. Not the swats, but the chemistry class," Campos joked.

"Actually, it turned out to be a turning point in my life. I fell in love with science and went on to eventually get my medical degree," Kevin replied.

"So why the hell are you working for the FBI?" Campos asked. "A doctor can make a helluva lot more money than what Uncle Sam pays us."

"I thought the FBI could use a few good men."

"I think you got the FBI confused with the Marines," Campos laughed.

"So do you really think they'd fire us for that mess in Santa Monica?" Kevin asked.

"Not fire us, but I wouldn't count on getting promoted anytime soon," Campos replied. "Besides, if it hadn't been for you who knows how many more would have died."

"Nobody should've died," Kevin insisted. "We screwed up."

"It wasn't our operation. We were just following orders. How were we to know Vasquez would have so much security?"

"It's our job to know things like that," Kevin replied.

"Vasquez even had a man on the inside. Samuelson tried to have you and Carlo killed," Campos said.

"Someday I hope to get the chance to pay him back for that," Kevin replied.

"We'll never see him again. He's living large in some hacienda on the beach down in Acapulco," Campos guessed.

"Not a chance. He's working like a slave for Vasquez unless they've already killed him," Kevin replied. "The cartels don't work that way anymore. Nobody gets a free ride."

"You know Akers thought I was the snitch. At least that's what he told me. I never would have figured it was Samuelson," Campos said.

"Too many people died needlessly," Kevin repeated. "We screwed up."

"It's Akers who screwed up. He'll go down for this one. He's the one who should've known how dangerous taking down Vasquez in such a public place would be.

They'll scold us, notate this in our files, and stick me behind some desk for a couple of months and you in some lab. Before you know it, we'll be back out in the field," Campos assured Kevin.

"I still can't believe you wrestled the clown into the water," Campos joked. "My kids will never forgive you. How did you know it was Vasquez and how did you know the other one was his bodyguard?"

"I don't know, the way he was paying more attention to who was coming and going than to the kids around him screaming for a balloon hat," Kevin replied.

"You know, you tackling the clown into the water was the most watched video on YouTube in the past three months."

"Please, don't remind me," Kevin pleaded.

"You avoided my question earlier. How is it a medical doctor who started out as a forensics expert and profiler end up working as a field agent?" Campos asked.

"I wanted the field experience and I didn't sign up with the FBI to be stuck in some lab all day sorting through evidence that someone else packaged for me to examine. I would rather be examining evidence in the field and packaging it for someone else to verify," Kevin explained. "When I'm at a crime scene it seems to talk to me. It tells me stories. I discover things about the crime I could never find out in the lab."

"Is that why you're always talking to yourself?" Campos asked.

"No, well, yes probably. It's a habit I picked up in high school. When I was trying to figure out a problem that was giving me trouble I would debate it with myself. Most people do it in their mind, I just happen to do it out loud. Kind of freaky, huh?" Kevin smiled.

"Maybe a little," Campos laughed, "but I've seen freakier."

"I don't want to know," Kevin laughed.

"Agent Bridges, Mr. Kaiser will see you now," the secretary said, opening the office door. "Please go in."

Kevin smiled at the secretary and walked briskly into the office.

"Agent Bridges, please take a seat," Deputy Director Kaiser said, standing as Kevin entered the room. "I believe you know Assistant Director Peter Hannah from your time at the academy."

"Nice to see you again Mr. Hannah," Kevin nodded and sat as instructed to do. Before Kevin settled into the chair the deputy director began, "Your file says you were once a Charismatic Christian. Are you still?"

Kevin was caught completely off guard. "I am a Christian, but I wouldn't necessarily consider myself an adherent to the Charismatic movement. I did attend one of their churches for a short time, but it wasn't right for me."

"Why not?" Hannah asked.

"I didn't quite understand their emphasis on speaking in tongues," Kevin replied.

"Like the Pentecosts?"

"Yes, but not nearly as extreme as some of them seem to be," Kevin said. "What does my faith have to do with what happened in Santa Monica?"

"What happened there wasn't your fault. That's not why we called you here," Kaiser replied.

"I don't understand. That's not what I was led to believe," Kevin said.

"That was done purposely," Kaiser snapped back.

"Do you remember Agent Caldwell?" Hannah asked. "He was in the same academy class as you."

"Simon Caldwell?" Kevin replied. "How could anyone forget Simon the Zealot?"

"Why did they call him that?" Kaiser asked.

"Simon was fiercely patriotic, just like Christ's Apostle, Simon the Zealot," Kevin replied, looking at the two men. "But you already knew that. What's this all about?"

"Agent Caldwell has disappeared while working undercover in Louisiana," Kaiser replied.

"We think someone inside the agency may have blown his cover. That's why no one but Mr. Kaiser and I know the real reason you're here. We want you to take over Agent Caldwell's investigation," Hannah explained. "We'll tell the Los Angeles bureau that you've been reassigned to the lab in Quantico. They'll figure it was because of what happened at Santa Monica pier. Several of the agents involved will be temporarily reassigned so it won't seem suspicious."

"What was Simon working on when he disappeared?" Kevin asked.

"A murder investigation," Kaiser said.

"It seems like the agency's going to a lot of trouble for a murder investigation. Isn't that something for the Louisiana State Police or our local field office to handle?"

"It's more than a simple murder investigation. It is a rather macabre serial murder case with complicated implications."

"Bodies with the missing heads. I read about that," Kevin recalled. "The headless serial murder case, they are calling it. If I remember correctly there were three bodies, two were found in Alabama and one in Florida, not Louisiana."

"Very good, Agent Bridges," Kaiser remarked. "But what you don't know, nor has it been reported to the media is that a fourth body has been found nor have the details about the autopsies or murder scenes been released."

"It would seem to me four bodies found without heads is the unifying detail in these deaths. I don't think you need an autopsy to tell you the cases are related," Kevin replied.

"No but the autopsies have revealed some other very interesting information common to all four victims."

"And that is?" Kevin asked.

"All four bodies had unusually high levels of poison in their systems. Not necessarily enough to kill them, but certainly enough to severely disorient them," Hannah explained.

"Let me guess, the poison came from a copperhead or a rattlesnake. That's why you asked about Pentecosts. The murderer probably used the poison as an anesthesia before chopping off the heads," Kevin surmised.

"Who said the heads were chopped off?" Kaiser replied. "Chopping off a head can be very messy and not necessarily too precise. The heads of our victims were surgically removed."

"While they were still alive?" Kevin asked incredulously.

"Apparently so," Hannah replied.

"It would take a very demented yet talented person to do something like that," Kevin explained, "with some form of medical training."

"Another reason Mr. Hannah thought you would be qualified for this case. You are a doctor which could work to your advantage in finding this killer," Kaiser said.

"Have you got any leads on this guy?" Kevin asked. "Are the victims related in any way, same neighborhoods, same occupations, same church? Did the local police find anything like that?"

"No, it seems the victims had no connections. However, we believe they were chosen because of their names." Hannah snapped.

"The Birmingham office has three agents already working the case and has come up with a couple of leads," Hannah said.

"And Simon was following one of these leads when he disappeared," Kaiser explained.

"Why the Birmingham office? Simon disappeared in New Orleans," Kevin asked.

"The first victim was a Mr. James Zeller from Birmingham, a used car salesman." Hannah said. "They found his headless body stuffed in the trunk of one of his cars. That was about eighteen months ago"

"The second man's name was Philip Connely from Muscle Shoals. His body showed up about ten months after James Zeller. What's interesting is how they found his headless body. He was crucified near a campground along the shore of Wheeler Lake Campground."

"Crucified?" Kevin blurted out.

Kaiser now spoke without answering Kevin. "Andrew Jackson Smith was the third victim found six months after the second victim. This is the one the media hasn't heard about yet. They found him headless and crucified on an X-shaped cross in the woods outside of Corinth, Mississippi. Forensics says he had been dead for a while before our murderer nailed him to the cross."

"St. Andrews Cross," Kevin replied. "Was the second victim also crucified this way?"

"No, he was nailed to a traditional shaped cross," Hannah replied. "And not long after his head had been removed."

"The fourth victim was found within a few days of the third, Matthew Davis. They found his headless body on the beach just outside Pensacola, Florida. He had a spear sticking out of his chest," Kaiser read from his notes.

"It's called a halberd," Kevin replied.

"How do you know that? I haven't shown you the picture yet." Kaiser asked.

"A halberd is a cross between a sword and a spear. It was commonly used as far back as 200 B.C. According to Christian writings, Matthew was slain by a halberd around 60 A.D. The same year the Apostle Andrew was crucified," Kevin explained.

"I told you Kevin would be perfect for this job," Hannah said to Kaiser.

"That's what you said about Simon if I recall," Kaiser replied. "And he ends up missing and most likely dead."

"Simon's not dead," Kevin interrupted, "or at least I don't think he is dead."

"What makes you say that?" Kaiser asked.

"When was the body of Matthew found?" Kevin replied.

"Approximately six weeks ago," Hannah replied.

"Then if I'm correct, this serial killer will hold onto Simon for a while before he kills him."

"How can you possibly know that?" Kaiser asked.

"Obviously, these murdered men have the names of Jesus' Apostles. There is a historically documented order in which they were killed and how they were killed. This murderer seems to be following that pattern," Kevin explained. "Five more apostles die before Simon is martyred."

"The Apostles weren't all beheaded. Even I remember that from Sunday school," Kaiser exclaimed.

"That is the one piece that doesn't seem to fit," Kevin admitted. "I'm also a bit confused about the time frame and the locations where the bodies were found. The Apostles were martyred throughout Europe, the middle-east and Asia over a thirty year period and John wasn't martyred. He lived to be 101 years old."

"Maybe some lunatic named John is behind these killings." Hannah ventured.

"More likely someone who thinks he is Judas Iscariot wanting to finish the job he started when he kissed Jesus revealing him to the Roman soldiers," Kevin speculated. "How long was it between the first and the second murders?"

"Around ten months. The third and fourth murders were about six months after that. We sent Simon in right after the body was found on the X-shaped cross. That was about two months ago," Hannah explained.

"What was the lead Simon was working on and how long ago did he disappear?" Kevin asked

"We lost contact with him about a month ago. He had gone to New Orleans to try to find some Voodoo 'spirit guide' who's known for supplying snakes to some of the Spiritual Churches in New Orleans. We also think he is supplying a Holiness Church just outside of Birmingham in an area called Sand Mountain in North East Alabama, somewhere near the city of Macedonia in Jackson County. Simon thought he had a lead with this church in Macedonia," Hannah explained.

"What'd he have?" Kevin asked.

"He never got the chance to share it with me," Hannah replied. "We only know about this snake charmer because the New Orleans office has a file on him."

"Have they spoken with him about Simon's disappearance?" Kevin asked.

"Yes, but he denies having ever seen Simon or anyone who vaguely resembles him," Hannah explained.

"I need to see a copy of their report. It's the only lead we have so I'll pay the man a visit," Kevin replied. "I'll also need to see the files on the first four murders."

"I thought you might," Hannah replied pulling a stack of files from his briefcase.

"Do we have anything on this church in Sand Mountain?"

"Sand Mountain is a general area, the town is Macedonia, but we're not sure the church is even in the town, it's just a few buildings scattered around the area," Hannah explained.

"I'll take that as a no," Kevin replied.

"Any idea as to how you plan on finding this maniac and getting Simon back?" Kaiser asked.

"Not until I study these files," Kevin replied. "What was Simon's cover?"

"Bridge inspector for whatever state he happened to be in," Hannah replied.

"I'll make sure I won't use that one as my cover," Kevin mused.

"Remember, you'll be on your own. We can't trust the regional field offices until we're sure there's no one leaking information," Hannah reminded.

"How long will that be?" Kevin asked.

"As long as it takes," Kaiser asserted, running out of patience.

"That won't do," Kevin replied.

"What won't do?" Hannah replied, somewhat taken aback.

"I'm not going in there blind without any quick access to information or resources that I may need in a hurry," Kevin explained.

"How dare you try to dict...," Hannah was interrupted by Director Kaiser

"What do you suggest," Kaiser interrupted.

"If you're moving agents around from the Santa Monica fiasco send Carlo Caressa to the Birmingham office to work the serial murder case. Carlo can be my conduit for progress the agency makes in the case. He and I can work out some sort of drop system when he has or I need information," Kevin explained.

"I think we can arrange that," Kaiser replied. Hannah wasn't so happy about the request.

"I'll expect you to check in with me every other day," Hannah ordered. "We'll track your movements through your phone's GPS system, so keep it on you at all times."

Kaiser slid an envelope across the table. "This is your new identity information. The usual stuff, driver's license, credit and ATM card, and the new cell phone. We left your first name the same but gave you a new last name."

"If you need anything else just let me know," Hannah added.

"Hold on a minute," Kevin replied, not feeling too sure about things.

"I'm going to be undercover. Checking in every other day isn't reasonable. I'll be in touch with Carlo and its Carlo who'll check in with you. I'll take the other stuff, but I can't say I'll use it. A cell phone may not fit in real well in the backwoods of Alabama, nor would a credit card and ATM card. Some of these sects think these items are Satan's doings and want nothing to do with them so until I'm in there, I won't know how to play it."

"I don't like it. Maybe you can hide the phone in your trunk so we can track you," Hannah suggested.

"Maybe," Kevin replied, "We'll have to see. Who says I'll even have a car? I just don't know yet."

Kevin opened the envelope; Kevin Jackson was his new alias. "You think the FBI could do better than that," Kevin wanted to tell the two men but thought better of it.

"Show him the video," Kaiser said.

"D-do you think that's necessary at this time?" Hannah stuttered slightly. "Our analysts still haven't figured it out yet."

"Damn right it's necessary. I want Agent Bridges to see what exactly he's up against even if we don't understand it."

Kevin's eyes widened like a deer in the headlights.

"Yes sir," Hannah replied to his boss and he turned his laptop to face Kevin.

"This was taken from a video camera monitoring the parade route during a local parade the weekend Simon disappeared. I think you'll recognize Simon." Hannah explained.

Kevin watched as Simon staggered into the frame from an alley on the left seemingly drunk. "He's been drugged. Simon doesn't drink," Kevin blurted out.

"Hold your comments and just watch the video," Hannah ordered.

Kevin watched as Simon wallowed helpless in the gutter and interacted with some of the passersby. He tried to read Simon's lips but that proved impossible.

"Here's where our stranger arrives," Hannah narrated.

A man walked into the frame from the same alley where Simon had seemed to come. He wasn't a large man, not nearly as big as Simon and his face was covered by a hooded sweatshirt. It appeared that he was speaking to Simon for Simon's head seemed to turn as if he were listening. The man reached down with one hand and easily pulled Simon into the air and onto his shoulder.

"That's impossible," Kevin exclaimed. "Simon weighs at least two hundred and twenty pounds and that man jerked him over his shoulder with one hand."

"Keep watching," Kaiser insisted.

Kevin didn't say anything else and watched as the man began to carry Simon away.

"It's coming up," Hannah said.

"Shh…" Kaiser shushed him.

Another group of revelers approached the man carrying Simon, but as they neared, the man lifted his hand towards the group and they seemed to fall aside as if they'd been shoved. They turned as if to confront the man carrying Simon, but a large trash bin pushed up against the building seemed to roll onto the sidewalk separating the revelers from Simon and his captor. It also blocked any further view the camera had of Simon.

"What was that all about?" Kevin said as the laptop screen turned black.

"We're still trying to figure it out. What do you make of it?" Hannah asked.

"None of it seems possible. First I don't know how anyone, even a world-class weightlifter, could jerk Simon so easily over his shoulder like that," Kevin started.

"Our experts say that is possible. It's the other stuff we want your opinion about," Kaiser said.

"I do know some martial arts masters claim to be able to stop attackers by focused energy though I've never seen it done. They call it Chi. It's a manipulation of this life force that allows one to be capable of feats which defy the normal bounds of human strength. As far as moving trash bins with telekinesis, that seems highly unlikely, but not necessarily impossible," Kevin offered. "I guess it's just a matter of directing your internal energy."

"As a medical doctor you actually believe that?" Hannah said mockingly.

"I'm a psychiatrist. I know the mind is extremely powerful. I've seen people move objects before, but never something as large as a trash bin," Kevin replied. "You know our government has an ongoing research project in telekinesis. We use such a small portion of our brains. Tapping into its infinite power could explain everything in that video."

"What about God's power?" Kaiser asked. "Would it be possible for a true believer in God to do what we just saw?"

"God's power is infinite," Kevin replied. "But from what I know so far about this case, I can't imagine God has much to do with it."

"I thought God controlled everything," Hannah interjected sarcastically.

"No," Kevin responded, "God created everything but doesn't control everything. He gave man free will to make his own choices, both good and bad."

"So did God give this man these incredible powers we see in the video?" Kaiser asked.

"I cannot believe that God or the Holy Spirit would do such a thing," Kevin replied.

"What do you mean Holy Spirit?" Hannah asked.

"The Holy Spirit is what God uses to give us his gifts," Kevin started to explain.

"What gifts," Hannah interrupted.

"The gifts are a matter of interpretation," Kevin said. "Some Christian sects believe there are only nine gifts of the Spirit, while other believe there are many more. I tend to think that a spiritual gift is something you do supernaturally well. The ability to work miracles, ability to heal, to prophesize, cast out demons, speak in tongues, these are some of the gifts."

"Then as a doctor, you have the spiritual gift to heal," Kaiser said.

"That's not how it works," Kevin said. "When the Bible talks about spiritual healing, it means the ability to heal by the laying of hands and God's power flowing through you to heal miraculously."

"So why don't we see a lot of this miraculously healing?" Kaiser asked

"We do, just not here in the United States, mostly in South America, Asia, and Africa, where Pentecostal Christianity is growing," Kevin replied.

"That's ridiculous, we have Pentecosts in the United States," Kaiser insisted.

"We also have doctors and that's where society has placed their faith in healing," Kevin replied solemnly. "Society feels we don't need miracles."

"Before we let you go I want to hear what you have to say about the killer. You were, or are, one of our top profilers. Tell me about the killer," Kaiser ordered.

"Based on that video I think we can safely say that the killer is not a woman. I know of no woman with that kind of strength, although, the killer isn't that big of a person either. The crimes are not sexual in nature. These are crimes based on a religious fervor of some sort. He's a very devout man in his forties or early fifties, white Anglo-Saxon protestant, probably born and raised in the south. He went to medical school, didn't necessarily graduate but stayed around long enough to learn some pretty advanced surgery. He has a reasonably high I.Q., is probably not a loner and is very talented in several other fields like writing, painting, music, and could be very athletic. He probably went to the seminary and dropped out. He is well schooled in the Bible. He may be a religious leader removed from his position who is seeking revenge," Kevin explained.

"What is he doing with skulls?" Kaiser asked.

"Most likely he's building a shrine of some sort. Historically conquerors have made necklaces with them, used them to crown their staffs, and even made chalices out of their conquered adversary's skulls."

"You said you don't think the crimes are sexual. How do explain the female DNA found on two of the victims?" Kaiser asked.

"The same DNA was found on two of the victims? I didn't see that in the reports," Kevin exclaimed.

"Of course, you haven't read them thoroughly, but would that lead you to believe the killer is a woman?" Kaiser asked.

"I don't believe a woman is strong enough to do what I just saw in the video, assuming that was the killer. Perhaps the DNA readings were lab errors." Kevin offered.

"Perhaps," Kaiser replied.

"Gentleman, if you don't mind, I'd like to conclude this meeting," Hannah interrupted, losing his patience with the turn the conversation had taken.

"Sorry," Kevin said.

"We meet with Carlo Caressa in half an hour and will inform him of his assignment. Be sure to tell no one of your assignment for as you are well aware the Vasquez Cartel has a two million dollar price on you and Agent Caressa's heads," Hannah droned.

Kevin wanted to say "Duh, you've moved us to temporary housing at Point Magu Naval Air Station for our protection and this is the first time we've been allowed off, do you really think we're going to announce our undercover plans to anybody, especially the Vasquez Cartel?" Sometimes Kevin couldn't believe how stupid the people he worked for could be.

"Tomorrow afternoon we will fly you out of Point Magu and into Birmingham-Shuttlesworth International Airport. We've arranged for an apartment for you on the military side of the airport. I'm sure there will be one available for Agent Caressa as well. It will give you a secure place to plan and organize your investigation," Hannah explained

"Any more questions?" Kaiser asked.

"About a million, but they can wait," Kevin joked.

Kaiser smiled but Hannah didn't think it too funny.

"Then that will be all Agent Bridges. Your plane leaves tomorrow for Alabama at 1:00 p.m. That will give you some time to get some of what you need in place. We'll be in touch," Hannah said curtly.

"I'm sure you will," Kevin replied, as he rose to shake both men's hands,

"Good luck, son," Kaiser said, with a firm handshake.

"Thank you, sir."

"Agent Bridges," Hannah replied nodding and turning avoiding Kevin's outstretched hand.

"This way Mr. Bridges," the secretary said, startling Kevin as she seemed to have appeared from nowhere, and gently grabbed his shoulder to guide him out a different door than the one he had come in.

"What a dick," Kevin said as the door shut behind him. "Oh my gosh, did I say that out loud?" His face turned red.

"I'm afraid you did," the secretary replied.

"I'm so sorry," Kevin apologized.

"Don't be," she replied. "You're not the first to say that today and you probably won't be the last. And to tell you the truth, I have to agree with you. Have a nice day." She closed the door and Kevin found himself alone in the hallway.

CHAPTER SIX

July 5, 1975 Jacksonville, Alabama

Once you have gently boiled away the hair, skin, fat, and muscle tissue and the remaining bones and gelatinous materials have cooled sufficiently there are only two moving parts that need to be reattached to the skull, the mandibles. Since the base of his chalice was to be brass he used brass screws to secure the lower and upper mandibles into place.

Of course, there is the problem of how to remove the brain. You want to remove as much of the brain as possible before you boil the skull to remove the skin and fat. The ancient Egyptians ran a wire up through the nose, whipped it around for a while and pulled the brains out through the nasal passage. Effective, but messy and time consuming. The other choice of course, was to remove the top of the skull and scoop the brains out, which needed to be done anyway so it only made sense to do this. However, the only problem with this was you had to peel back the hair and skin to get a clean approach with the Gigli's Wire.

A Gigli's Wire had been around since 1894 and was still one of the preferred methods for removing sections of the skull. In the case of Emily Sue's skull the entire upper portion was to be removed. He measured and drilled a series of tiny holes around the circle he had drawn. He carefully threaded the wire through the first hole and caught it with the bent sharpened needle attached to the second wooden handle. With the wire blade attached he slowly began the process of removing the top of her skull. When finished, the top would be ground into a fine powder to be mixed with a clear resin that would seal the inside of the skull making it water tight and camouflage the screws required to connect the skull to its ornate brass stem and base forming the perfect chalice. It was a beautiful piece, but not the kind of object you could leave sitting around for others to admire, nor was it intended to be kept and admired. This chalice was the trial piece for what was to come in the future. A seeker had come calling and Satan had offered him the challenge and the opportunity to grow strong.

     The chalice was traded to a Haitian Botanica shop in the Ninth Ward section of New Orleans. It is what would be considered one of the real Louisiana Voodoo shops. Nothing at all like the tourist shops located in and around Bourbon Street.

     Her headless and badly decomposed remains would be found almost eleven months later. Identification of the body was made by her mother through the jewelry and clothing Emily Sue always wore. She was buried in the back of the Holiness Church with Signs Following in Macedonia, Alabama. The church her step-father had pastored since 1969.

CHAPTER SEVEN

"Do you know they were going to send me to Anchorage, Alaska? Anchorage, freak'n Alaska for goodness sakes. I could've been stuck there for years," Carlo complained.

"This is only temporary, you still might be," Kevin joked.

"Thanks a lot. For a psychiatrist you sure don't know how to cheer a guy up, do you?" Carlo complained.

"You should thank me. If I hadn't insisted you join me you'd be…"

"I know, I know, and I'm really grateful," Carlo interrupted. "I'm just so damn pissed off that we have to hide like this because of the Vasquez Cartel."

"Give it five or six months and it will all blow over."

"You really think so?"

"They can't afford to waste the manpower or time to search for us. That would be bad business and Vasquez can't look like he's running a bad business. It would make him look too weak. And if he looks weak someone will try to take him out," Kevin explained.

"So Hannah told me you'd fill me in on this assignment. I can't believe we're both working undercover."

"Whoa, there partner," Kevin replied, "I don't recall Hannah saying anything about you working undercover."

"Well not out in the field, but under a false name at the office and as a kind of free-lance agent out of Washington. I get to call my own shots," Carlo said gleefully.

"This sounds like trouble."

"No, no trouble. I'm to follow up on what you tell me to follow up on, keep you informed on how the investigation is going and on any new information we turn up, and keep in touch with Hannah," Carlo replied.

"How often?" Kevin asked

"How often what?"

"How often do you have to call Hannah?"

"Every day," Carlo replied, sheepishly.

"Every day!" Kevin exclaimed. "We'll talk about that. So what am I supposed to call you this trip?" Kevin asked.

"Charlie," Carlo said softly.

"Charlie. What kind of southern name is Charlie? What last name did they give you?" Kevin prodded.

"D...," Carlo muttered an answer to soft to hear.

"What did you say?"

Carlo just shook his head and handed his new set of fake ID's to Kevin.

"Charlie Daniels! Doesn't anyone at the FBI have a brain? Don't they know where they're sending you? Charlie Daniels. He's like a legend in the South. The idea of undercover work is to go unnoticed. You tell someone your name and five seconds later they're supposed forget it. That's how it's supposed to work. But this. They will never forget your name. Charlie Daniels! What were they thinking?" Kevin raged.

"I know, I tried to tell Hannah but he wouldn't let me get a word out," Carlo said, hanging his head.

"It's like he wants you to screw up," Kevin said. "Did they show you the video?"

"Yes, but I really didn't understand it all. Only that whoever was under that hood was pretty damn strong to lift Simon like that. The rest of it was just nonsense," Carlo replied. "Have you got a plan for us?"

"I'm working on it," Kevin replied. "After we get settled in at the airbase I'm going to want you to see what you can find out about that snake salesman in New Orleans. There's got to be some connection we're missing between these victims."

"You mean besides their names?" Carlo replied.

"Wait a minute, what's the name of that snake salesman?" Kevin asked.

"Rastas Bart Smith," Carlo replied, thumbing through the file.

"I'll bet you ten bucks that Bart is short for Bartholomew," Kevin deduced. "That would make him an eventual target."

"Before or after Simon?" Carlo asked.

"That's the problem, nobody knows when Bartholomew was martyred, only where and how," Kevin explained. "And that is something that we may be able to use to our advantage."

"Maybe," Carlo replied, "but there's got to be quite a few Bartholomews living in the South, wouldn't you guess?"

"Something you need to find out," Kevin replied smiling. "But right now, I need to catch up on my sleep, so why don't you catch up on these files and wake me when we get to Birmingham Charlie. I've already read the files twice."

Kevin tried to rest but immediately spoke up.

"What do you think about the woman's DNA on two of the victims?" Kevin asked.

"I think that the victims knew each other and were seeing the same woman," Charlie replied. "Are we missing something?"

"Read them again and see," Kevin ordered.

"Yasuh Bossman Jackson," Carlo replied in a very bad attempt at a southern accent.

"Please, don't ever do that again."

"Sorry," Carlo replied sheepishly.

"You've seen too many old Burt Reynolds movies. The South isn't like that anymore. At least, I hope it isn't," Kevin reflected, as a sly grin appeared on his face.

"What's so funny?"

"I was just thinking that maybe I've been watching too many Burt Reynolds' movies myself. Now let me get some sleep. We've got a lot of work to do when we arrive in Birmingham."

"I was getting tired of the beach anyway," Carlo replied. "Too many pretty distractions."

"I take it you've never been to the South."

"Sure I have, if you consider Quantico, Virginia the South."

"I guess sleep is overrated anyway. Let's talk business. As corny as it may seem, they got it right in *Silence of the Lambs* when they said the first murder of a serial killer is usually close to home or meaningful, which would lead me to believe the first victim, James Zeller, either knew the murderer or had some kind of confrontation at one time or at someplace with the murderer. Maybe they were disgruntled neighbors, possibly business rivals, or maybe they both chased after the same girl in college. Who knows, but in some way I bet their lives intersected in a negative way. I want you to concentrate on finding out everything you possibly can about Mr. Zeller. Secondly, I expect the next murder to happen within the week at one of the prominent churches here in Birmingham. Actually, the murder will have taken place elsewhere and I doubt we will be able to do anything about it. The head will have of course been removed but the body will have been seriously stoned causing massive broken bones and contusions. That I'm guessing will come after the head has been removed. The broken body will be brought to this prominent church or temple and the body will be thrown from it in some manner, so look for a church with a large steeple or bell tower. Of course, this is all predicated on if the murderer follows his established pattern, which we have no reason to believe he won't. The local field office should have a list of all the men in Birmingham with the first name of James and the middle initial or last name beginning with A or the middle name James with the last name beginning with A, at least everyone who has a driver's license. Now you just need to edit that list to all men smaller than the first victim. I would also be willing to bet that there is a connection between some of these men that has been overlooked. I'm not suggesting the Birmingham office isn't doing their job, but if our killer is as clever as I think he is, some of these victims should be connected somehow."

"What about Vasquez?" Carlo asked.

"What about Vasquez? Does the hit he has out on us still worry you?"

"I wouldn't think his network extends this far into the South."

"I think we both would be surprised how far his network extends," Kevin replied. "Just don't spend a lot of time hanging around the Birmingham field office and as much as I hate to say it, I don't think Samuelson is the only one at the bureau who is dirty."

"You think it's Hannah?" Carlo asked.

"I would if Hannah wasn't such a bumbling idiot."

"Maybe that's part of his cover."

"Part of your cover maybe, but I doubt Hannah would be that shrewd," Kevin joked. "We'll just have to watch our backs until this cartel thing blows over."

"If it blows over."

"Trust me, Vasquez can't afford to let something like this drag on. He either whacks us right away or he lets it go," Kevin explained. "Now that we've disappeared from Los Angeles I'm sure he's just going to let it go."

"I sure hope so," Carlo exhaled.

"But like I said, let's just watch our backs for a while anyway," Kevin reaffirmed.

"Yasuh Bossman Jackson. I'm just kidding, I'm just kidding," Carlo said with a big grin, even causing Kevin to laugh.

CHAPTER EIGHT

At least he was still alive. Simon had been floating in and out of a haze for quite some time. Today was the first day he could make any sense of his situation. He had a pretty good idea why his captor had not yet killed him, but when you're dealing with a psychotic serial killer you're never quite sure about anything.

Quite a bit of Simon's recent memory was blurry at best. He knew at times he had been heavily drugged. He also knew he was in the South trying to catch a serial killer. The problem was the serial killer also knew this and had caught him. He was sure the FBI would have other agents working the case by now, but from what he had seen so far, this was no ordinary case.

He had been placed in a cage in a basement of what appeared to be an older brick building. One of the side walls was the original brick but the floor and the other walls were all cement. The cage was also set below the level of the floor so there was about three feet of cement before the steel bars began. He did have a toilet and a cot had been provided to make his stay more comfortable. On the back wall and side cement wall were rings positioned to cuff the prisoner if it became necessary. Simon hoped it would never become necessary.

Simon heard the door being unlocked and sat up on his cot.

"Agent Caldwell, I see you're finally awake," the killer said as he entered the room.

"Don't think for a moment I've forgotten what you've done to those poor souls you've tortured and murdered," Simon said.

"How could you have not forgotten when you haven't even witnessed," the killer replied. "I'm about to give you that opportunity."

"You saved my life. I don't understand how such a brilliant man allows himself to do such inhumane acts," Simon reasoned with the murderer.

"Shut up, I'm trying to work," the man replied, carefully polishing the mirrors and steel operating table.

"God has given you such marvelous gifts of the Spirit. You could do so much healing, save so many lives, change so many lives," Simon continued.

"I've changed plenty of lives," the man giggled. "And how do you know it's God who has given me these gifts? Perhaps they are 'deeds of the flesh' not 'gifts of the Spirit'."

"Because I know, beneath your callous façade your heart cries out for Christ," Simon replied. "I know you want to be saved."

"And I know it's you who are saying whatever you can in hopes of saving your own ass," the man laughed. "Don't worry, it is not yet your time to meet your God. At least six more heads must fall before I add yours to my collection."

"You are a very sick person," Simon began.

"No, I'm not!" he snapped right back.

Simon knew he had discovered a weakness.

"Oh yes you are. A very sick person who needs to see a psychiatrist," Simon continued, hoping to find a way to break the man down.

"I am not *shamnada hydakom* freak'n *glorybedaGoda alleluia* sick," the killer replied jerking violently.

Simon stared in disbelief. "You really are sick."

"Shut up, shut up," the man yelled holding his ears and continuing to jerk, "I do not need to *glorybedaGoda* see a doctor *shamnada*."

"You have Tourette's syndrome. I can get you help. We can make the pain go away," Simon said soothingly.

The man raised his outstretched hand towards Simon. His face twisted as though bewitched by Satan himself. As the killer began to slowly clench his fingers Simon's hands shot to his own throat trying to remove the invisible hand that seemed to be choking him.

The man lifted his arm and Simon rose off the ground in his cage.

"I told you I *glorybedaGoda* don't need no god damned doctor," the man said through gritted teeth, moving his arm sharply to the left slamming Simon against the brick wall of the cage. The killer straightened his arm dangling Simon for a moment a few feet above the floor. Simon continued to gasp for breath before the killer jerked once again and Simon dropped roughly onto the cage floor.

Simon lay motionless. The killer took several deep breaths to gain his composure then hurried up the stairs and out of the basement. He had left the door ajar and Simon could hear what sounded like preparations for a meal in a kitchen.

"Man, I thought Darth Vader was the only one who could do that and that was just in the movies," Simon said to himself, making sure no bones had been broken.

"It's going to take a lot more than a few FBI agents to solve this case. I remember my dad always talked about spiritual warfare but I never realized how serious he was when he said we must all take up the battle against evil. I guess there is a lot more to Christianity than just admitting your sins to Christ and saying you've been saved. Lord, you've opened my eyes and solidified my faith, so I am down on my knees and pray for you to bring forth your spiritual warriors and let the battle begin."

"Praying for salvation or for a quick death?" the killer said carrying a tray of food down the stairs.

Simon didn't answer, but slowly stood trying to decide if now would be his best chance at overtaking the killer. His hope was that he could grab the cuff of the killers pant leg and jerk the one leg between the cell bars and break the leg before the killer could use his mental Chi to overcome Simon. If all went as planned Simon could then beat the killer to death before he could either kill Simon or heal himself. Then with any luck someone would find Simon before he starved to death, although, he could always eat the killer if it came down to it.

"Please step back away from the bars," the killer warned, as he approached the slot designed to insert the food tray.

Simon shuffled back slowly. As the killer's gaze turned slightly away, Simon pounced grabbing the man's pant cuff and pulling.

"Fool," the man said, turning his foot slightly and bracing it on the outer edges of the steel bars. He raised his hand with fingers outstretched as before and immediately Simon's throat was constricted. "I should just kill *glorybedaGoda* you now," he yelled as his body once again began to jerk. He released Simon and removed the food tray from the ledge of the cage then hurried to a shelf on the wall where he removed a wooden box. Simon lay semi-conscious on the floor in the middle of the cage too weak to move.

"I thought you might enjoy a little company," the killer said as he tossed two rattlesnakes into the cage. Within seconds Simon had been bitten three times.

CHAPTER NINE

When the HC-130 finally landed at the Birmingham-Shuttlesworth International Airport there was no one from the local field office there to greet Kevin and Carlo.

"You think they'd at least sent a car to shuttle us to our apartments," Carlo complained.

"You forget, I'm here under cover, and you're to remain about as low key as possible while investigating this case. Remember Charlie?"

"Yes Mr. Jackson."

Just then a jeep pulled up next to the two agents with two MPs inside.

"Are you the two special guests the CO said would be staying with us a while?" the driver asked.

"I believe that would be us," Kevin replied. "I'm Kevin Jackson and this is Charlie Daniels."

"Charlie Daniels, no kidding, is your name really Charlie Daniels?"

"My whole life," Carlo replied. "Believe me; I hear it all the time."

Kevin could barely keep from laughing.

"They delivered your cars about an hour ago. One of you sure got the short end of the stick," the other MP said.

"What did your CO tell you about why we're here?" Kevin asked.

"All we know sir is that you are with a government agency here on an undercover operation and you are high priority targets of a drug cartel," the MP replied.

"That's just great," Kevin moaned. "how many people did your CO share this information with?"

"Just us sir. We are basically your body guards while you are on this base. Once you exit onto East Lake Street you are no longer our responsibility," the driver explained.

"Let's just make sure no one else learns our secret. Is that understood?" Kevin ordered.

"Understood perfectly sir," both sergeants replied.

"But sir, just so there is no misunderstanding," Sergeant McClellan began. From that information alone, it is obvious you are here working on the Apostle serial murder case and since you are high priority targets, you Agent Jackson must be Kevin Bridges and you must be Carlo Caressa, Agent Charlie Daniels."

Sergeant Boone laughed. "Who ever thought up that name for an alias didn't know much about the South."

"Was it that easy to figure out?" Kevin said.

"You two are still a big hit on YouTube and the papers had plenty to say about the hit the Vasquez Cartel has ordered on you. When the CO said an HC-130 from Pt. Magu was coming in with two VIPs for a little extra protection it didn't take much to put two and two together. If I could offer a suggestion, you might consider growing a beard or at least some sideburns."

"I think he's got a good point Charlie. Why don't you grow a beard and let your hair grow out? I'll get a crew-cut and grow some sideburns. It will go along with my car," Kevin said.

"Which car is yours?" the MPs asked, as they loaded the luggage into the jeep.

"I ordered the beat-up '80 Nova," Kevin replied.

"Then the sideburns will work but you should really consider a mullet," the MPs laughed.

"When did they start calling it the Apostle serial murders rather than the headless serial murders? I guess some hot-shot investigative journalist up in Montgomery found out about a fourth murder that the FBI had been keeping quiet. Some guy named Andrew was crucified on an X-shaped cross. Didn't take her long to figure out the killer's victims had the names of the Apostles. It's been all over the news today," the MP explained.

"Her?" Carlo said.

"That's going to make your job a little more interesting Charlie," Kevin said to Carlo. "This could lead to some mass hysteria if we get reporters turning into amateur investigators predicting the name of the next victim and even possibly where the next murder will take place."

"You've been on that plane too long," the MP said. "Every newspaper in the South is already warning every man with the first name of James and the last initial A to watch his back because he could be the Apostle killer's next victim."

"This has to be some kind of a joke," Carlo said as the jeep pulled up next to the base apartments.

"It was meant to be a joke," Kevin said, as Carlo jumped out of the jeep and opened the door on the black 89 Pontiac Trans Am, "but now I'm afraid it will be too much of an attention grabber."

"Not a chance," one of the MPs said. "A third generation Trans Am is a classy car here in the South, especially one with the 'Firebird' on the hood, but unless it was a 77, 78, or a 79 nobody down here would pay much attention,"

"Well it sure got my attention," Carlo replied.

"Don't get too cozy with it because it's only a loaner while we're working on this case. Any dents and the repairs come out of your paycheck," Kevin warned.

"I'll treat her with kid racing gloves," Carlo joked.

"That's what I was afraid of," Kevin moaned.

"So gentleman, here are your apartments during your stay with us in Birmingham. There is a door connecting the two apartments inside. My name is Sergeant McClellan and this is Sergeant Boone. We will be staying in the apartments right next door to you. The CO said you are welcome to help yourself to any of the base facilities which include the gym, dining hall, and lounges. Sergeant Boone or I will be happy to show you any of those in the morning. Is there anything else I can get you this evening?" the MP asked.

"How about a couple of big maps of Alabama," Kevin replied. "Like the ones you would get at a bookstore, maybe a Borders or a Barnes and Noble."

"There's a Barnes and Noble up at the Summit Shopping Center," Sergeant Boone replied.

"And a couple of cheeseburgers with fries and cokes or maybe something a little stronger," Kevin said. "I'll buy."

"I'll drive," Carlo offered, "if you boys show us the way."

"It'd be our honor," Sergeant McClellan replied.

"Perhaps a little tour of the city and its hot spots while we're at it," Kevin suggested.

"You couldn't have picked two better guides," Sergeant Boone replied. "Just allow us to change out of these uniforms."

CHAPTER TEN

"You're just jealous," the assistant editor said.

"Of course I'm jealous. Who wouldn't be? This is the kind of story that comes around once in a lifetime. The kind of story that lands you that network anchor job that we all dream of," the reporter replied. The two of them watched through the window as the editor of the Montgomery Beacon and star reporter Paige Eliot carried on a candid conversation.

"Well keep dreaming because she's got this story wrapped up tight," the A.E. replied. "And you're right; if she follows through she's got everything it takes to secure that network position, brains, beauty, and tenacity."

"You left out no morals, no ethics, and no feelings for her fellow man," the reporter added.

"Like I said, you're just jealous," the A.E. repeated.

"And you're as bad as she is if you fail to recognize what she did to that poor man and his family to get this story," the reporter insisted. "She seduced him to gain access to secret FBI files, which in itself should be a crime, and in the process ruined his marriage."

"If it was a crime she would have been arrested," the A.E. insisted.

"It's a crime what she did to that family," the reporter replied.

"I cannot defend her moral actions, but who is to say the relationship wasn't already on the rocks," the A.E. said.

"Whatever," the reporter huffed, "but you know how Paige is and if you really believe that, then I'm sorry to say, but I question your sense of ethics and morals as well."

At that moment the door to the editor's office opened and a smiling Paige strutted out.

"Hold down the fort for a while boys, I'll be out of town on assignment," she gloated.

The entire news room felt like cheering, for they had already grown tired of Paige's antics and were happy to see her go.

"Working on the Apostle Murder Case no doubt," the A.E. asked. "Where are you headed?"

"Now Honey, why would I want to go and tell my secrets in front of all these other reporters who'd like nothing more than to scoop Paige Eliot?" Paige purred, rubbing her hand through the A.E.'s hair causing him to blush.

Paige wasn't from the South but when needed, she could fake a decent southern accent. She was born and raised in Costa Mesa, California and had worked her way through the University of California at Berkeley School of Journalism, honing the skills that she had now perfected to attain whatever she wanted by whatever means necessary, regardless of the costs, as long someone else was paying.

"Going to be gone long, Paige?" One of the other reporters asked.

"As long as it takes to get the story," she replied.

"You planning on catching the Apostle Serial Killer yourself?" another one joked.

"If that's what it takes to get the story you're damn right I am," she replied.

"Paige," the editor yelled from his door, having heard her last comment, "don't do anything stupid, and everything, and I mean everything, is cleared through me before it's released, do you understand?"

"Of course I understand," she replied, with her most disarming smile.

"That goes for you too," the editor said to the assistant editor. "Anything she gives you, you clear through me first, no exceptions."

"No exceptions, boss," the A.E. replied.

"The boss says I'm to check in with you every two days to let you know how things are going," Paige said to the A.E. as she headed out the door. "I'll be in touch."

CHAPTER ELEVEN

Simon drifted in and out of consciousness for several minutes before finally opening his eyes. Through his blurriness he could make out the bars of his cage and could tell he was lying on the cot that was bolted to the floor. He tried to lift his left hand to wipe away the cloudiness of his eyes but his left arm refused to move. It was strapped tightly to his body and his body was strapped to the cot. He tried his right arm and his hand moved freely allowing him to wipe away some of the cobwebs of confusion the enveloped him.

"What the hell happened?" he said to himself.

Then he remembered the two rattlesnakes being tossed upon his limp body and the feeling of the fangs sinking into his skin. His right hand immediately went to his left shoulder where the first bite had occurred but he felt no pain there. Next he felt for his left hand which was also bitten. Here he felt the bandages.

"What's all this?" he said to himself.

"It's a lesson I hope you have learned," a voice said out of the darkness.

"What, am I supposed to thank you again for saving my life from the rattlesnake bites I received from the snakes you tossed on me?" Simon said sourly.

"No, I did that out of anger. I need to learn to control my anger. You could've hurt my snakes and that would've made me really angry," the killer said softly.

"So what happened to my hand?"

"Ah, your hand," the killer mused.

"You shouldn't have tried to pull my leg through the bars of the cage," the killer lectured. "If you continue such behavior I'll just kill you and find another Simon when the time comes. As it stands now, you still have a year to live. Perhaps I will be caught before it becomes time to kill you. Why take that chance? Have a little faith in your fellow agents."

"You didn't answer my question, what happened to my hand?" Simon repeated.

"I removed your thumb. That way you won't be grabbing for anything with your left hand anymore," the killer replied. "I hope it's a lesson learned."

"You're a sick human being," Simon said.

"I warned you, if you want to live, d-d-don't m-m-make *shamnada hydakom* me angry." His body started to jerk violently.

Simon lay quietly, thankful that he was strapped down and the cot was bolted to the floor as the killer took several deep breaths to calm himself down.

"I'm very disappointed in you Simon," the killer began. "I had hoped to share the beauty and perfection of the martyrdom of Apostle James the Lesser with you, but obviously you have proven you are not worthy of such an honor."

Tears began to well up in Simon's eyes. A psychotic killer was announcing his plans for his next ritualistic torture and beheading and there was absolutely nothing Simon could do about it.

"Aren't you curious as to what I do with the skulls?" the killer asked, as he unlocked a large safe standing against the far wall.

"Isn't it beautiful? This once belonged to James the Greater," the killer said holding a skull chalice in the air.

Simon could barely see the chalice as the killer twirled it in his hands before placing it back in the safe.

"Do you have a hobby Agent Caldwell?" he asked.

The killer pulled a large blank canvas from a stack of several neatly piled in the far corner of the room.

Simon didn't answer.

"Painting is my passion. I make a very fine living off of my paintings. I bet you didn't know that," the killer laughed. "I bet there's a lot you don't know about me. Maybe we can get better acquainted over the next twelve months. I'm a very interesting person once you get to know me. Try to get some rest and I hope the music doesn't keep you awake, but I do like to play it loud."

Simon continued to stare as the killer climbed the stairs. Moments later the walls vibrated to the Allman Brother's *Whipping Post*.

CHAPTER TWELVE

Paige had written several breaking stories in which she named the killer the Apostle Serial Killer and the media followed her lead. She had garnered considerable information about the killer from one of the Assistant Special Agents in Charge of the Atlanta Bureau who supplied her with copies of the files of the three previous victims which contained enumerable details not yet released, including the file of a fourth victim which the FBI was keeping under wraps. Her breaking story accusing the FBI of a cover-up had all of Washington a buzz and the FBI scrambling for damage control. Paige still had a few cards to play but knew the FBI would be all over her if she didn't disappear from Montgomery in a hurry. She knew about Simon being captured and she had heard another agent would be going undercover in his place but her source had no idea who it might be. He did know that a request had been made for two unmarked cars to be delivered to the Alabama Army National Guard at the Birmingham-Shuttlesworth International Airport for use by this agent. The FBI was fairly certain that the next victim of the Apostle Serial Killer would turn up in Birmingham. Paige wasn't quite sure how they had arrived at this conclusion but she was determined to find out before the prediction became fact. The FBI also predicted it would occur within the next few days leaving little doubt that Birmingham was her new residence.

In her line of business it was wise to have an alternate set of identification paper's and even though the Montgomery Beacon wasn't willing to recognize the production of such as a legitimate expense account item, Paige was able, for a considerable sum, to have a counterfeit set produced. Counterfeit only because they contained a fake name, social security number, and address. Real in every other aspect.

    Before she left town she rented a car using her fake credit card and arranged for a month's lease on a furnished apartment in Birmingham under the name of Jessica Stowe. She wasn't sure how long she would be gone, but hoped it wouldn't take an entire month for the FBI to solve this case. She had bigger plans and spent the hour and a half drive to Birmingham dreaming of that network anchor spot.

    When Paige arrived, she spent the afternoon having her hair colored and the style changed feeling certain it would be enough of a disguise to avoid the FBI. She couldn't possibly be that high of a priority on their list.

    After the hairdresser she took a drive along East Lake Boulevard to see if she could get on to the National Guard Base or at least get a look at the black Trans Am the undercover agent would be driving. As hard as she tried she just couldn't come up with a good enough story to convince the guard to let her pass and she could tell when she had reached the point where if she didn't back off it would become an issue.

    "Well maybe next time, it will be you and me who hook up down at Banana Joe's and I promise not to lose your number." Jessica smiled her, see what you could of had smile, and made the U-turn around the guard booth and back onto East Lake Boulevard.

"Damn, now what?" she said to herself. It was beginning to get dark. "It's a big city to cruise around looking for an 89 Trans Am."

She took a hard left and headed around the west side of the base thinking she might get a glimpse of the housing area. There wasn't much traffic so she could go fairly slowly but she still missed the overpass that gave her a view into the base until she was past it.

When she finally found a place to turn around and head back there was no place for her to pull over to stop to have a look without leaving her car in traffic, so again she had to drive on by. This time there was a road not more than a hundred yards up ahead. She made a U-turn at Burgin Road and pulled into the grass off the road just past the overpass that concealed the tunnel that connected the two parts of the base. The sign said no parking but Jessica wasn't about to let a sign stop her, especially with so few cars on the road.

She hurried across the street, jumped the railing, climbed through the overgrown weeds down to the fence, and as if it had been planned all along, there in front of the base apartments sat a black Pontiac Trans Am and a Chevy Nova.

A broad smile appeared on Jessica's face which was immediately replaced by a frown when she heard the whoop of a police siren.

"Damn," Jessica yelped, as she quickly headed back towards her car.

"Having a problem?" the officer called, shining his light in her eyes from across the road.

"I wasn't until you blinded me with that light," she replied, waiting for a car to pass before re-crossing the road.

"You know there is no parking anytime here, "the officer said sternly. "May I please see your license?"

"I know," she replied, turning on her charm, "I was hoping I could do it just for a moment when it wasn't busy so I could try to find the hubcaps to my car."

The officer looked down at her car. "It looks to me like you have all your hubcaps."

"This is a rental car," she replied, knowing the cop probably already knew that. "Last week some guy in a pick-up side-swiped me and my hubcaps went flying off into the weeds over there. I was hoping to find them to save some money."

"Shouldn't his insurance pay for that?" the officer asked.

"He never stopped."

"What about your insurance?" the officer asked.

"I've reported enough to my insurance and have a rather high deductible. I have a friend fixing my car."

"You know by law you're required to report all accidents," the officer lectured.

"Yes sir, I'm sorry sir," Jessica replied coquettishly.

"There's a place just off the Stephen's Expressway on University, actually it's on Twenty-third, but you take University. It's called Hubcap Heaven. Ask for Mike, and tell him Officer Hansen sent you."

"Thank you, Officer Hansen, I'll be sure to do that," Jessica replied. As always Jessica was working the officer like she had worked so many other men in her past. It was her gift, but as she continued her innuendo of flirtation her concentration was shattered as a black 89 Pontiac Trans Am with a red Firebird emblazoned on the hood, roared by with four men inside, causing her to completely lose her composure and distracting her from her problem at hand.

"And Ms. Stowe, Ms. Stowe," Officer Hansen repeated.

"Oh, I'm so sorry, that car startled me," she replied, falling back into her poor vulnerable me façade.

"As I was saying, no more parking in restricted zones. Is that understood?" He said as he returned her license.

"Perfectly understood," Jessica replied, climbing back into her car and signaling before pulling away.

"Damn, damn, damn," she cursed, trying not to speed, knowing Officer Hansen was right behind her, "I'm going to lose them. They have to be headed for the freeway."

But as luck would have it, and with a police car driving right behind you, you don't run yellow lights, so the Trans Am was gone.

"Now what?" Jessica said as she pulled onto Interstate 20 headed for downtown Birmingham. "Four guys in a car are either headed for dinner or headed out drinking, or both," she concluded.

She knew enough about Birmingham to know that the Southside had more than its share of good bars and eateries. It was the most logical choice so she would spend her time searching there. She had to start somewhere.

Just about the time Jessica reached the Southside, Carlo had reached the Summit Shopping Center.

"There's your Barnes and Noble," Sergeant Boone said pointing out towards the left.

"Great," Kevin replied, "this shouldn't take me but a few minutes. Any suggestions on where to eat?"

"Personally sir, I hate to mix dinner with my liquor. If it's a cheeseburger and fries you want, Johnny Rockets is fast and easy. After that we can show you the real hotspots of Birmingham and do some serious drinking, which believe me cannot be found at the Summit Shopping Center," Sergeant McClellan explained.

"I think that's an excellent idea," Carlo said.

"And I agree," Kevin concurred. "I'll meet you at Johnny Rockets. Charlie you know what to order for me."

"Would'ja look at this," Sergeant Boone said picking up a flyer lying on top of a stack by the entrance.

"What's it say?" Charlie asked.

"Says 'Show 'em you're not afraid. Free drinks all night long at Banana Joe's if your name fits the Apostle Serial Killer's next victim. Must have proper ID to prove your first name is James and your middle or last initial is A. Must be twenty-one or older to participate.' Sounds like the place you guys need to be," Sergeant Boone said.

"I doubt if our killer will show up there," Charlie laughed.

"I wouldn't count it out," Kevin replied. "I'd be curious to know how many of the local James A's show up."

"So you think Birmingham is the sight of the next killing?" Sergeant McClellan asked.

"Do you think it is?" Kevin replied.

"I have no idea, sir. I'm just going by what that newspaper lady Paige Eliot said," the sergeant replied.

"She said it was Birmingham?" Kevin asked surprised.

"No, but it was one of the four cities she had narrowed it down to and said the exact city would be in Sunday morning's paper."

"This lady not only knows how to use people but actually might be smart," Kevin admitted. "Birmingham is where the next body will be found, probably within two or three days, but let's keep that between the four of us. Is that understood?"

"Yes, sir," both sergeants answered simultaneously.

"She's probably already here in Birmingham looking for the Apostle killer," Charlie said to Kevin.

"I've no doubt she's in Birmingham, but my guess is she's looking for the new FBI undercover agents not the serial killer," Kevin replied.

"That's impossible, nobody knows we're here," Charlie replied.

"Too many people know we're here or at least know you're here," Kevin replied. "Everyone associated with the case knows the agency had to send someone down to replace Simon. That's why when they asked me to come work undercover I knew it wouldn't work unless a second agent came along, one that wouldn't be too undercover."

"So I'm just your cover? That's why you got me the Trans Am," Charlie said a bit perturbed.

"No, you are my lifeline, but yes, the Trans Am was to make you stand out just a little and keep the focus off of me," Kevin replied. "My life is in your hands, Buddy."

"Safely in my hands," Carlo assured him.

"Hopefully, nobody but you and our two friends here know anything about me. That's the only way anyone was going to be able to work this case. I'm depending on you to keep me informed and to check out information I come across. We know there are too many leaks in the organization. I don't want to end up like Simon and I'm depending on you to make sure that doesn't happen," Kevin explained.

"So what's the next step?" Charlie asked as the cheeseburgers arrived.

"Could you boys excuse us for a moment? Kevin said to the two sergeants.

"Not a problem, sir," they both replied, stepping away from the table.

"I need to get back to the apartment and prepare for a little trip. I'm leaving early for Sand Mountain," Kevin began. "I need to have a look around there and then I'm heading down to New Orleans to have a talk with the Voodoo store owner."

"I thought you wanted me to talk to him," Carlo replied.

"I do, but after I have a look around," Kevin replied. "I need you to be here when the next body appears."

"And you expect that to happen soon?" Carlo replied.

"Very soon. It's probably already too late, but I still want you to check on all the James A's in the Birmingham area like we talked about on the plane. And a good place to start would be at Banana Joe's tonight. Who knows? Our killer may even show up there and it's a pretty sure bet that the reporter will be there. See what you can find out about her, but be careful. She's a smart one and my guess is she will be there trying to do the same thing with you," Kevin warned.

"I know when I'm being worked," Carlo replied.

"You'll be fine just as long as you remember she is there to work you for information. Use that to your advantage. Let her think she's hooked you, but be forewarned, this lady knows what she is doing. She has already taken down a senior supervising agent and who knows how many others. She's ruined families and careers with no remorse and you would be nothing more than another notch on that gun handle."

"Kevin, you've got nothing to worry about. I know how to handle this reporter lady," Carlo replied, as he went to tell the two sergeants to come join them again.

"That's exactly what I was afraid of," Kevin said, as he watched Carlo walk away.

CHAPTER THIRTEEN

Just like with Kevin and Carlo, it didn't take Paige long to discover the special Banana Joe's was running that evening for anyone with the name of the Apostle serial killer's next victim.

"Boy is this place going to take some serious grief from the local citizenry when the next victim shows up on the streets of Birmingham after this little publicity stunt," Paige mused as she read the advertising flyer.

She had been cruising the streets and parking lots of downtown and the Southside of Birmingham for almost two hours searching for the Trans Am with no luck. She considered going back to the airport and trying to see if she could get another glimpse of the National Guard apartment building, but decided that would be too risky. After another twenty minutes of searching Paige decided to let the agents come to her. It was still early and after driving by Banana Joe's several times and seeing the clientele it seemed to cater to, she wasn't about to hang out all night waiting there. She had driven past a restaurant only a couple of blocks away from Banana Joe's called the Highlands Bar and Grill that offered a good view of traffic coming and going from several of the clubs and restaurants in the area. It also gave a perfect view of one of the busiest intersections in the Southside, where Magnolia, 11th Avenue, and 20th Street all came together. It was a good place for dinner and a good place to await her prey.

After burgers Kevin had Charlie and the sergeants run him back to the apartments so he could prepare for his trip early the next morning. He had purchased several different maps of Alabama, one world map, and a large world atlas which he wanted to study before his early departure. He didn't like the idea of leaving Carlo to fend for himself against what he knew would be hostile agents at the Birmingham office. No one appreciated the federal office sending in someone else to work a case in their jurisdiction because they were unable to make any progress in solving it and being blamed for outing an undercover agent made it about a thousand times worse.

Kevin had told Carlo to inform them that the next victim was going to show up in Birmingham, but knowing that the newspaper would be announcing that fact he would look pretty silly doing so. So now he was to confirm what she says in the article and fill in the details about where they can expect to find the body and the kind of shape it will be in unless she has figured that out as well.

Kevin had purchased a box of colored push pins along with his maps. He hoped the Alabama National Guard wouldn't mind a few holes in the apartment walls. He tacked up the world map and next to it he selected and tacked up one of the Alabama regional maps.

He pulled out four white push pins and placed two on Birmingham and on the world map placed the other two on Jerusalem.

"Okay, now we have our home base," Kevin said out loud.

Kevin had a habit of talking through his problems out loud to himself. It helped him focus but sometimes led to some rather embarrassing situations as his sanity was more than once called into question. If he wasn't so successful at his job it might have become even more of an issue.

"Okay these will be numbers one and five," he said as he wrote the tiny numbers on the heads of both sets of white pins. "Damn, I wish there was some way I could stop five but that would take a miracle at this point."

He grabbed two red pins from the bag. "You guys will be number two. You go here," he said sticking one pin in the vicinity of Hierapolis, Turkey, "and you go here." He stuck the second red pin in the Alabama map near Muscle Shoals where the second body was discovered.

Next came two green pins, one placed near Edessa, Greece and the other at a place called Gobbler's Knob near Corinth, Mississippi where the third body was found in the woods on an X-shaped cross.

The fourth victim, Matthew Davis, was found speared and headless on the beach near Pensacola, Florida. Kevin pushed the blue pin into the map in the general area. On the world map he stuck the corresponding blue pin in the upper left region of Ethiopia. "I'll have to work on that one later," he said, not liking the proportions of the blue pins compared to the others he had placed.

It was victim number six that Kevin hoped to save. According to the Apostle Killer's time table Kevin had about two months before Peter would be beheaded and crucified upside down.

"You will be number six," he said pulling two more red pushpins from the bag and writing tiny number sixes on their heads.

The first one was easy to place. Peter was crucified in Rome, so Kevin placed the first pin in the center of the dot representing Rome on his world map.

"Now the tough part," Kevin began. "This would have been a whole lot easier if these maps were the same scale, or if I had remembered to have bought a ruler."

Using the legend on the maps Kevin was able to make a ruler and in just a couple of minutes had figured out where the other red pushpin should be placed and stuck it into the other map.

"Why there?" Kevin asked. "It's in the middle of nowhere. Peter was one of the most important apostles and was crucified in what was considered the center of the world, the place where Christianity flourished. It doesn't make sense that such an important apostle would be left in such a remote place. I've got to think about this."

Kevin stared at the map for another moment and then headed for the bathroom.

"Now for the tough part," he said, staring at his neat California styled coiffure and his Hollywood three-day-stubble.

Kevin had borrowed a pair of scissors from one of the sergeants before they had left and he began cutting away at his wavy hair. When most of the length was gone he pulled out his beard trimmer and continued to attack his hair until its length nearly matched that of his facial stubble. He then pulled out his razor and carefully trimmed away the stubble leaving long straight side-burns like the ones Elvis wore.

Before he left Pt. Magu he had stopped by a thrift store and picked up two older white long-sleeved shirts, a pair of khaki pants and a pair of worn dress shoes, along with a beat-up bag to carry everything in. He hoped when he reached Sand Mountain he would fit right in. In a few hours he would know.

"So this is the place to go if you're looking to party in Birmingham?" Charlie asked the two sergeants.
"Yeah, but you don't ever go there alone," Sergeant McClellan replied.
"Or unarmed," Sergeant Boone added.
"Are you kidding me?" Charlie replied.
"No sir. This used to be a great place to drink and meet women. I guess it still is, but lately it has gotten a bad reputation for attracting trouble. Don't get me wrong, it's still a fun place and a lot of women still come here, but all over the Southside there seems to be more trouble happening these days," Sergeant Boone explained.

Just as she had hoped, the black Trans Am with the red firebird on the hood rumbled down Magnolia and turned up 20th Street South towards Banana Joe's in perfect view of the Highlands Bar and Grill. Her only concern was this time there only appeared to be three men in the car.
"Perhaps I was mistaken the first time," she said to herself. "No, I'm sure there were four men in the car the first time I saw it. Different car? Not likely. No, that's got to be them, whoever them is. Okay, it's show time," Paige said, with a smile. "Waiter, could I get my check, please."

"Here's your first real test Charlie. They check everyone's ID before you get in here," Sergeant Boone laughed.

"Great," Charlie said, as he fished out his fake Alabama driver's license.

The bouncer at the door looked at the license and up at Charlie's face making sure the picture matched and started to hand it back to him when the name on the license registered. "Charlie Daniels! You ain't Charlie Daniels," the doorman said causing everyone within ten feet to turn and stare.

"I shaved my beard." Charlie replied, snatching the license out of the doorman's hand. "Makes me look younger. Boys see if you can find me a table."

"Yes sir, Mr. Daniels," both the sergeants replied, playing along with Charlie's game and acting the part of his body guards clearing a path through the crowded club. They were definitely built for the part and the doorman was so stunned he had two of his security personnel make sure a prime table was made immediately available and drinks were provided on the house.

"So what was it you were saying about my alias?" Charlie teased Sergeant McClellan.

"I don't know how long you can pull this off, sir, but it'll sure be fun while it lasts," he replied as several curious onlookers, mostly very attractive curious onlookers, began drifting closer to their table.

Paige had also changed into her alter ego, Jessica Stowe, and had entered Banana Joe's just as those women intoxicated by their desire to be close to the rich and famous or those who appear to be rich and famous began to make their move on Charlie.

"Please, Mr. Daniels is here to enjoy the music," Sergeant Boone said, herding a group of women away from the table, "perhaps, when the band takes a break."

The club security got the hint and kept people from bothering Charlie.

"What'ja do that for? There were some good looking women in that group," Charlie said to Sergeant Boone.

"Trust me, it will only make us more desirable later," he said with a wink. "Besides, it gives you a chance to look around without being bothered for a few minutes."

"Good thinking, thanks," Charlie replied.

"Who are the three men over there getting the star treatment?" Jessica asked the bartender.

"Somebody said it's Charlie Daniels and two of his bodyguards, but the guy looks too young to be Charlie Daniels to me," the bartender replied.

"That's not Charlie Daniels," Jessica replied. "But the guy does look familiar."

"And those two guys with him are built like bodyguards," the bartender replied. "What would you like?"

"Whatever light beer you have on tap will be fine," Jessica replied. "How many James A's did you get in here tonight?"

"I heard only three, those two sitting down at the end of the bar and the guy sitting at the table up by the dance floor with the two girls." He pointed for Jessica to see. "I can't imagine there are that many in Birmingham in the first place. That'll be four bucks," he said sitting the beer on the bar in front of her.

Jessica pulled out a five, "Keep the change," she said, as she picked up her beer and headed into the crowd.

She began systematically circling the club looking for groups of three or four men who most likely would be the FBI agent or agents she was looking for. After two passes around the room and deflecting several passes directed at her, the task was proving more difficult than she expected. She returned to her starting position at the bar to rethink her approach.

"Another beer?" the bartender offered.

"Still sipping on this one. How's Charlie Daniels doing?" she said, watching the women hovering like flies attracted to a flame.

"I swear that ain't Charlie Daniels," the bartender replied.

Jessica quickly swung around as if stung by a bee, "No, that ain't Charlie Daniel's, but I think I know who it is," she whispered to herself.

Just as she thought, the two supposed body guards both had military haircuts. "They're just showing him the town. He's here because of the flyer just like I am."

Jessica sat her beer on the bar and headed straight for the group surrounding Charlie and the two alleged bodyguards only to be stopped by club security like all the other women.

"Charlie, Charlie," she called, "You want to meet the James A's or you going to sit on your butt all night. Or maybe you'd like to dance?"

She did know how to get a man's attention.

Charlie turned to see who had called him knowing it had to be the reporter just as Kevin had warned him.

"I think I'd like that dance," Charlie replied, excusing himself from the two sergeants and disappointing at least a half dozen other women still gathered around.

"Who thought up the lame Charlie Daniels alias?" Jessica asked.

"My momma named me Charlie," Charlie replied. "I guess I shouldn't take advantage of it like I do when I go to bars like this, but it sure is a good way to meet ladies."

"Cut the southern hick crap," Jessica exclaimed. "Do you want to know who the three James A's are or not? I'm here working just like you are Mr. FBI."

"Okay who are they? " Charlie conceded.

"See the two guys sitting at the end of the bar," Jessica said.

"Yeah," Charlie replied.

"And the guy acting all nervous with the two women sitting at the table by the dance floor."

"Let's go dance. The two at the bar are not the next victim," Charlie replied.

"How do you know?" Jessica asked.

"They're too big. James A will be a small man. At least smaller than James Z. and he wasn't that big," Charlie explained.

"I hadn't thought of that," Jessica replied.

Charlie grinned, "I guess you can't think of everything."

The two made their way to the dance floor just as the band finished *Can't You See* by the Marshall Tucker Band which had the crowd going crazy.

"We're gonna slow it down for ya'll with a little song by Little Feat entitled *Dixie Chicken*," the front man announced

"Man, I haven't heard that one in years," Charlie said.

"Then you haven't been in the South," Jessica replied, pulling Charlie close as the singer began to croon.

"I don't think that's our James A either," Charlie said staring into Jessica's eyes.

"I really don't think it matters," she replied, pulling his lips to hers.

For the rest of the evening nothing really seemed to matter to Charlie either.

CHAPTER FOURTEEN

"Damn," Kevin said the second his eyes opened. He knew something wasn't right and he had a good idea what it was.

The door between his and Carlo's apartments was still open. Carlo had not returned from his night on the town.

Kevin double-checked the clock, "Yep, 5:00 a.m., just as I thought."

He opened the door and looked out front. "No Trans Am. That's not a good sign."

He walked over to Sergeant Boone's apartment and pounded on the door.

"Hold on, hold on, I'm coming," came a response from inside.

The door open and a groggy Sergeant Boone stood half-naked in the doorway. "I bet you're wantin' to know what happened to Charlie Daniels?"

"I am a bit concerned," Kevin replied.

"Charlie knows how to party, that's for damn sure. He had half of Birmingham believing he was the real Charlie Daniels and that he'd just shaved his beard. We got the star treatment all night long and talk about women, whooeee!" Sergeant Boone began to rant.

"Sergeant," Kevin said brusquely, "where's Charlie?"

"Charlie told us he hooked up with that newspaper reporter and was going to see what information he could get out of her," Boone replied. "But to tell you the truth, sir, I don't think it was information Charlie was planning on getting from her tonight if you know what I mean."

"How'd you and Sergeant McClellan get back here?" Kevin asked.

"Sir, I don't think Sergeant McClellan has made it home yet either. Charlie attracted women like cow dung attracts flies. There were more than enough women to go around," Boone replied. "I was just dropped off at the front gate about an hour ago."

"Well I'm glad you all had an entertaining evening," Kevin replied. "I had hoped to speak to Charlie before I left but let him know I'll give him a call later tonight or tomorrow."

"Yes, sir," Boone replied. "Is there anything else, sir, because I can barely stand up right now?"

"No, sergeant, get some sleep and thanks for all your help."

"My pleasure, Mr. Jackson."

"There is one more thing," Kevin said. "Keep a close eye on Charlie. Try not to let him get into any trouble."

"Will do, sir," Boone replied," as he shut his door and staggered back to bed.

As Kevin stood looking out towards Birmingham the darkness seemed to hang heavy that morning as though awaiting the impending depravation about to befall upon the city. Even Kevin thought he could sense evil lurking in the gloom.

A shiver ran through Kevin's body.

"I need some coffee," he said, glancing at his watch, "and I need to get on the road."

As the coffee was brewing he shaved one more time to try to define his new sideburns as much as possible.

Kevin pulled out some of the clothes he'd picked up at the thrift store in Pt. Magu and dressed as he believed the adherents to the Pentecostal Holiness Church were known to dress. He wore a long sleeve white shirt and the khaki slacks but decided to pack his levis in case this church accepted the wearing of them. He put on the older dress shoes but took his running shoes as well. He didn't wear a ring, so that wasn't a problem but did remove his watch and place it in the bag for now.

He placed his shaving kit in the bag along with his extra clothes. His gun and two extra clips he wrapped in a towel. These he would have to hide somewhere in the car. His cell phone created somewhat of a quandary for him. It was a convenience that would be nice to have, especially considering the situation Charlie had seemed to have gotten himself into, but even turned off the FBI had the ability to track his movements and with a traitor in the organization, that wasn't a very pleasant thought.

"No, the cell phone stays here," Kevin decided. "Chances are I'll have poor or no reception up in the mountains anyway."

The coffee was ready and Kevin sat down to have one last look at his maps and files before he headed out.

"If I leave these here, chances are pretty good the newspaper lady will see them within a couple days," Kevin began debating with himself.

"Then again, she has already seen copies of these files so it really doesn't matter."

"But she hasn't seen my maps," Kevin thought as he pondered the gravity of her discovering the maps.

"But she's already figured out the name of the next victim and that he would be dumped here in Birmingham, which would lead me to believe she's smart enough to know that Peter is the next Apostle Serial Killer's victim and how he will die."

Kevin smiled broadly. "But is she smart enough to figure out where and when the next victim will be discovered?"

Kevin picked up the red push pin with the number six written on it and stuck it in Tyronza, Arkansas, proportionally and directionally correct in comparison to the previous Apostle Serial Killer murders.

The last thing Kevin did before he left was MapQuest the directions to Sand Mountain.

"An hour and fifty minutes to get there. That will put me there around seven-thirty assuming I don't get lost and can even find the place," Kevin said.

He jotted down the directions and then carefully wrapped his laptop in a towel and walked back over to Sergeant Boone's, where for the second time in the last half an hour he pounded on the door.

"Now what?" Boone growled from inside as he opened the door.

"Sorry to bother you again, but I need you to hold on to this for me until I get back next week?" Kevin asked.

"What, you don't trust Charlie?"

"I'd trust Charlie with my life," Kevin snapped back. "It's that I don't trust Charlie's new friend who I have no doubt will be dropping by for a few visits."

"Just lock the door between the rooms. That will keep her out," Boone suggested.

"Maybe I want her to come in and look around," Kevin replied.

"You FBI guys are smarter than I thought," Boone replied. "Don't worry, I'll take care of it and say nothing to Charlie."

"I'd appreciate it and sorry I woke you again," Kevin said.

"No problem, sir and have a safe trip wherever that may be."

"I'll do that," Kevin answered, as he threw his bag into the Chevy Nova and headed for Sand Mountain.

About twenty minutes away in another part of Birmingham another man carefully placed the case of his 1963 Fender Telecaster behind the seat of his pick-up truck. And on the floorboard on the passenger side he placed a wooden box with three timber rattle snakes. He too was on his way to Sand Mountain.

Kevin's trip went smoothly until he exited the I-59. Expecting to find the Alabama-35 he found Glenn Boulevard and Lowell Barron Highway. When he finally did turn he was facing a sign that had Alabama State-35 road designations going both directions and he wasn't sure which direction he was to go.

"I've got to work on my handwriting," Kevin bemoaned.

He finally made it back to where he exited I-59 and pulled to the side of the road to decipher his scribbles. As he sat there a white pick-up shot past that seemed to know where it was going but there was only a single driver. Soon two other cars drove past that looked to be carrying 'church-going' people. At least that's how they looked to Kevin. He quickly pulled behind the second car and followed along.

"Alabama-35 North, hot dog, I'm on the right road," Kevin yelped as his scribbles finally matched his actual course. When the cars in front turned left onto Main Street South he knew he was almost there.

Several more cars had fallen in behind Kevin and when they reached an old church building just off of CR-43, Kevin was surprised at the number of cars already there, including the white pick-up that had passed him earlier.

"Welcome to the Holiness Church with Signs Following brother," a pretty woman greeted him as he entered the long meeting hall type building.

"I'm new here," Kevin began to explain.

"Yes I know, "she interrupted. "This is the first or second time here for many of these people. Just like you they are here because they can feel the darkness coming. Evil is upon us and God has called us to be his spiritual warriors."

"Welcome brother," she had turned to welcome another worshipper.

Kevin shuffled away from the doorway awestruck by the gravity of the situation. He had felt it that morning in Birmingham. Charlotte had warned him about it back in Los Angeles. The Apostle Serial Killer was no random psycho. He was a powerful disciple of Satan with demonic powers bent on spreading evil throughout the South.

Suddenly, Kevin's thoughts were shattered by the driving hypnotic beat of a rhythm guitar. Within seconds the band picked it up and the entire church was standing and rocking to what Kevin had to admit was one of the best bands he had heard in years.

"These guys are terrific," he said to the pretty girl who greeted him, but she was lost in a trance, as were most of the worshippers gathered.

The room was electric. Kevin had never experienced such a feeling of 'Living in the Spirit'. He had been to many Pentecostal services where the momentum would build and eventually people would be speaking tongues, some would be laying hands on others to heal, and some would be 'slain in the Spirit' where they would pass out, but nothing like this. This was instantaneous.

Immediately people were praying, shouting, and singing in tongues. People were jumping, rolling, and dancing seemingly uncontrollably.

Kevin caught two people who were 'slain in the Spirit' before they hit the floor and through it all the band continued to amaze. It was impossible to be a passive observer and Kevin was filled with the Holy Spirit. Kevin had been bouncing around dancing for almost forty-five minutes when he decided he had to take a break outside and cool off.

"Wow, I can't believe what I just experienced," Kevin said to himself as he went to sit on the hood of his car.

"The Holy Spirit can do some pretty amazing things," a voice answered startling Kevin. "Sorry I didn't mean to scare you. I thought you were talking to me."

"No, I have this bad habit of talking to myself. I guess I did look a bit startled. Hi, my name's Kevin Jackson."

"I'm Virginia Lee Turner, but folks round here call me Ginny Lee."

"Well it's a pleasure to meet you Ginny Lee," Kevin replied.

"So you're new to these parts. Don't ever recall seeing you before."

"What gave it away, the Canadian license plates?" Kevin joked.

"No, I hadn't even noticed the plates. It's just that I would have remembered if I had seen you before," she said a bit flirtatiously.

"You been going to this church long?" Kevin asked, trying not to blush.

"My whole life. My daddy founded the church more than thirty-five years ago," Ginny Lee said.

"Your daddy still the preacher?" Kevin asked.

"No, Daddy died going on ten years now. He's buried out back behind the church. These days most of the elders share the preaching duties."

"Who takes care of the church?" Kevin asked.

"I do what I can off the little bit of offering the folks round here can afford to give, which isn't a whole lot. Daddy first built our house up on the hill there where he used to hold services. As the congregation grew he built the meeting hall down here on the flat part of our property. I think he planned it that way all along so nobody could ever take his church from him," Ginny Lee explained.

"Why would anyone want to take away his church?" Kevin asked.

"A lot of people still don't care much for the way we worship the Lord," Ginny Lee replied. "I'm sure you understand or you wouldn't be here."

The band had stopped playing for a moment and the front door was shut.

"I think we should head back inside," Ginny Lee said. "We have to use the back door now."

"That worship band is one of the best bands I've ever heard." Kevin said. "The guitar player is amazing."

"His name is Casper. I know of no other who has received the gifts of the Spirit more than Casper. He has the power to do God's miracles," Ginny Lee replied less than enthusiastically.

As if on cue, the band suddenly kicked into another blues dominated gospel rock song that would have made the Rolling Stones jealous.

As they entered the building the presence of the Holy Spirit was overwhelming. It was no wonder so many people came here. It made you feel so alive and forced you to move your body to the rhythm of the music.

Kevin saw immediately why they had to use the back door. The open area where he had danced earlier still held dancers but now the dancers held a variety of poisonous snakes in their hands.

"Come join in if the Spirit moves you," Ginny Lee offered as she headed to the front of the hall.

Kevin stared in fascination as young and old alike passed and tossed rattlesnakes, water moccasins, and copperheads back and forth and across the room. And through it all the faithful continued their prayers, their speaking, praying, and singing in tongues, their laying of hands, their shouting, their fainting, and their uncontrolled exuberance for the Lord and the Holy Spirit.

It was an intoxicating experience that grabbed Kevin's spiritual essence and refused to let go. When it ended he felt as if it had just begun.

"How are you feeling, Kevin?" Ginny Lee asked, as she walked over to where Kevin was sitting.

"I feel absolutely incredible," Kevin replied, "Although the service seemed to end rather quickly."

Ginny Lee laughed.

"What's so funny?" Kevin said.

"You were 'slain in the Spirit' during the service," Ginny Lee said. "You were out for over an hour. I kept checking on you to make sure you were still breathing."

"I passed out?" Kevin said.

"No, the Holy Spirit took over your body. That's why you feel so incredible. You probably have some gifts of the Spirit you didn't have before," Ginny Lee explained. "You do know about the 'gifts of the Spirit'?"

"I do," Kevin replied, still feeling rather foolish for having passed out regardless of the reason.

"You know we also have a Wednesday night service here at the meeting hall and some of the members hold services in their homes on other nights if you're interested," Ginny Lee said.

"I'll be sure to be here next Wednesday," Kevin replied, "but I don't know about any other nights. I'm still looking for work."

"Well, if you haven't found a job by Wednesday, why don't you come up early. I could use some help around here. I can't pay you a lot, but I can offer you lunch and dinner," Ginny Lee offered.

"I'll do that even if I do find a job," Kevin assured her.

"I'll look forward to Wednesday," Ginny Lee replied, with a cheerful smile

"As will I," Kevin replied.

"Ginny Lee," a voice boomed with impatience.

Ginny Lee's smile quickly disappeared. "What is it now Chester?"

Chester Cunningham came into the meeting hall glaring at Kevin. "I've been waitin' almost twenty minutes for you to come along outside, Ginny Lee. Did you forget that the Sunderlands invited us over for lunch?"

"Chester, I'd like you to meet Kevin Jackson. Today was his first time at the church and no, I didn't forget."

"How do, Mr. Jackson?" Chester said out of obligation.

"Kevin, Chester is our local doctor. He's got an office just down the road in Boaz and one in Birmingham. He's also a guitar player in the worship band."

"Pleasure to meet you Chester," Kevin said, his interest piqued for a number of reasons.

"Chester, I'll be right out," Ginny Lee said prodding Chester reluctantly towards the door. "Did you remember to get your snakes?"

"Yes, Ginny Lee, I got my snakes," Chester replied.

"I better be on my way," Kevin said. "I didn't mean to keep you."

"I'm afraid I was using you as an excuse to try to avoid going with Chester. It seems everyone in the church thinks Chester and I would make a good couple. That is everybody but me. I've prayed about it, but the Holy Spirit has so far guided me away from Chester. I don't know why but I know to trust in the Holy Spirit," Ginny Lee explained.

"Sounds like Chester agrees with the rest of the church," Kevin remarked.

"Chester thinks we're already a couple no matter how often I put him off. I don't know where he comes up with his crazy ideas," Ginny Lee remarked

"Crazy ideas?" Kevin said.

"Chester's a good man but a little odd and a might possessive and a bit old for me," Ginny explained. "Then again, lots of hill folk around here are a little odd."

"Well certainly none that I've met," Kevin said, smiling at Ginny Lee. He wanted to ask her more about Chester but thought it better to wait until Wednesday. "You'd better get going. I don't want Chester getting jealous."

"It's way too late for that," Ginny laughed. "See you Wednesday."

Kevin watched as Ginny Lee hesitantly scurried out the door to keep the date she wished she hadn't made with Chester.

Still beaming with the Holy Spirit Kevin helped stack the chairs away and decided to look around the outside of the church for things that needed to be done on Wednesday when he returned.

"Those face boards need to be painted and they could sure use some guttering," Kevin said to no one.

"Oh, but first something's got to be done about the graveyard. The fence in falling down, weeds are taking over, and the gravestones are starting to lean," he complained.

He tried to open the gate and it came off in his hand. "This gate needs a little work too."

He walked in and looked at several of the grave markers.

"Pastor Franklin Lee Turner, that must be Ginny Lee's father. I wonder if her mom is alive?" He looked near the pastor's grave but found no other Turners. "Maybe she is alive," Kevin guessed.

He looked at a few more graves reading the names and imagining what the people were like. The one's that died young always bothered him the most.

"I only hope they had time to come to the Lord," Kevin said, and he began to cry.

CHAPTER FIFTEEN

Charlie awoke with a hangover like none he could remember. His head throbbed and his eyes ached too much to open them. He slowly moved his hands away from his body and felt nothing but sheet.

"At least I'm in bed alone," he thought. "I think that's a good thing."

"Drink this," a voice said from above. "It's an old family recipe guaranteed to knock down that battle going on in your head."

Charlie slowly opened one eye and slowly focused on the goddess standing above him holding a warm concoction in her hand.

"Here, take it. I'm freezing my butt off out here," Jessica replied.

Charlie forced open his other eye to gain a sense of depth perception and reached for the cup. As he sat up to drink Jessica slithered back under the sheets next to him.

"Hurry up, that will help you sleep for another hour or so and you will wake up feeling fine," she explained.

Charlie did as she ordered and pulled the covers back over both of them.

It became quickly obvious that the potion did more than just get rid of hangovers.

Jim Arnold was beside himself with fear, pacing back and forth across the room.

"For Christ's sake would you sit down and relax," one of his buddies said. "Have a beer and enjoy the game."

Jim couldn't enjoy the game. Jim couldn't enjoy anything. He was certain he was the next victim of the Apostle Serial Killer.

"Did you see this morning's paper?" Jim raged. "Look at the headline. 'Birmingham site of killer's next victim'. Birmingham! How much more proof do you need? Expect to find victim within days."

"Dude, there are hundreds of men in Birmingham with the first name James and the last initial A," the friend replied.

"Yes, but how many of those men knew two of the other victims?" Jim said softly.

"You knew two of the other victims?" another of the men in attendance asked.

"At least two, hell, I might have known all four," Jim answered almost in tears. Now he had everybody's attention.

"Where...? How...? When...?" They all were asking questions at once.

"I sort of ran into them in Jacksonville back in 1970," Jim started to explain. "I had gone down there to watch a Jacksonville State football game with a couple of buddies then play with my band at a fraternity party. One of the guys in my band was James Zeller, the Apostle killer's first victim. There was a lot of drinkin' and a lot more horny guys than there were women. One thing led to another and before you know it we got caught up in this group that was gang raping this nursing school student."

"Oh Christ," one of his friends moaned. "What happened?"

"Of course, when she sobered up she raised all sorts of hell. I was sure we were all going to jail. We got out of town as fast as we could, hoping nobody would remember our names, but of course they did. The police contacted us a couple of days later just to ask if we knew anything about a rape in Jacksonville, but before they called, an attorney called me who had been hired by Andrew Smith's parents. Andrew was in my band but he was also some big shot student down at Jacksonville State. They told us everything had been taken care of and the girl, Emily Sue, had decided not to file charges. I heard later they paid her a shitload of money."

"So you think the Apostle Serial Killer is this chick Emily Sue taking revenge on all the guys who raped her?" one of his buddies asked.

"That's what's weird; Emily Sue was murdered back in 1975. When they found her body the head was missing, too," Jim explained.

"Does the FBI know this?" another friend asked, "because I've seen nothing like this in the papers."

"You'd think they'd know about it. They're the FBI for Christ's sake. They know about everything," Jim replied.

"Then why the hell haven't they come here to talk to you or protect you?" his buddy asked. "I think you should give them a call and tell them what you just told us."

"Sounds to me like this Andrew's parents buried all the information when they worked the deal with that Emily Sue. There's probably no record of the rape anywhere for them to find that would link you all together," another buddy offered.

"Do you know who the other guys were?"

"The only ones I knew are both dead," Jim replied, which wasn't exactly true.

"I'd make the call or get the hell out of town," his first friend said.

"I'd get out of the country if I were you," the other friend added.

"You guys are making me feel a lot better," Jim sighed. "I can't afford to just run away, I'd lose my job, my boat, and my house."

"Better than losing your life, buddy."

Two hours after drinking her tonic Charlie awoke headache free and although a little foggy, remarkably refreshed. As like last time when he moved his hands away from his body, he felt nothing but sheet. He looked around and realized he wasn't at the military apartment.

"I hope the sergeants made it home safely," he said softly.

It was then that the aroma of coffee waft into the room.

"Breakfast will be ready in fifteen minutes," a voice called out. "There are clean towels on the sink by the shower. Coffee is almost ready. I'll bring you a cup in the shower as soon as it's done. Do you take cream and sugar?"

"Just cream," Charlie replied.

Three minutes into his shower a hand reached through the curtain with a steaming cup of Jamaican Blue Mountain Coffee.

"There's a shelf right outside the back where I usually sit the cup," Jessica recommended. "Don't be long."

"This is great coffee," Charlie declared.

"It better be, it cost me over sixty dollars a pound," Jessica replied.

After his shower Charlie found his clothes folded neatly on the foot of the bed.

As he began to dress a voice startled him almost causing him to lose his balance as he pulled on his underwear.

"I had to wash them," Jessica said. "I couldn't stand the smell of smoke and liquor all over them."

"I wasn't expecting a sleep-over so I didn't bring a change of clothes," Charlie replied, "so thank you."

"You're welcome," Jessica replied smiling. "Let's eat breakfast."

"Can I finish getting dressed first?" Charlie kidded.

"If you must," Jessica sighed then laughed.

As Charlie sat down the morning paper lay next to his plate with the headline blazing, 'Birmingham site of killer's next victim'. He knew Jessica waited with bated breath for his reaction to the headline.

"Wow, did you see this, the Yankees beat the Cardinals in extra innings last night. That's unbelievable," he said grinning, as he sat down the paper and started eating his breakfast.

"Okay, smart guy, what great plan does the FBI have for stopping the Apostle Serial Killer?" Jessica asked a bit annoyed.

"By the way, that's a great name you came up with for the killer," Charlie congratulated.

"I didn't come up with that name, Paige Eliot did. She's a reporter for the Montgomery Beacon," Jessica replied, with a smirk.

"She must be one smart woman," Charlie replied. "I bet it was her who figured out that the next victim would be found here in Birmingham as well."

"So I ask again, what's the FBI's next move?"

"You should probably ask an FBI agent that question," Charlie grinned. "Just kidding," Charlie added when he saw Jessica's annoyance level beginning to build.

"We both know what's going on here and I think we can help each other out as long as no laws are broken and no careers are put at risk. I very much enjoyed your company last night but don't feel obligated to repeat the behavior just for the purpose of information gathering. Fair enough?" Charlie asked.

"First answer a few questions for me," Jessica replied.

"Fair enough"

"Is your name really Charlie Daniels?"

"No, but I can't tell you my real name just yet," Charlie replied.

"Are you the FBI agent Washington has sent out to work the Apostle Serial Killer investigation?"

"Yes I am," Charlie replied, thankful for her wording.

"When do you expect the killer to strike next?"

"Today or tomorrow?"

"What do you plan to do about it?"

"I haven't even checked in with the local bureau yet. Remember, I just arrived last night. I plan on checking in as soon as breakfast is over," Charlie explained.

"One more question," Jessica said. "The Trans Am was for you. Who was the Chevy Nova for?"

"An agent working on another case," Charlie replied.

Jessica caught the twitch of his eye. His last answer was a lie. There was more information she needed to get out of Charlie and she knew the best way to do it.

"Last night was wonderful for me too. If we can help each other out we should make it as pleasurable as possible," she purred.

Charlie smiled, "I better call the bureau."

"Can it wait another hour?" Jessica said, grabbing his hand and pulling him towards the bedroom.

Charlie smiled and followed her lead.

CHAPTER SIXTEEN

"This guy knows nothing about who was involved," the private detective said to his partner after listening to the devices they had planted earlier in the house. "This is a waste of time."

"Who knows, maybe we'll catch this Apostle Serial Killer. Besides we're getting paid well, so quit whining."

"You really think this guy's the next victim?"

"Our employer seems to think so as does the guy himself. If I were him I'd take his friend's advice and move out of the country, today," his partner replied.

"You got that right. Wait...he's making a phone call."

"Hello, you've reached the Birmingham office of the Federal Bureau of Investigation. If you know your party's extension you may dial it at any time, otherwise press 0 for the switchboard,"

"It's a recording," Jim announced.
"Well what's it say?"
"Says to press 0 for the switchboard."
"Then press 0 for Christ's sake," his friend moaned.
Jim pressed 0.
"FBI how can I help you?" a man asked.
"I think I need protection," Jim began.
"Protection from what?" the agent asked.
"From the Apostle Serial Killer. I'm his next victim," Jim replied.

The agent switched on a recorder. "What makes you think you're the Apostle Serial Killer's next victim?"

"My name is James and my last name is Arnold. It starts with an A," he began.

"Several men are named James and have last names that start with A," the agent replied.

"Yes, but I knew two of the previous victims and may have known the others as well," Jim explained.

The agent became very attentive. "How did you know the other victims?" But before Jim could answer the FBI switchboard began ringing again. "Hold on a second James."

"Damn, I get no calls all day and now when I get a break in the case the phone starts to ring." He thought to himself.

"FBI please hold," the agent said impatiently.

"So how did you meet the other victims James," the agent asked again.

"We all were involved in a rape of a nurse back in 1970," James said.

"Tell me a little more about it," the agent said.

"Look, I need protection. You get me some protection and I'll tell you everything I know about it. He's coming for me I know it. You've got to help me," James begged.

"Is there someone with you now?" the agent asked.

"I have three friends over at the house keeping me company, but they're going to be leaving soon and I'm scared man, really scared," Jim pleaded.

"I'll get someone up there as soon as I can. Try to keep your friends around until an agent or an officer arrives do you understand?"

"I understand," James replied. "Just hurry."

The agent wrote down James' address and phone number and was about to call his boss at home when he saw the hold button still flashing.

"Sorry to keep you on hold so long, this is the FBI how can I help you?" the agent asked.

"This is Special Agent Charlie Daniels from Washington sent down to oversee the Apostle Serial Killer case," Charlie said trying to sound official in front of Jessica.

"My gosh am I glad to hear from you," the agent replied and proceeded to rehash the phone conversation he had just completed with James A.

"Do you have any agents on duty?" Charlie asked.

"I'm it here at the office. There are a couple on call that I can get here in about an hour, but this guy sounded pretty desperate."

"Give me that address again. I'll pull it up on a computer and head over there. Hold off on calling in those two agents just yet. I hate to pull them away from their families on a Sunday," Charlie said.

"Keep in touch and welcome to Birmingham Agent Daniels. I'll contact Supervising Agent Billings and let him know you're in town and about the James Arnold call."

Jessica could tell something was up by the tone Charlie's phone conversation had taken. She waited patiently, tempted to copy the information Charlie was writing down, but willing to give him the opportunity to share it with her on his own.

"So what's going on?" she asked as he hung up the phone.

"The agent on duty just took a call from a James Arnold who claims he is the Apostle Killer's next victim," Charlie related.

"So what makes him think he's next?" Jessica asked.

"He claims to have known at least two of the previous victims and they were all involved in the rape of a nurse back in 1970," Charlie said.

"These murders are payback for a 1970 rape? I don't believe it. That kind of information would have turned up long ago if it were true," Jessica insisted.

"Unless it was somehow dismissed or buried or expunged from the public records," Charlie replied.

"According to the agent the guy sounded desperate and was begging for protection. I have to check it out," Charlie replied.

"I'm going with you," Jessica insisted.

"I thought you might say that," Charlie replied. "I can't stop you, but we have to take separate cars and you have to let me check out the situation first. I'll talk with him. If I think he needs protection I'll bring him to my apartment at the National Guard base, where we both can question him. If I decide not to bring him in I'll call your cell and you can join us at the house. Fair enough?" Charlie asked.

"I guess," Jessica replied hesitantly.

"What's wrong?" Charlie asked.

"It just doesn't make sense. This is much bigger than a few revenge killings and I can't imagine a female having the strength to stage the murder scenes or overpower the victims."

"I'm sure she could overpower the victims, but I agree setting up the crosses with the bodies attached would take considerable strength," Charlie replied. "Here's the address. Do you know how to get there?"

"No, but I'll print out the directions while you finish getting dressed," Jessica replied.

A white van drove by where the two private detectives were parked watching James Arnold's house.

The Molly Hatchet song *Flirtin' with Disaster* was blaring from the truck vibrating everything within fifty feet.

"Somebody needs to tell that idiot to turn that crap down," one of the investigators shouted to his partner.

"Damn, it screwed up our equipment. I'm getting nothing from the house," the other man complained.

"Give it a minute; I'm sure it will come back."

"Hey look, the van is pulling into Arnold's driveway," the first investigator said. "Get some pictures of that guy."

His partner started snapping away. "Looks like another friend. They let him right in."

"You getting any audio yet?"

"No nothing."

"Damn, then we'll just have to wait."

"FBI open up," the man called out as he knocked on the door.

"That was fast," Jim said ushering the man in. "What's in the box."

The man looked around the room. "Your friends can leave now," he said coldly.

"Shouldn't he show you some sort of identification or something first before we leave, Jim?" one of the friend's said and the other two nodded.

"Oh yeah, could I see some kind of identification," Jim repeated.

The man sighed deeply. He sat the box he was carrying down and in a swift movement pulled a rattlesnake out by its head, its fangs sprung forward and he plunged them into Jim's neck. He then tossed the snake on the floor by the three other men and touched Jim's forehead causing his knees to buckle and slump to the floor.

"I wish you would've left when I gave you the opportunity," the man said.

The men started to rush towards him but he lifted his hand and they all fell backwards onto the couch.

"As a famous southern band once sang, *'When we gamble with our time we choose our destiny'*, and unfortunately boys, you took a bad gamble."

He lifted his hand and began to squeeze. All three men's hands flew to their throats trying to stop whoever or whatever was choking them. Unfortunately, none were successful and within minutes all three were dead.

"I still got nothing," the investigator complained, "the vibrations must have fried something."

"Look two of them are leaving now," his partner said. "One looks drunk."

"They've been sitting around drinking all day. You'd expect they'd be drunk by now."

"Probably one of the friends was too drunk to drive and somebody came to pick him up now that the FBI is coming," the investigator guessed.

"That makes sense."

"Okay, we're getting close. You cruise the area until I call and tell you what's happening," Charlie told Jessica over the phone.

"Better idea, leave your phone on so I can hear what's going on and don't leave me waiting long. I'm not very good at it," Jessica insisted.

"Okay I promise," Charlie replied, pulling into the driveway.

"Looks like more company," one of the investigators noted.

"Nice car, must be another one of his 'good ole boys'," the other investigator replied.

"Charlie," Jessica called over the phone before he reached the door, "something's going on out here."

"What is it?"

"Two guys who look like cops watching the house. Looks like they have eavesdropping equipment and cameras," Jessica reported. "Don't look this way."

"Try to get their license and wait for me," Charlie said.

"What if they leave?"

"We'll worry about that if it happens," Charlie said, as he knocked on the door.

"James Arnold, it's Special Agent Charlie Daniels with the FBI, please open the door."

Charlie waited and listened but heard nothing from inside.

"I don't like this Jessica. Nobody's answering and I hear no noise inside," Charlie said, "I'm going in."

"Be careful," she warned.

"I swear that guys talking to somebody. We should think about getting out of here," the investigator said.

"Are the microphones picking anything up yet?"

"Nothing but static."

"Look, he's pulling a gun. You think that's the killer?"

"Well how many FBI guys drive a Trans Am. It must be the killer."

"What do we do?"

Charlie eased through the door. "I hear something inside like an electric current," Charlie said to Jessica

He had barely taken two steps into the room when a rattlesnake sprung towards his leg sinking its fangs into the folds of his levis.

"Bam, Bam," two shots exploded from Charlie's 9mm Beretta ripping the snake in two.

"Those were gunshots. Call 911," one of the investigators yelled to his partner.

"Are you sure we want to get involved? That's not what we're being paid for.

"Charlie, are you okay," Jessica was screaming into the phone.

"Hang up and call 911. There are three bodies here and possibly more poisonous snakes. I'm coming to check out the two guys you saw," Charlie ordered.

"He's coming out the door. Should we go after him?" the first investigator said.

"You guys aren't going anywhere," Jessica said coming up behind them holding a shotgun. "Lay flat on the ground with your arms spread."

"Lady you're making a big mistake. You're letting the Apostle Serial Killer get away. Didn't you hear the gunshots?"

"That was Special Agent Daniels with the FBI. He's on his way here to have a word with you boys right now about the three dead bodies he found inside the house you've been watching."

"Three dead bodies? We know nothing about any dead bodies," the first investigator replied.

"Who you talking to?" Charlie asked as he walked up holding his gun.

"The lady with the shotgun," he replied.

"What lady?" Charlie replied, smiling. "What are you boys doing here?"

"We're private investigators hired to watch the house and see what we can find out about James Arnold," the man in charge replied.

"What kind of information were you looking for?" Our client wanted to know if he knew who else was involved in a rape that happened back in 1970. We were just supposed to listen and write down names."

"And did you?"

"He never mentioned any names or the rape until right before he called the FBI. We've been here for three days monitoring the house."

"So how did everybody die?" Charlie asked.

"Right before you got here a white van drove by blasting some music. Knocked out our equipment. We thought it was another one of his buddies dropping by, just like we thought you were till we heard the gunshots. What were the gunshots?"

"I'm the one asking the questions?" Charlie replied.

"The guy walked in like he was a friend, stayed about ten minutes and left with another person who looked drunk. We figured he came and picked up somebody too drunk to drive home. They'd been drinkin' all day and with the FBI on its way up and all."

"You've got pictures of this guy and the van?

"Yes, the cameras on the front seat," he replied.

The first police sirens could finally be heard.

"Who are you two working for?" Charlie asked.

"We took the job over the phone. Never met our client. He insisted we not know his name. Normally we would pass on a job like that but he paid double our regular fee and we needed the job,"
the investigator explained.

"How are you paid?" Charlie asked.

"Cash delivered by courier. And before you even ask we can't contact him, he contacts us," the investigator replied, tiring of the questioning.

"You guys packing?" Charlie asked.

"We got two 45's locked in the trunk."

"Leave 'em there," Charlie replied. "And follow me down to the house."

"I did a preliminary search of the house. Three bodies on the couch no one else inside. Watch out for snakes I had to shoot a rattlesnake that struck at me," Charlie explained to the police, the FBI, and multiple forensic teams that had gathered. "We believe the Apostle Serial Killer abducted his fifth victim from the house, a Mr. James Arnold. We may have caught a break because someone had hired the two private investigators standing over there to watch the house. I need one of you," he said pointing to an FBI agent, "to collect all of their information. It could be the break we've been looking for. Anybody have any questions?"

"Who's the woman standing next to the Trans Am?" one of the FBI agents asked.

"The Trans Am is mine. When the agent on duty notified me about Mr. Arnold calling in she was with me and I didn't take the time to drop her off," Charlie explained.

He knew it wasn't a very good answer but it was all he had at the moment.

"So if there are no more questions, we've got about another hour of daylight before we need to move some lights in here. This is a multi-agency investigation but the FBI is in charge so if you have any questions follow your department protocols but include an FBI agent in the loop," Charlie concluded.

From the back a voice called out, "Is your name really Charlie Daniels?"

"In Washington my name never seemed to be a problem, but here, everywhere I go, nobody seems to believe that's my real name. Well you boys better get used to it because that's what Mr. and Mrs. Daniels wrote on the birth certificate. Now let's see if we can catch ourselves a serial killer."

CHAPTER SEVENTEEN

It was still early afternoon when Chester's white pick-up truck pulled back into the church parking lot.

"What's his car still doing here?" Chester grumped.

"Now how would I know that Chester? I've been having lunch with Luke and Emma Sunderland this afternoon," Ginny Lee replied impatiently.

"You were having lunch with me too Ginny Lee," Chester reminded her.

"Well of course I was Chester, but it was only lunch, so don't go thinkin' it means we're dating, 'cause we're not. I have no interest in being in any relationship except my relationship with God and the Holy Spirit and you are just going to have to honor that," Ginny Lee demanded.

"Well, I'm hoping someday you'll change your mind. I pray about it every day and I hope you do too," Chester replied. "Do you want me to see what that boy is still doing here?"

"No, I can handle him. Besides Ver Dell and Ida are still cleaning up inside if I need anybody," Ginny Lee replied. "I thought you needed to get back to Birmingham this afternoon."

"I do. I have a lot of paperwork to catch up on to make sure I get those government payments," Chester explained.

"I'll see you Wednesday then," Ginny Lee said, as she jumped out of the car.

"Take care Ginny Lee and watch that guy. He looked a little rough to me."

Ginny Lee just smiled and waved then scampered into the church.

"Where's Mr. Jackson?" Ginny Lee asked obviously disappointed he wasn't inside.

"What 'ja say?" Ida replied shutting off the vacuum.

"I asked if you'd seen Mr. Jackson?" Ginny Lee replied.

"Don't know no Mr. Jackson. You know Mr. Jackson, Ver Dell?" Ida asked.

"No, ain't never heard of no Mr. Jackson neither," Ver Dell replied.

"Well his car is parked out in the lot still," Ginny Lee said perplexed.

"Oh, you be talk'n 'bout Kevin. Kevin out back work'n," Ida replied.

"Yeah, Kevin out back work'n," Ver Dell confirmed.

"Thanks," Ginny Lee said heading out the door.

Ver Dell and Ida weren't the smartest members of the church and pretty much typified what the outside world thought inbred hillbillies would be like. But they were God loving people who were raised in and filled with the Holy Spirit. Two people who would sacrifice their lives to save yours. True spiritual warriors of God.

"Kevin, what are you still doing here?" Ginny Lee asked.

"After you left I decided to have a look around and see what kind of repairs the place needed that I could help out with on Wednesday. One thing led to another and before I knew it I was cleaning up the graveyard. I hope you don't mind," Kevin said.

"Of course I don't mind. It looks terrific," she replied.

"Ver Dell showed me where the tools were and helped me lift a few of the heavier headstones back in place. Mostly it was just pulling weeds, stacking rocks back into the wall, and fixing the gate. I'm just about through here anyway for now," Kevin explained.

"I thought you had to head off to find a job," Ginny Lee said.

"I do, but everything will be closed until tomorrow, so I figured there was no need to hurry," Kevin said.

"Then let me fix you dinner. It's the least I can do," Ginny Lee said.

"No, you just got back from lunch and it's way too early for dinner," Kevin replied.

"Then let me fix you some lunch," Ginny Lee offered.

"Ver Dell and Ida shared their lunch with me so that won't be necessary. Actually, I do need to get back to Birmingham, but I promise I'll be back bright and early on Wednesday," Kevin assured her.

"Remember we do have small groups that meet other nights. I have a group that meets at my house on Tuesdays if you're interested," Ginny Lee smiled.

"I appreciate the offer but I do have to find a job," Kevin reminded her.

"If you work as hard Wednesday as you did today maybe I can talk the church into hiring you. Lord knows we need someone fulltime around here," Ginny Lee declared.

"I'm not sure Chester would be too pleased about that," Kevin joked.

"The Lord gives me extra grace to deal with Chester," Ginny Lee explained. "And in turn I give extra grace to Chester. Some people just require that grace and the Lord provides. Thank you Jesus."

"I straightened your father's headstone, but I didn't see one for your mother. Is she still living?" Kevin asked.

"Momma's in a home over in Scottsboro. She suffers from dementia. I took care of her as long as I could but it got to be too much with running the church and taking care of Momma," Ginny Lee murmured.

"I'm sorry to hear that," Kevin replied.

"She was a mighty woman of God in her day. When her and Daddy were together the Holy Spirit burned bright in this church, much like it is again today."

"So the church hasn't always been so strong?" Kevin said.

"Heavens no," Ginny Lee replied. "There was a while there when Ver Dell, Ida, me and two or three others were 'bout the only ones you could count on."

"What changed things?" Kevin asked.

"Casper," Ginny Lee said. "He showed up one day started playing his music and people just started coming in and the Holy Spirit came along."

"I thought you told me the people started coming when a sense of evil came to the South?" Kevin said.

"I did," Ginny replied. "When the Holy Spirit arrived Satan sent his evil demons to fight against it. The battle grows larger every day. This Apostle Serial Killer is leading Satan's battle. We need a warrior to fight against him,"

Ginny exclaimed, seemingly to look into Kevin's very soul and challenge him to be that leader.

A shiver ran down Kevin's spine.

"I should be going," Kevin said, not sure how to respond to Ginny's last statement.

"I'll see you Wednesday and I'll keep you in my prayers," Ginny Lee said, "and thanks for cleaning the graveyard."

"I'll finish it on Wednesday," he said, as he climbed into his car. "Thank Ver Dell and Ida for me. Goodbye."

As Kevin pulled away a thousand questions were swirling through his mind as were a thousand feelings very unfamiliar to him.

"As an undercover investigator I'm going to be no good to anyone if I spend even a part of the time passed out on the floor of the church," Kevin said as he drove back towards Birmingham.

"But then again, being 'slain in the Spirit' may be what Charlotte was talking about when she said 'God had glorious plans for me'. Ginny Lee did say I may now have some gifts of the Spirit I never imagined possible. It's just all so confusing," Kevin continued to debate with himself.

"Possible suspects: Chester would be the perfect suspect if he wasn't such a wimp. Wait maybe that makes him a perfect suspect. Medical training, familiarity with poisonous snakes, office in Birmingham. Carlo needs to check him out. Who else: Ver Dell, not a chance, not the brain power. Ginny Lee, I doubt the killer is a woman, although it is possible. She's smart enough, but I don't know if she's strong enough. She does handle snakes. It's a thought. Casper: He was smaller than Ginny Lee and I didn't see him handling snakes. I don't think a guitar player of his talent would risk that. Ida: She's big enough to manhandle the victims and smarter than Ver Dell, but smart enough to perform the surgery required to severe a head? I don't think so. So that leaves about seventy more in the congregation I need to check out. Obviously Simon discovered a likely suspect. Given time, I'm sure I can too. I just need to do it without meeting Simon's fate."

CHAPTER EIGHTEEN

Simon awoke with his head throbbing to the now silenced beat of the Allman Brothers Band. The house or building or place of confinement, whatever it may be was eerily silent. Either his captor was asleep or he was gone.

Simon tried to move his hand. He felt more of a tingling sensation than pain where his thumb had been removed. The killer had obviously given him drugs, probably morphine, to help him sleep and deal with the pain. He was still strapped to the bed in the cage. The odor of paint still lingered in the air.

"That's right, he told me he was an artist," Simon whispered.

Simon tried to look around the basement but the straps limited his head movement and the light was too dim.

"What could I do anyway," Simon sighed, and closed his eyes to try to sleep.

"I should stop and buy one of those throw away cell phones," Kevin said. "Something tells me I need to check in on Carlo."

He was still over an hour outside of Birmingham and beginning to worry.

"Everything will be fine as long as he doesn't blow my cover," Kevin kept reminding himself.

"I'm sure he's spending a relaxing day driving around Birmingham, probably with the newspaper woman, looking at churches where the Apostle Serial Killer will dump his next victim. He'll pick out three or four likely spots and will stake them out. If we're lucky it will all be over in a few days. Gosh it's great to be so optimistic," Kevin congratulated himself.

"Problem is, I got a bad feeling the reality of the situation is far from the picture I just painted," Kevin said, and pushed on the accelerator.

"What do you mean all three victims strangled themselves?" Charlie said, "Is that even possible?"

"No it's not," the coroner replied, "but until I can get full autopsies on them that's my preliminary finding. Beats the hell out of me how they did it."

"Let me know when you find what really killed them," Charlie asked.

The coroner just raised his arm signifying he heard Charlie and walked away shaking his head.

"We only found the body of the one snake inside and only part of its head," one of the police forensic scientists reported.

"What happened to the rest of the head?" Charlie asked.

"That's what I came to ask you. You said it struck your pants and you shot it. Is that correct?"

"Yes, I shot it right in the head," Charlie replied.

"Show me where it struck you."

"Right he..." Charlie stopped mid-sentence.

"That's what I thought," the forensic person said, pulling out a bag and forceps. "The fang and rest of the head is still caught in your pants. That was a pretty risky shot so close to your leg."

"Those were pretty big fangs coming at me. It was worth the risk," Charlie replied.

"Charlie," one of the agents questioning the private investigators called. "You need to see this."

"These are the pictures they took earlier in the day when the guy's buddies first arrived."

"You mean the three dead ones inside?"

"Right. Now here are the pictures of the van that we believe the Apostle Serial Killer drove up in and left with our victim."

"They're all blurry. You can't make anything out," Charlie bellowed. "What the hell happened?"

"We didn't change anything," the private investigator said. "When the van went by we lost all our audio also."

"Doesn't make any sense," the agent said.

"Nothing here is making any sense," Charlie replied, exasperated.

Standing about five feet behind Charlie the entire time was Jessica frantically taking notes about everything that was being said.

"Jessica we need to talk," Charlie said.

"You're not going to be able to report everything you've just heard, at least not quite yet," Charlie said.

"Look Charlie," Jessica started, "there's a little thing called freedom of the press and if..."

Charlie interrupted, "Jessica, I know I can't stop you from doing it. I'm just asking you to hold off a little while. You still have plenty for an exclusive on this and if you work with me here I'm sure there will be plenty more in the future. Why screw up your shot at the big story?"

Jessica tapped her foot up and down impatiently for about ten seconds while she thought. "You're right. You can edit out what you think needs to be kept quiet, but I want to send this out within the hour so keep that in mind," Jessica replied.

"That sounds like a reasonable compromise," Charlie agreed.

"Simon, we have a guest."

At first Simon thought he was dreaming but then he heard a door close in the room above and footsteps that seemed to be laboring under some sort of weight.

"Simon are you awake? I said we have a guest."

The door at the top of the stairs opened and the killer carefully slid the unconscious man slowly down the steps. Once at the bottom with a quick one handed jerk he pulled the man up and carried him to the steel operating table in the middle of the room.

"Do you know who this is Simon?" the killer giggled.

Simon remained quiet.

"Come now Simon, you know the bible, tell me who this is," he ordered.

"This is the stand in for James the Lesser son of Alphaeus," Simon replied.

"Very good, Simon. Do you know why they called him the Lesser?"

"Because he wasn't physically as large as James the Greater," Simon replied.

"And do you know how he was martyred?"

"I know for a fact that he wasn't beheaded," Simon snapped.

"D-d-don't upset me, Simon."

"He was beaten and stoned to death and thrown off the temple in Jerusalem," Simon replied.

"And such will be the fate of James Arnold," the man said solemnly.

"Tell me, what will happen when you gather all the chalices of the twelve apostles?" Simon asked.

"He will come of course," the killer replied.

"Who will come?"

"The antichrist, it is he who guides me," the man explained. "He will come drink from the chalices and the apostles will be resurrected to lead the armies of the antichrist."

"I don't understand. I've seen you powers. I've seen your gifts. They are not 'deeds of the flesh'. They are 'gifts of the Spirit'," Simon expressed.

The bands binding Simon to his cot suddenly burst loose and Simon was lifted into the air. He could see the man was shaking with anger.

"Never s-s-speak *shamnada hydakom* to to me about *glorybedaGoda* gifts of the *bedasakom* Spirit again, do do do you *doGodo* understand?"

But Simon couldn't answer. It felt like someone had grabbed his tongue and was squeezing it so hard it was about to explode. In fact, he could feel the individual blood vessels begin to explode and blood begin to trickle down his lips and throat that soon turned into a steady stream. Then without warning, his body dropped back to the cot and the pressure on his tongue eased.

"You'd better put some cold water on that right away," the man said as he stormed out of the basement.

"He's still not here," Kevin complained as he pulled his Nova in front of the military base apartment.

Sergeant Boone heard the car pull in and came out to have a look.

"I wasn't expecting you back for a couple of days, the way you was talking when you left here this mornin'."

"Got a late start from my last stop so I thought I might as well stop here instead of pay for a hotel room further down the road," Kevin replied. "Charlie been around?"

"Ain't seen hide nor hair of 'im since last night at Banana Joe's," Boone replied. "Ain't seen Sergeant McClellan either fer as that goes."

"Just what exactly happened at Banana Joe's last night?" Kevin asked.

"As I told you, Charlie had everybody believin' he was the real Charlie Daniels. We was getting free drinks, women was all over us, we had to have security hold 'em off," Boone explained.

"I'm sure Charlie liked that."

"Pretty soon, this gorgeous woman shouts over to Charlie something like, 'you wanna meet the James A's or you wanna dance?' Charlie said he reckoned he'd like to dance. At that point McClellan and I figured we was free to join the party as well, so frankly I don't remember a hell of a lot after that."

"You think this woman who called to Charlie was the newspaper lady?"

"I'd only be guessing, but with a come-on line like that it sounds like a pretty good call," Boone replied. "Charlie did ask if we could arrange to get another ride back to the base."

"I assume you were both able to?" Kevin said.

"There was a lot of women there last night and they all thought we were Charlie Daniel's personal bodyguards. It wasn't a problem, believe me."

"Thanks for the information. I guess I'd better give Charlie a call."

"You want your computer back?" Boone asked.

"Not just yet. I'm not sure how long I'm going to be around," Kevin replied.

"It's safe with me and here when you need it."

"Thanks," Kevin said, heading into his apartment.

Nothing had been moved, but he hadn't expected that it would be since Charlie hadn't yet returned. He went to the drawer where he placed his cell phone and switched it on. The first thing he noticed were several missed calls from Charlie.

"He's either feeling guilty or something's gone down," Kevin said as he dialed Charlie's number.

Charlie had his phone on vibrate because he didn't want Jessica to know when he received any calls. Especially, this call.

Charlie looked around for Jessica and saw she was over listening to an agent interview the two private detectives. He walked behind a van but kept his eye on Jessica before he answered his phone.

"Kevin, am I glad to hear from you," Charlie said. "Things are crazy here."

"Crazy where? What's going on?" Kevin asked.

"We just missed the Apostle Serial Killer by a few minutes. We discovered his next victim. We were on the way to pick him up but the killer beat us there. Two private investigators were even watching the house and he pulled off the kidnapping and three murders right under their noses," Charlie began.

"What about the newspaper lady, she there with you? She's here at the scene but not with me now. She knows nothing about you, don't worry." Charlie tried to ease Kevin's concern.

"Charlie, it's imperative she know nothing about me. That could blow the whole investigation," Kevin scolded.

"I've got her under control. You have no need to be concerned," Charlie insisted.

"You may have her muzzled for now Charlie, but trust me at some point she's going to turn on you and when she does she will try to rip your throat out. So just remember what I've said," Kevin warned. "Now what else you got?"

"The newest victim, James Arnold, knew two of the previous victims."

"And we didn't know this?" Kevin said in disbelief.

"Back in 1970 he, James Zeller, and Andrew Smith, were part of a group that gang raped a nursing student down in Jacksonville," Charlie began.

"That should have come up when we did background checks on the victims," Kevin interrupted.

"The reason it didn't was somebody's wealthy parents bought off the victim and the whole thing got swept under the table and off the record books," Charlie said.

"I can't believe these Apostle Serial Killings are payback for some rape that happened thirty-five years ago. The removal of the heads, the tie-ins to the type of deaths, the names. Those aren't the markings of a revenge killer," Kevin insisted.

"I agree, but we have the connections," Charlie stressed.

"So we have no idea who the other men involved in the rape were?" Kevin asked incredulously.

"Not quite. Two private detectives were hired by someone, who we believe was involved in the rape, to see what James Arnold knew about who was involved. Problem is, the two investigators either aren't being very cooperative or were duped into working for someone they didn't know," Charlie continued.

"What about the rape victim? Could she be our Apostle Serial Killer?" Kevin asked.

"Not according to the private investigators and I also heard the tape. James Arnold was telling his buddies about the rape before he called the FBI for protection. He said that the girl they raped, this Emily Sue Whitman, was murdered and beheaded in 1975. He said they never found her skull," Charlie reported.

"Did you say Emily Sue Whitman?" Kevin said.

"That's right, you heard of her?"

"I just pulled the weeds from around her grave site this afternoon," Kevin replied.

CHAPTER NINTEEN

"Okay, so what can't I include in my report?" Jessica asked when she and Charlie finally left James Arnold's house.

"Well you already got a jump on every other news agency in the country about the kidnapping and the three murders," Charlie reminded her.

"Yes, but now my readers will want details. I need details," Jessica repeated.

"You can say the three victims found in the house were strangled."

"The Apostle Serial Killer was able to strangle three men without them fighting back?"

"I didn't say who strangled them," Charlie replied.

"Well they didn't strangle themselves. Or did they? No, it's impossible to strangle yourself," Jessica insisted, once she thought about it. "What kind of crap are you trying to feed me Charlie?

"I'm telling you exactly what the coroner told me. I'm making none of this up."

"I can't tell my readers that, they'll think I'm crazy."

"You could play up the rape of the nurse angle. What was her name?"

"Emily Sue Whitman."

"Yeah, that's right. Maybe a story about her would stir up some memories and even stir up a few new leads. You could do it a lot better than we could. Word is that when she was found murdered in '75 she had also been beheaded. Something we're going to be looking into."

"What about these private detectives? Who are they working for?" Jessica asked.

"I think they're too dumb to know for sure, but you better believe we'll be working overtime to find out. My guess is it's another one of the men involved in the rape who is running scared. Possibly one who has a lot to lose if his name comes up as a possible victim," Charlie guessed. "Again, that's where you can help us out. Newspaper articles are bound to jog memories."

"What about where the Apostle Serial Killer plans to dump James Arnold's body? We know it's going to be thrown off some temple or church somewhere here in Birmingham. Shouldn't we get that in the papers and stir up some vigilante surveillance of all the possible sites?" Jessica suggested.

"As a member of the law enforcement community I condemn any form of vigilante activity," Charlie stated. "But the harder we squeeze this guy's balls and make his life more difficult the happier I am."

"Well Charlie, if you don't mind, I could use a little time alone to do some work," Jessica said, cuddling up close. "I like that your beard is starting to grow back."

"Maybe I won't be hassled so much about my name when we go to the bars if it gets a little longer," Charlie replied. "I do need to get back to the base. I haven't even unpacked yet. I sure hope Sergeants Boone and McClellan made it home safely."

"They looked like they were doing just fine when we left last night. Why don't you call me in a couple of hours and we can get back together. Maybe your place tonight," Jessica said.

"Sounds like a right fine idea," Charlie replied.

"Until then," Jessica said, pulling Charlie close and kissing him passionately.

"It's about damn time you got back here," Kevin complained. "Where the heck have you been? You've got lipstick all over your mouth," Kevin said wiping it away with his finger.

"I've been going over what Jessica can and can't release to the newspapers," Charlie explained.

"Jessica, I thought her name was Paige," Kevin snapped.

"It is Paige, but she goes by Jessica like I go by Charlie."

"She doesn't know your real name does she?" Kevin asked very concerned.

"Not at all," Charlie replied.

"Not at all as least as far as you know," Kevin corrected.

"Well, yeah," Charlie replied. "But even the local agents down here don't know my real name."

"For Christ's sake Charlie the two MP Sergeants were able to figure out who we were. Don't you think Paige and the local agents will eventually figure it out too?

"I guess you're right," Charlie agreed.

"Of course I'm right, and that is why it is so damn important that none of the local agents, or Paige, or anybody down here finds out about me. Do you understand?" Kevin preached.

"Of course I understand," Charlie said. "You're like a brother to me."

"Some way, somehow, somebody blew Simon's cover and the Apostle Serial Killer now has him. We can't afford for that to happen to me. I think Simon was on to something at the church up at Sand Mountain. I'm sure of it now that you told me about the nurse that was raped but there still has to be a tie-in with that houngan, or Voodoo priest down in New Orleans. I'm going to head down there in the morning and I may want you to follow up later this week once James Arnold's body shows up."

"You may want to leave for New Orleans tonight. I thought you had already headed that way so I invited Jessica over here for the evening. If I try to change it she'll start asking questions," Charlie tried to explain.

"You know that's probably a good idea. I need to be back in Sand Mountain on Wednesday anyway. I'll pick up one of those throw-away cell phones so we can keep in touch," Kevin said.

"Why not take your company phone?" Charlie asked.

"I don't like the company knowing where I am every second of the day. You might want to think about that yourself." Kevin paused. "I need you to check someone out for me, a Dr. Chester Cunningham; he has a practice here in Birmingham and one up in Boaz."

"Think he might be our guy?" Charlie asked.

"I just think he's worth checking out is all," Kevin replied.

"I told Jessica she could release an article about the body being thrown from a temple or church somewhere in Birmingham within the next few days," Charlie said.

"That ought to stir up the residents," Kevin replied.

"That was our hope. I also told her to run with the rape story thinking maybe it will stir up old memories and supply a few new names and leads," Charlie said.

"At least you're putting her to good use."

"Simon, Simon, Simon, whatever am I to do with you?" the killer sighed. "Well I know what I'll eventually do to you, but what am I to do with you until then? I try to be cordial and share my thoughts with you and you either physically attack me or you try that psychology crap that you know only angers me. And my anger always causes you such pain. By the way how is your tongue?"

"Hnbrrf," Simon tried to answer but his tongue was so swollen he could barely move it in his mouth.

"It will be swollen for several days. You will have to drink your meals for a while I'm afraid. I will be covering your cage tonight while I perform the surgery on James the Lesser. I had wanted to share it with you but I don't feel you are quite ready yet and I couldn't tolerate interruptions. I'd have to kill you. I'll get you something to drink for dinner and then I think it best if you be strapped in the cot for the night. I'm sure you understand."

As Kevin got back on I-59 South heading for New Orleans he actually thought Carlo had handled the situation with Paige better than he had expected. She was going to get her information one way or another and at least Carlo seemed to have some control over her at least for the moment and was using her for the benefit of the investigation.

"I just hope he made it clear that the bureau had nothing to do with the warning about the body showing up at one of the churches in Birmingham. We don't want to be accused of stirring up a bunch of vigilantes," Kevin mused.

But what troubled him the most, as mile after mile of blacktop raced by, was the gravesite of Emily Sue Whitman.

"Could she actually have been the first victim of the Apostle Serial Killer and why is she buried at the Holiness Church in Sand Mountain? It must connect somehow to the recent murders. That would mean someone who has been at that church since before 1975 is probably the murderer. I wonder how long Chester has been around. I wonder if he could have made it to Birmingham that fast. Yeah, he had plenty of time to get there and nab James," Kevin decided as he continued to debate himself.

"What doesn't make sense is that these murders are simply to cover-up someone's involvement with a thirty-five year old rape," Kevin said.

"Obviously, there is a connection of some sort but with the taking of the heads it goes way beyond that. And from what James Arnold said two of the first four victims had nothing to do with the rape. I wonder if Emily Sue has any living relatives? Ginny Lee will be able to tell me that on Wednesday. I've got to make sure Carlo and Paige don't drop by the church on Wednesday."

Kevin's brain was going a mile a minute, which was about half as fast as he was driving.

"Whoa, I don't need to go blowing my cover to some Mississippi state trooper just to get out of a speeding ticket," Kevin said, easing back on the gas.

He was just entering the outskirts of Meridian, Mississippi and decided it was time to take a break. He was approaching State Route 39 and saw a slew of motels off to his right.

"This looks as good as any," he said pulling off and into the Hilton Garden Inn.

Kevin still had about a three hour drive till he reached New Orleans. He figured he could probably sleep in and still get to the Market Botanica before it opened. What he didn't know was that Market Botanica wasn't like the typical Bourbon Street tourist shops that stayed opened till three in the morning and didn't open till noon. Market Botanica was a serious shop that catered mostly to Haitian immigrants and others who took their voodoo very seriously and practiced it religiously. Something he was about to find out the next morning.

As promised the killer brought Simon a large plastic cup of chicken broth with a straw. It would be several days before Simon would be able to let anything larger than that straw past his tongue and even that was a struggle.

"I'm going to try something new this time," the killer said excitedly to Simon.

"I'm going to videotape James' expression when he sees his head pop off. It is always a look of absolute sheer terror that defies description. If you're good I'll show it to you later," the man said, as though he was promising a child a treat for good behavior.

"I may even release it to the news media. I know, I know what you're thinking. You're thinking no one would ever broadcast such a horrific thing and of course, you may be right. However, if I upload it onto the internet, how can they stop that? They couldn't could they? Then everyone could see what sheer terror looks like," the killer giggled.

The body on the table began to moan.

"Oh good, he is starting to come around. I guess we will be starting soon. I'm going to cover your cage and if you choose to cry out you will only hurt your tongue, for I won't be able to hear you over the music. You know I get to break several of his bones before I remove his head. The original Apostle James the Lesser was clubbed and stoned to death before he was tossed from the temple. That should be quite painful for my James the Lesser and I think I will enjoy this one more than the others," the man gloated.

He had come a long way from the small cabin back in 1975 when he first successfully accomplished his miraculous surgery of allowing his victim to witness their own beheading. That first time took several hours and his tape player ran out long before the procedure was completed. Now he had it almost perfected. Fifty-one minutes and fifteen seconds!

Fifty-one minutes and fifteen seconds. The body is strapped into place and the neck device is secured. Video recording is up and running although it won't be necessary till the final few seconds.

"Where am I?" James Arnold asked through his haze.

"Oh come now James, you know where you are. You've been expecting this since James Zeller was sacrificed," the man in the surgical gown answered.

"We didn't mean to hurt her. It just got out of hand. You understand that don't you?" he pleaded. "I didn't want to rape her."

"Th-th-his is not about *glorybedaGoda* that night James," the man replied jerking violently.

"Who are you? Were you there?" James asked

The man jerked violently again.

"Are you sick or something?" James asked.

Without answering the man picked up a small bat and slammed it hard against James' forearm, breaking both the radius and the ulna.

James began to shriek in pain.

The man moved quickly to the kneecap and with one swift swing shattered it. Almost before James' pain receptors could register the pain from the kneecap his tibia and fibula were broken right below it.

"You know the ribs are designed to protect your inside organs. They take a hit and disperse the pain but unfortunately suffer significant damage in doing so," the killer said as he slammed the bat several times hard into both sides of James. Each time eliciting the distinct crack of bone as the ribs served their protective purpose.

James was no doubt in agonizing pain and gripping the edge of the table tightly.

"People tend to use a closed fist or like to grip something tightly to help deal with their pain I've noticed," the killer said as he smashed his bat onto James' right hand breaking several of his fingers in multiple places.

Immediately James balled up the other hand.

"I always wondered which hurt more," the man said smashing the bat onto the closed fist, "but I guess you'll never get the chance to tell me."

James Arnold was reduced to semi-consciousness and was barely capable of moaning.

"Let me lessen your pain," the man said and started a morphine IV. He also placed several other IVs in place in final preparation for the surgery.

Fifty-one minutes and fifteen seconds!

Three times seventeen minutes and five seconds, the length of the 60's psychedelic rock band Iron Butterfly's classic hit *In A Gadda Da Vida*. The man had timed it perfectly. He had looped it three times onto his tape machine and left a ten second click track to allow him to start the machine and get back into position with scalpel in hand as the opening of Don Ingles Vox organ arpeggios set the scene for the song and the macabre operation. Next the entire band kicks in with the continuous ten note ostinato line over two measures that is carried by Lee Dorman's bass throughout the song. The meat of the song allowed the man to get down to the meat of the surgery, the cutting and cauterizing of all the minor veins and arteries in the neck. But as great and hypnotic as that line may be, it is the long middle section of solos by Erik Brann on guitar, Ron Bushy on drums, and especially Doug Ingle on organ that took the man's mind and twisted it into the darker places than most people dared not imagine. Those places that one cannot find on their own but must be led there by a more evil and deviant power. Swift precision the result of having performed the operation five previous times, paced perfectly to the music, each slice to the precise strum of Brann's guitar, each release of the morphine or adrenaline to Bushy's kick of the bass drum. Precision, scripted to perfection to the music building to the final repeat of the Ingle's opening arpeggio the third and final time through the song building to the climax of not the entire ten note ostinato pattern but only the first six notes of the pattern all played in unison. All played in one measure when the adrenaline rushes into James Arnold's body, his eyes pop open in awareness, he looks straight up at the mirror above him, his eyes are given a second to focus as the final four notes are played in the measure leading up to and setting up that final downbeat of silence when James is momentarily totally aware and the killer pushes a button and James watches in terror as his head pops away from his body. A horrific vision seared onto the retina of his eyes as he realizes he witnessed his own beheading an instant before he dies.

CHAPTER TWENTY

"You sick perverted bastard," Simon thought when the music ended and all he could hear was the giggling coming from beyond his cage. He was still strapped down so couldn't even turn.

"Simon, it was beautiful. I so wish you could have seen it," the man said pulling back the canvas that had covered Simon's cage.

"Did you enjoy the beating I gave him? I found it quite pleasurable. Have you considered how I'll eventually kill you? You know there are differing opinions on how Simon the Zealot was martyred. Some say he was crucified. Others say he was sawn in half," the man lamented. "Sawn in half is rather intriguing don't you think? It really won't matter because you'll die when I take your head just like I do with all the others."

"Speaking of heads, would you keep an eye on James' head while I dispose of the body?" Simon was holding the head by the hair behind his back and now opened the cage and sat it on the table in the cage next to Simon's head.

"Normally I wouldn't be in such a rush but some reporter seems to be better than the FBI at figuring out what my next move will be. I'm sure as soon as this morning's paper comes out people will be watching every church and temple in Birmingham hoping to catch the Apostle Serial Killer. I won't be long."

As much as Simon didn't want to, he couldn't help but stare at the decapitated head sitting on the table next to him. If someone didn't do something it would be his head sitting there soon.

"So whose room is this?" Jessica asked as she wandered around Charlie's military base apartment.
"No one's I guess," he replied. "But if it is I don't want them walking in on us in the middle of the night," he said pulling the door shut between the adjoining apartments and locking it.
He wasn't sure Jessica bought it, but it was the best he could do at the spur of the moment.
"So what do you think, should we bother checking out churches tomorrow to look for likely dumping sites?" Charlie asked.
"I think we should concentrate on the Emily Sue Whitman rape angle," Jessica replied. "We should head for Jacksonville and see what we can dig up. There's got to be some kind of record. If we can find out which fraternity we would have a huge list of possible suspects."
"I do need to check in at the bureau in the morning so I won't be able to get away too early," Charlie replied. "Remember, I am in charge of this investigation so I need to tell these guys what I want them to be doing even though I would rather spend all my time with you. I will have to spend some time working."
"When you're with me you're working too," Jessica smiled.
"You got that right."

He was always amazed how much lighter the body was when the head had been removed and most of the blood had been drained away. Then again after each killing he grew stronger and since he was already stronger than any mortal man, the weight of the dead body was insignificant.

"Now where am I going to leave you?" the man puzzled.

He wanted to avoid cameras so the suburbs would probably be best. Somewhere with no twenty-four hour gas stations or markets with their security cameras always running and preferably no banks with their ATM machine cameras capturing vehicles passing by in the dead of night. Avoid if possible but not absolutely necessary. He knew his image could not be captured clearly by any of these cameras. He considered it one of his 'deeds of the flesh', but in his heart he knew it was part of a gift he had tried to deny yet twisted to meet his perverse needs.

"The suburbs it will be, and I know the perfect church, easy freeway access, no cameras, not too big, but big enough."

"Didja see dat," Stu said to the wife driving the van, as he tossed three papers onto the sidewalk of the Liberty Park Baptist Church.

"Jus' like the paper said id be," she replied. "That there's a body."

"Yep, jus' like the paper said. A body wit' no head. We better call 911," Stu said.

"Yeah, call 911," his wife agreed. "Dat must be the Apostle Serial Killer victim the paper talk 'bout."

"Better call Otis, too, somebody's gots to deliver these papers. Police is gonna wanna talk to us," Stu said.

"Yes sir, police are gonna wanna talk to us," his wife repeated. "Dat body has no head. Mercy, mercy, mercy!"

CHAPTER TWENTY-ONE

"It's been almost three weeks. Why are Carlo Caressa and Kevin Bridges still alive?" Vasquez screamed at Meathook.

"We got million dollar hits out on both of them but they seem to have disappeared *Jefe*."

"Where's that *pendejo* Samuelson? He should know what the FBI did with them. They can't just hide them somewhere and pay them for doing nothing like I do with his lazy ass. Go find me Samuelson," Vasquez ordered one of his foot soldiers.

"Boss wants to see you, now," one of the lower echelon bodyguards said when they found Samuelson laying out by the pool.

"You wanted to see me," Samuelson said, entering the bosses living room.

"It's been three weeks and still those two agents are alive. I want them dead," Vasquez explained.

"Then have your men find them and kill them," Samuelson replied.

"Easy as that, huh? Just find them and kill them. Why didn't I think of that? Meathook, why didn't we think of that? Are we that freakin' dumb that none of us thought of that?" Vasquez was growing irate. "You stupid arrogant *pinche gringo*. You worked for the FBI smart guy. Where would the FBI reassign them? Are they behind some desk in Washington? I don't think so because my people there tell me they're not. So where are they, working undercover someplace using different names?"

"That's a possibility," Samuelson replied.

"You hear that Meathook, that's a possibility," Vasquez taunted.

"Maybe they've been reassigned to counter-terrorism and shipped out of the country," Samuelson suggested.

"Well I don't think so," Vasquez replied. "I think they're working undercover and you're going to go find them for me."

"How the hell am I supposed to do that? Samuelson asked.

"You're the smart college boy, you figure it out. Do some research, then pick five of my men and take care of it. Just bring me back proof," Vasquez said.

"What kind of proof?" Samuelson asked.

"I'd prefer to have their heads on a platter but pictures and confirmation from my boys will suffice," Vasquez replied. "But remember this, if you fail me it will be your head on the platter. Whatever you need and when you're ready to go let Meathook know, 'cause I don't want to see your face until the job is done."

Samuelson knew this day was coming. He could either make a break for a country that had no extradition treaty with the United States or do what Vasquez asked. If he surrendered to United States authorities he would most certainly be put to death or meet with an accident before the trial even occurred. Life with Vasquez was tenuous at best but it was life. He had considered trying to get to the Russian Federation. There he at least had a good chance of blending in and eventually learning the language. Getting that far would be the challenge as would getting to his second choice, Viet Nam.

Actually, if he could weather this storm and kill Carlo and Kevin, getting to Russia just might prove to be in the cards.

It was time for Samuelson to get serious about being an investigator again.

CHAPTER TWENTY-TWO

The Market Botanica was nothing like Kevin had anticipated. He had expected a cross between a dingy pawn shop, souvenir shop, and reptile store. What he found was closer to the health food markets that dominated the landscape of Southern California. At least the main room felt that way filled with bins holding various grains, roots, and herbs. There were shelves of Haitian and other ethnic foods normally not found in your local chain super markets.

"This can't be the right place," Kevin muttered as he wandered the aisles. No one seemed to notice him nor did anyone seem to care that a white man was wandering around a store that was filled predominantly by black women and children.

He began to notice that some of the customers moved freely through a beaded curtain into a separate section of the market without being challenged. Kevin boldly stepped through the curtain.

Suddenly, Kevin's inconspicuousness became a blazing flare as every eye in the room darted towards him suspicious of his actions. People purposely moved away as he neared them as if he carried a deadly disease.

"Eh mon, wat you need" a dreadlocked man asked as he approached menacingly. "You scarin' my customers."

"I'm just looking," Kevin replied.

"Well maybe you look someplace else, okay mon," the man replied.

"Maybe I'm looking for something I can only get here," Kevin said, continuing to look around the room.

The shelves in this room contained smaller containers, mostly sealed, with strange names or graphics on them. There was a refrigerated area of various and unusual animal parts that one normally wouldn't even think about saving for dog food or sausage.

Now that the dreadlocked man was with Kevin the other customers seemed to have calmed down and paid less attention. However, most were still wary and kept their distance.

"Whazit you look for?" the man asked.

"My church needs snakes," Kevin semi-whispered.

The man laughed loudly causing several people to turn and stare. "You one of dem snake handlin' church people. I taut you look like dem," he grinned.

"Mr. Bart got plenty o' snakes. What kind how many you want?"

Things had moved a little faster than Kevin had expected.

"I'm not buying them for the church. I'm buying them for me to take to church so I only need two," Kevin replied trying to figure what he was going to do with two deadly poisonous snakes.

"Follow me mon," Bart said.

Kevin followed as Bart walked behind a counter opened a door and headed down into a basement.

"I thought these places didn't have basements because of the water table," Kevin said.

"Don't know mon," Bart replied. "Always been a basement. You got a box?"

"No, I didn't bring one," Kevin replied.

"Box cost you an extra twenty, mon," Bart said.

The basement was even stranger than the room above. There was an entire wall of shelves that contained nothing but bones, including several skulls and what looked like a stringer of dried human ears. What caught Kevin's attention was one skull in the middle that had been made into a chalice.

"What kina snakes you want, mon?"

"I'll take two rattlesnakes," Kevin replied.

"Mon, what kina rattlesnakes? You want cheap or you want expensive?"

"I want cheap," Kevin replied.

"Cheap, you get timber rattlesnake, it local," Bart replied.

"Where's the expensive from?" Kevin asked.

"Expensive come from California, Sidewinder and Desert rattlesnake, but you don't want Sidewinder, they bite," Bart said.

"You want to sell that skull chalice over there?" Kevin asked.

"You can buy those down on Bourbon Street," Bart replied. "It's just tourist crap."

Bart used a snake stick and reached into a pit that held several snakes. "You like that one, mon?"

"That one looks fine," Kevin replied.

With a flick of his wrist Bart snatched the rattler up and dropped it into a wooden box he had pulled from the shelf.

He grabbed another without even asking.

"That will be thee hundred and twenty dollars, mon," Bart said.

"Expensive snakes," Kevin replied, pulling out his wallet and handing over the cash.

"Catch them yourself next time, mon," Bart replied.

Kevin looked around the room one more time before Bart ushered him back up the steps.

"Anything else you need, mon?"

"No, just looking around," Kevin replied.

"Well, don't look long, da snakes scare my customers."

Kevin got the message and was headed for the curtain when a painting caught his eye. It was a religious scene of Christ on the cross but there were black women in Haitian dress performing some sort of ritual which included a skull chalice like the one he had scene in the basement.

"Who did the painting? I kind of like it," Kevin asked.

"I don't know mon. Some local artist traded it to me to help pay off a bill many years back. A woman I tink. Ain't seen her for years," Bart said.

Kevin could tell Bart was lying. That was one of the specialties he had learned in his FBI training. Identifying those facial twitches that always occur when someone tells a lie and Bart's face just showed that twitch.

"Thanks for the snakes," Kevin said as he headed out the door.

Kevin wasn't sure if he should put the snakes in the trunk or on the passenger floorboard in front. He finally decided in front so he could see if they somehow managed to get out he too could get out fast.

"I've got to get Carlo down here with a search warrant. Some of those skulls were the real thing and there's no way I'll find a chalice like that one in a shop down on Bourbon Street. That was the real thing, no doubt about it," Kevin said. He had Bart's home address and drove around the Lower Ninth Ward until he found the house. It was an older two story on Tennessee Street surrounded by trees and bushes.

"I'd love to get a look inside that place," Kevin muttered, as he stopped his car to stare at the house.

"Whachu wan, mon? You lookin' fo' meth? I got meth and I got weed. Whachu wan?" a tweaked drug dealer said pounding on the passenger window.

"I want nothing, get out of here," Kevin said.

"You in my hood, punk," the dealer yelled. "You either buy or die."

Kevin's gun was under the seat and going for it would not have been a smart move considering there had to be other gang members around.

Kevin not wanting any more trouble floored the gas pedal, popped the clutch and steered the fishtail into the dealer throwing him off balance.

"Punk bitch," the dealer yelled grabbing a loose brick and bouncing it off Kevin's rear fender.

"I guess that's my cue to head back to Birmingham," Kevin said.

"So much for your vigilante idea," Jessica fumed.

"What are you talking about?" Charlie said, coming out of the shower.

"It's all over the news. The Apostle Serial Killer already dropped the headless body of James Arnold at some church outside of Birmingham. A newspaper delivery man found the body and called it in around 5:00 a.m."

"The guy's smart. He must have known we would put that information out and didn't want to risk getting caught," Charlie said.

"What do you mean we? I thought the FBI wanted to stay clear of anything to do with vigilantes," Jessica said.

"We do. I should have said your story, forgive me," Charlie said.

"You're forgiven for that," she replied. "But..."

"But what?" Charlie interrupted.

"But don't go trying to ditch me today when you head into the bureau to work. You promised you would keep me informed about the progress made in this investigation," Jessica reminded him. "I should know about any leads my articles generate, especially those related to the rape of Emily Sue Whitman."

"I promised you I would and I will keep that promise," Charlie assured her. "I'll drop you back at your apartment and call you later. Maybe we can meet for lunch or get together for dinner."

"You better damn well meet me for dinner," Jessica said. "I need to know what's going on."

Although she didn't say it, Charlie could tell that if he didn't keep her up to date with the investigation she would find someone else who would. Charlie had no idea who that might be, but he had no doubt in her ability to do so.

"I'll call you," he said as they both climbed into the Trans Am. It was going to be a long uncomfortable ride back to her apartment.

The ride back wasn't as bad as Charlie anticipated, mostly because Jessica pouted most of the way.

"Can you give me a card or something so I can check out James Arnold's house?" Jessica asked.

"I can if the forensics team is through with it," Charlie replied.

"Shouldn't they be by now?" Jessica whined.

"Here," Charlie said, pulling a business card from his wallet and scribbling something on the back. "Just show this to the cop guarding the house. If forensics is gone it won't be a problem. What are you looking for?"

"Just background information or maybe a human interest story on the victim. I'm not sure," Jessica replied.

Anything that would keep her happy for the time being Charlie figured and the request seemed mundane enough.

CHAPTER TWENTY-THREE

"Whoever hired those two idiots was a pro, no doubt about it," Agent Parker explained to Charlie.

"What did you find?" Charlie asked.

"All calls were made on different throw-away cell phones. Cash was sent one time in the form of used bills by FedEx, using a drop off location in Washington D.C. which had no video surveillance. There were no usable finger prints on the envelope but we are checking the drop box. Plenty of DNA and cocaine residues on the bills, but impossible to track it all down. Whoever paid these guys is a ghost."

"You think it's somebody in the trade?" Charlie asked.

"We're taught this stuff at the academy, but this is the kind of thing the CIA or NSA does," Parker replied. "They knew way before we did who the Apostle Serial Killer's next target was, which makes me think it had to be one of them."

"What about someone who was part of the rape? Maybe he was trying to find out if James Arnold was about to out him." Charlie suggested.

"It would still require somebody with some special skills and knowledge," Agent Parker replied.

"What about a politician or government official? Would one of those agencies be authorized to cover his butt to protect his reputation?" Charlie asked.

"You know as well as I do that stuff like that happens all the time," Parker replied.

"So this is a dead-end with these investigators," Charlie said.

"Yes, but it has given us a plethora of possibilities regarding a possible cover-up in the Emily Sue Whitman rape," Parker said.

"And murder," Charlie added. "She quite possibly is the Apostle Killer's first victim. Here's what I need you to do. I want everything you can find out about Emily Sue Whitman. I also want you to find out all you can on a Chester Cunningham. He's a doctor here in Birmingham."

"Is he a suspect?" Parker asked.

"Possibly," Charlie replied. "I also want you to go back to our victims and dig deeper into their pasts. We obviously missed some connections the first time around. We don't want to make those mistakes again. I'm going down to Jacksonville to see what I can dig up on the rape. Somebody has to remember something."

"Can I help you miss?" the officer said as Jessica approached.

"I'm with the FBI," Jessica said, handing him the card Charlie had given her.

"You're welcome to go in miss, but please don't touch anything or move anything around," the officer ordered.

"Of course not Honey," Jessica replied in her most disarming voice causing the young officer to blush.

He watched her for a few moments while she looked around the living room of the house until he realized that she might take it wrong and report it to his boss, so he went back out and left her alone.

"I still don't understand how anyone could choke themselves to death, it's just not possible," she said staring at the tape marks showing where the three bodies were found on the couch.

The house had been thoroughly gone through by the forensics' team but Jessica was hoping to find something they may have missed. She walked down the hallway looking at the few pictures and in the bedrooms scanning the walls but to no avail. Sitting on a shelf next to the stereo she discovered what she was looking for though it wasn't what she had expected.

In a five by seven inch frame was a picture of a long-haired James Arnold sitting behind a set of drums. On the bass drum head was emblazoned the name The Jackson Smith Band.

"Where have I heard that name before?" Jessica thought.

She started looking in-between each album cover until she found what she had hoped was there, a full eight by ten inch glossy promotional photograph of the Jackson Smith Band.

She turned it over and read, "Andrew Jackson Smith, lead guitar and vocals, James Zeller, bass, vocals, Chester Cunningham, rhythm guitar, James Arnold, drums. They just didn't stop by that fraternity party, they were the entertainment at the fraternity party," Jessica said, slipping the photo into her purse.

She immediately called her assistant editor's voicemail at the newspaper. "It's Paige; I need you to find out everything you possibly can on a guy named Chester Cunningham. I'm guessing he still lives in the Birmingham area but maybe not. I need everything and I need it right away, thanks."

"Thank you officer for letting me in. I think I saw all I needed to see," Jessica said.

"Anytime miss," the officer replied, continuing to stare as Jessica climbed into her car.

Charlie didn't recognize the number that was calling his phone and debated answering just for a moment.

"Charlie Daniels," he finally answered.

"Don't even think about not answering your phone just because you don't recognize the number," Kevin scolded.

"How did you know I thought about not answering?" Charlie asked.

"Because you always answer in the first two rings," Kevin replied. "And from here on out I'll be using these throw away phones so I can't be followed on GPS."

"Why are you worried about that?" Charlie asked.

"You talk with Hannah today?" Kevin asked.

"Like I had a choice," Charlie replied.

"Exactly, how many times did he ask where I was?" Kevin said.

"That was about half of our conversation," Charlie replied.

"I figured it would be but I just don't know why for sure. He seems to be overly interested in this investigation," Kevin commented.

"He did lose an agent and it was one he had assigned. He's probably feeling pretty guilty about that," Charlie speculated.

"I don't think Hannah's the type to feel much guilt. You just make sure to answer your phone when I call."

"Okay, I answered so what's bugging you?" Charlie asked.

"I just visited the Market Botanica in New Orleans and there is more to it than meets the eye. The basement is full of snakes for sale and there is a shelf full of skulls. I need you to get a federal warrant and have the New Orleans office move in there today and pull out all those skulls for DNA testing," Kevin ordered.

"What grounds do we use for the warrant?" Charlie asked.

"I doubt that he has a license to sell poisonous snakes or that it's even legal to keep them in a public store in New Orleans, but if he does and it is legal, make something up. I want those skulls out of there today," Kevin insisted.

"Are you sure he sells the snakes?" Charlie asked.

"Positive, I've got two of them sitting on the floor next to me," Kevin replied.

"I'm on it right now," Charlie said.

"Anything on Chester Cunningham yet?" Kevin asked.

"I just assigned it a couple of hours ago. Give it a day," Charlie said.

"I'd like a little something by tomorrow morning before I head back to the church," Kevin said. "How's it going with Jessica?"

"She wasn't real happy that James Arnold's body was dumped before the papers hit the stands telling them where it was going to be dumped," Charlie explained.

"I can't imagine she was," Kevin replied.

"She's over going through his house to get background on a human interest story about him," Charlie explained.

"That's a load of crap," Kevin replied. "She's not the least bit interested in a human interest story. She's looking for clues that we missed and I'll bet you she found some. Keep an eye on her, she'll be up to something. You can bet on it."

Charlie felt like he'd been had.

"What about the two private investigators?"

"Dead end. Whoever hired them knows how the game is played. We're guessing CIA or NSA," Charlie replied.

"That changes things," Kevin replied. "Somebody with a lot of influence and access is concerned about the investigation. No wonder Hannah wants you to call every day. Somebody's got his balls in a vice."

"Is it okay if Jessica hears about the skulls?" Charlie asked.

"Why, would it be a problem keeping it from her?" Kevin asked.

"I'll have to head to New Orleans immediately and coordinate the warrant on the Market Botanica on my drive down. We had planned on driving to Jacksonville and seeing what we could dig up on the Emily Sue Whitman's rape. I was going to strong arm the police and college while she talked to the local papers and see if we could find out the fraternity involved. Telling her that the trip was off would not go over well at all, but telling her we had to make a detour, especially when I told her what it was for, might pay big dividends," Charlie explained.

"By big dividends I assume you mean what she was up to inside James Arnold's house today," Kevin snapped back.

"Oh yes, of course, exactly right," Charlie chided.

"I'll be at the apartment tonight, but will be leaving for Sand Mountain early in the morning. Call me when you get the skulls. The New Orleans lab can run the DNA tests but we need to find out if there are any DNA records on Emily Sue Whitman. If not, or even if there is, start looking for family members because we may need to exhume the remains," Kevin said. "Oh, make sure they get the skull that is made into a chalice. I really want it checked out. I got a strange feeling about that one."

"I know all about your strange feelings. I'll put that one at the top of the warrant. You know, I can't believe you saw her grave. What a coincidence," Charlie commented.

"I wouldn't call it a coincidence; I'd consider it the hand of God intervening in our investigation. This is more than just a crazed lunatic bent on killing people. This is evil itself spreading across the South," Kevin began to explain.

"Whoa there partner. Don't get too carried away with this spiritual warfare battle idea of yours," Charlie warned. "If Hannah heard you talking like that he'd think you'd gone nuts."

"Do you think I've gone nuts?" Kevin asked.

"Not one bit," Charlie answered without hesitation. "There is no logical or scientific explanation for some of what I've seen so far in this case and even though I don't share the fervent Christian beliefs you hold, your explanation makes more sense than any other as far as I'm concerned. You know I trust your judgment. You've got the gift man."

Kevin wasn't quite sure what Carlo meant by 'the gift' but he knew he was his most trusted friend and ally.

"I'll see what I can find out about Emily Sue when I work at the church tomorrow. Ginny Lee has lived there her entire life. She's bound to know about Emily Sue Whitman," Kevin said.

"You never mentioned Ginny Lee before," Charlie replied. "Is she a new friend?"

"I think she would like to be, but only as an excuse to get Chester Cunningham off her back," Kevin explained. "I may be wrong about that. You know I'm not the best at reading a woman's intentions. Maybe she does really like me."

"Yeah, like Jessica really likes me," Charlie teased.

"Ginny Lee is very devout and I can assure you Ginny Lee will never 'like' me in the same way Jessica 'likes' you," Kevin guaranteed Charlie.

"Somebody's got to do it," Charlie replied.

"Jessica still knows nothing about me, right?"

"Not a thing. She did ask me who the Chevy Nova was delivered for and I told her another agent working a different case."

"Did she believe you?"

"She hasn't mentioned it again."

"Okay, I'll talk to you later. Call me when you get the skulls, but make sure she doesn't know you're calling me," Kevin reminded Charlie. "Oh, one more thing. There was this painting on the wall in the back room of Christ on the Cross. You can't miss it. Get a couple of pictures of it for me will you?"

"Will do, and don't worry I'll be careful," Charlie replied. "Talk to you later."

Kevin closed the cell phone.

"She already knows about me," Kevin said trying not to be angry. "There was nothing Charlie could have done. She knew about the two cars being delivered to the base and about two agents coming in almost as soon as it had been arranged. It would only stand to reason that she knows our real names as well. If we're not careful this thing is going to blow up in our face worse than the Vasquez fiasco in Los Angeles."

Kevin called Charlie back.

"See it only took me two rings."

"Charlie, I've been thinking. Jessica has to know that there is another agent on the case. She knew about the two cars being delivered to the base and that two agents were coming in. I'm betting she even knows our real identities. Hell, the sergeants even figured that out."

"So what are you trying to tell me?"

"Don't let her out of your sight if you can help it. Keep denying that I'm involved but do what you have to do to keep her happy. I'm afraid if information became scarce and she needed a story she just might let our real identities slip. Besides blowing my part of the whole operation we would have Vasquez to contend with."

"I'll do what I have to do, don't worry," Charlie said. "I'm on my way to pick her up now. We're headed for New Orleans. The Market Botanica closes at eight and we plan on serving the warrant at seven or as soon as Jessica and I arrive."

"Good luck," Kevin said.

"Adios," Charlie replied.

Now Kevin had one more matter to deal with that day. What to do with the two timber rattlesnakes sitting in the box on the floor of his car.

CHAPTER TWENTY-FOUR

"So what's the rush," Jessica said, as Charlie whisked her out of the apartment.

"We have to make a bit of a detour on our way to Jacksonville," Charlie replied.

"How far is a bit of a detour?" Jessica asked.

"New Orleans."

"New Orleans! Why in the world are we going to New Orleans? That's like six hours in the opposite direction from Jacksonville."

"We are exercising a warrant on a Haitian Voodoo parlor that has several human skulls for sale in a hidden basement. We're going to pick them up and run DNA tests to see if any match our victims," Charlie explained.

"I didn't know it was illegal to sell human skulls," Jessica replied. "I thought I'd seen those in shops before."

"It is legal with the proper permits and perhaps he has the proper permit. I don't know," Charlie conceded.

"Then what is the warrant for?"

"The keeping and selling of poisonous and dangerous reptiles without a proper permit," Charlie replied. "The basement is full of poisonous snakes."

"So how did you find out about this place?"

Charlie knew Jessica was trying to catch him about a second agent being involved in the operation.

"We've known about this guy for quite some time. One of our agents discovered the snakes and the skulls over a month ago," Charlie explained.

"Would that be the agent that disappeared in New Orleans while working the case undercover? The agent you are here to replace," Jessica said, waiting for a reaction from Charlie.

"It seems you are better informed than I thought," Charlie replied. "Why haven't you released that story through your paper?"

"FBI agent working undercover on Apostle Serial Killer murders turns up missing and presumed captured as future victim of serial killer. It's a great story. I'm just waiting for the right time to release it. What is he now, five victims away?"

"And when will that time be?" Charlie fumed.

"When you stop giving me stories that keep the networks attention focused on me," she replied. "The Apostle Serial Killer is my ticket to the big-time."

"It was going to be a long five hours until they reached New Orleans," Charlie thought.

"I hope you two didn't talk about me while I was gone," the killer joked as he came back into his basement. "Oh that's right your tongue is too swollen to allow you to talk Simon. I guess it was a one way conversation." The killer laughed even harder.

"I brought you a nutrition drink that will help keep your stamina up until the swelling goes down," he said, opening the cage and setting the drink on the table.

"Sorry to take you away from your friend, James, but I have a bit more work to do on you," the killer explained grabbing James' decapitated head by the hair and carrying it out of the cage locking the cage behind him.

He carried the head over to a workbench at the far end of the basement.

"Oooooh," Simon moaned.

"Sorry," the killer said and lifted his hand causing the restraints binding Simon to the cot to release. "Enjoy your lunch."

Over the years he had experimented with various methods of removing the tissue from skulls, including using beetles to eat the rotting flesh. He had settled on hot water maceration as the preferred method. The primary drawback was that if not properly monitored there was the potential for damage to the skull and almost always there would be some degree of shrinkage. Cold water maceration would have eliminated both of these problems but the killer lacked the patience required for the extended time this method required.

"You know Simon, this part is kind of like peeling an orange. I just have to be very careful not to nick the bone," the killer explained as he used a scalpel to carefully peel away layers of facial skin and tissue from the decapitated head.

"Can you think of anyone who could use this? He giggled, cutting off the nose and tossing it into the cage. "I can."

"I know someone who collects human ears. I'm sure I could've accumulated a tidy sum by now if I was willing to sell them to him," he said as he sliced the two ears off the head with quick motions. "But then he'd know too much and I'd have to kill him sooner than I'd like."

He made three quick slices and peeled Mr. Arnold's entire scalp off the skull.

"The more tissue I remove now the quicker the maceration process will be," he explained.

"Now this part you'll really enjoy. This is just how the ancient Egyptians used to do it. You stick the wire up the nose scramble it all around and then pull the brains back out through the nose. The Egyptians did it to preserve the brain in a separate jar. Can you guess why I do it? No guesses? Then I'll tell you. If I didn't remove the brain it could expand during the hot water maceration process and split the skull. If that happened I'd have to find myself another James A and that would throw off my entire time table," the man explained.

He continued peeling away as much of the skin and tissue as possible.

Kevin carried the box containing the two snakes into his apartment at the military base and sat it in the middle of the living room floor.

"Now what?" he said.

He noticed that the door between the apartments had been closed and looked around to see if anything had been disturbed. All looked just as he had left it. He was sure Charlie had kept Jessica out of the room last night but he knew Charlie couldn't do it every night. In fact, he was counting on it.

He tried to ignore the box sitting in the middle of the floor but the harder he tried the more difficult it became.

"This is worse than the elephant in the room that nobody wants to talk about. I'd be happy to talk about it if somebody was here to talk to," Kevin said.

"Ginny Lee said they handle snakes only if the Spirit moves them. The Spirit has said nothing to me about dumping these two out on the floor and picking them up so I guess I'll just stick them in the bathroom shower stall for the evening," Kevin announced to himself.

"Maybe I can donate them to the church tomorrow," he thought.

"Then again, maybe not. I've got to give that one some thought." Kevin continued his debate as he carried the box to the bathroom.

"See that didn't take long at all," he said, pulling the skull from the pot of hot water.

He gently shook the skull as fluid ran out the eye and nasal cavities. He sat the skull on a towel on the workbench and picked up the pot with two pot holders.

"Let's see how many teeth we lost shall we?"

He carefully poured the putrid water through a sieve which collected the lower and upper jaw as well as three teeth that had fallen out during the maceration process.

"Mr. Arnold didn't see his dentist as often as he should have," the man laughed. "Looks like I'll have some cosmetic dental work to perform as well."

He pulled the pieces from the sieve and set them aside.

"You know the first time I did this part I did it by hand using a tool called a Gigli's Wire. Have you ever heard of it?" As he was speaking he was securing the skull firmly in a specially designed clamp and setting up to perform some sort of work. "Some brain surgeons still use them today. However, I've found that a Dremel tool works much more efficiently for my needs."

The high-pitched whine of the tool's motor filled the room and Simon could see a cloud of fine dust rise up from the top of the skull as the man began carving away at what was left of James Arnold.

CHAPTER TWENTY-FIVE

"The warrant says nothing about ears," the local supervising agent said.

"You're kidding right?" Charlie replied.

"No suh. The warrant specifically says we're to pick up skulls and any objects made with skulls. As perverse as that stringer of ears may be we have no right to take it at this time," Supervising Agent Markham insisted.

"What about the snakes? Charlie asked.

"We're probably going to get our asses kicked for that one as well. The warrant lists this place being in violation of Animal Control ordinances 4-19 and 4-20. 4-19 is about harboring poisonous snakes in an apartment house, which this obviously isn't and 4-20, let me quote this, *'It shall be unlawful to own, keep, possess, maintain or harbor any dangerous animal.'* This one we may squeak by on enough to justify confiscating the skulls, but don't expect to keep them for long," Markham warned.

"Then you better get them DNA tested ASAP," Charlie replied. "Especially the one made into a chalice."

"What's so important about the skull made into the chalice?" Jessica asked.

"It seems to me to fit in with the Apostle Serial Killer's overall theme," Charlie began bluffing. "The chalice was such a major religious icon especially with the Apostles at the Last Supper. The Holy Grail. I think it's reasonable to think he may be using the skulls to make chalices or these Holy Grails. I know that was often done with the heads of the losing generals in religious wars during the crusades. I don't know, it's just a thought."

His bluff must have worked because he could see Jessica's mind going a mile a minute with possibilities.

The owner of the Voodoo store said he's had that chalice for over twenty-five years. Maybe that skull belongs to Emily Sue Whitman," Jessica said excitedly.

"That's something the FBI is considering. We're trying to contact next of kin to have her remains exhumed to compare DNA samples."

"Why didn't you tell me this?" Jessica demanded.

"I just did. Besides, it's better if you figure it out as we go along. It's not as if I was going to do anything without you being there," Charlie replied. "We just have to systematically take these things in order."

"So what's our next systematic step as you put it?" Jessica asked tersely.

"Next, you stand over here by this painting while I take a couple of pictures," Charlie replied.

"Why this painting?" she asked.

"It has a chalice in it just like the one we confiscated. There may be a relationship," Charlie replied. "But I don't think Bart feels much like discussing artwork at the present. Perhaps it's something to talk about at a later date."

"So what do we do now?" Jessica asked.

"The DNA results won't be ready until the morning so I've always wanted to eat at one of Emeril Legasse's restaurants, so why don't we check into a nice hotel near the French Quarter and I'll make dinner reservations."

"I think it's a great idea as long as you give me about forty-five minutes to file a story."

"Just as long as your story won't interfere with our investigation," Charlie replied.

"Oh, it won't. I just find your chalice idea rather provocative and worth a tie-in with this raid on the Haitian Market."

"I see no problem with that," Charlie said.

"And if there was a problem?" Jessica challenged.

"I'm sure we could work something out between us."

"I'm sure we can," Jessica replied, with a gleam in her eye.

Kevin awoke early for his return trip to Sand Mountain. He had much on his mind and much to accomplish that day. He had forgone his normal middle of the night trip to the bathroom not wanting to face the rattle snakes but the time had come and he had to face the inevitable task of dealing with the snakes.

"I wonder if they need to be fed," Kevin said, as he grabbed a broom from the kitchen and headed to the bathroom door.

"Let's do this real slow," he said, pushing ever so gently on the door.

Once the door was open barely a crack, he tentatively stuck his hand in at the level of the light switch trying to turn on the light waiting at any second for fangs to plunge into his wrist.

"Now maybe I can see what I'm doing," he said, as he slowly pushed the door open with the broom.

Despite all his expectations, the box holding the two rattle snakes sat firmly in the center of the shower stall with the lid solidly attached.

"Well, that was easy," Kevin said.

He carefully picked up the box, trying not to disturb the snakes inside, and carried them out into the living room. This time he placed them in the closet by the front door.

"It'll only be for a few minutes guys while I shower and dress," Kevin said, talking to the snakes, "then we'll be on our way."

Twenty minutes later Kevin grabbed his snakes and headed out for his car.

Both Sergeants Boone and McClellan were outside the apartments that morning to greet him.

"Mr. Jackson, good to see you again. Need help with that box?" McClellan said making a move towards the box.

"I don't think so but thanks anyway," Kevin replied, as one of the snakes suddenly began to rattle, causing McClellan to jump back.

"Sergeant Boone told me you had quite of bit of fun the other night with Charlie," Kevin said to McClellan who was still staring at the box.

"Sir, that was an evening and day I can honestly say I will never forget or for that matter remember much of," McClellan laughed. "I know you're a Godly man sir so I won't go into details, but if someone told me they had been with that many women I would call them a bold face liar. I could no longer say that, sir, if you get my drift."

"I believe I understand what you're trying to say," Kevin replied.

"I can't get him to shut up about it," Sergeant Boone said.

"Have you seen Charlie" Kevin asked.

"He stayed here night before last with his lady friend from Banana Joe's. I believe she is that newspaper reporter Paige Eliot, but he calls her Jessica. We never got the chance to talk with him," Sergeant Boone said.

"Have you seen today's paper?" Sergeant McClellan asked, "It's her newest article about the Apostle Serial Killer."

"No, what's it say about him?" Kevin asked.

"Talks about an FBI raid on a place called Market Botanica down in New Orleans that deals in lots of Voodoo items including rattlesnakes," McClellan said," looking past Kevin and at the box Kevin had been carting. "Says the FBI confiscated several human skulls from the place for DNA testing to see if there is a link to any of the killer's victims. Talks about one in particular that had been made into a chalice that they believe is most likely tied to the Apostle Serial Killer."

Kevin wasn't liking all the information he was hearing. This was even more than he had given Charlie. This Jessica had taken the little bits she was able to squeeze out of Charlie and extrapolate it into a major part of the investigation.

"Does it say anything else?" Kevin asked.

"Yeah, it says the skull made into the chalice is thought to be possibly linked to the murder of a nursing student named Emily Sue Whitman back in 1975 whose headless remains were found about nine months after her disappearance. An autopsy report from the time describes an almost surgical removal of the head, which is very similar to the recent Apostle Serial Killer's *modus operandi*. It goes on to say how the FBI plans to exhume the body to compare DNA."

"It doesn't say where the body is does it?" Kevin asked.

"No, I didn't see that anywhere," McClellan replied.

"Guys, thanks for the information and remember never mention anything about me in front of the reporter lady. Understood?" Kevin said.

"Understood sir," they replied in unison.

"Thanks guys, see you later." With his snakes safely on the floor of the front seat, Kevin headed for Sand Mountain and what he hoped would be an enlightening day.

"Oh man, turn off the bells," Charlie moaned as his cell phone ring sounded like his hotel room was located in the bell tower of the St. Louis Cathedral.

"Hello," Charlie barely got out, when he finally managed to answer his phone.

"Agent Daniels, this is Supervising Agent Markham."

"Good Morning Agent Markham," Charlie muttered.

"Sounds like you enjoyed some of our famous New Orleans hospitality last night, Agent Daniels," Markham laughed.

"No sir, just waking up slowly is all," Charlie replied. "Any news on the DNA results?"

"No matches what-so-ever to any of your Apostle Serial Killer victims or any other records in our data bases. Looks like we missed on this one," Markham replied. "We're going to have to return the skulls to the owner."

"I'm going to want that chalice for a few days until we can exhume the remains of the nursing student," Charlie insisted.

"I can arrange that, but for no more than a week. If we have no match by then, it too has to go back, understood?"

"I understand," Charlie said. "I'll stop by your office and pick it up on my way out of town."

"Take your time; it's still across town at the lab." Markham replied.

"I think it will be a little while yet," Charlie wheezed.

"I kind of got that impression," Markham laughed. "Bourbon Street can do that to you."

"Oh yeah," Charlie replied, hanging up the phone.

Charlie turned and looked at the figure completely covered by a sheet next to him. Jessica even had a pillow pulled tight over her head to block out sound.

"Time to get up," Charlie said, pulling the sheet off of her.

"Oh, I've got the hangover of doom," Jessica moaned.

Charlie was staring at her.

"What's wrong?" Jessica asked.

"How did you get all of those necklaces?" Charlie asked.

"Jessica looked down at her naked body. There were at least fifty brightly colored necklaces draped around her neck.

"If you can't remember, don't ask," she said. "Let's go eat breakfast. We have a lot of work to do today."

Charlie's head hurt too much to disagree with anything Jessica said, but he certainly did remember how she got them.

CHAPTER TWENTY-SIX

"What kept you? I was expecting you an hour ago," Ginny Lee said, as Kevin pulled his Nova into the gravel lot.

"Expecting me or just hoping for me?" Kevin teased.

"Well the pancakes are gettin' cold," Ginny Lee whined.

"You didn't say anything about breakfast or I would have for sure been here earlier. All you promised me was lunch and dinner for a day's work," Kevin replied.

"Then I guess it was more hoping than expecting then wasn't it," she replied with a smile, sitting the plate of pancakes in front of him.

"What would you like me to start on?" Kevin asked, after finishing the stack.

"I really liked the way you were cleaning up the graveyard out yonder, but I noticed the fencing is all busted up and needs replacing," Ginny Lee began.

"Yeah, I did what I could but you're going to need to buy some posts and wire to keep animals from tearing it up," Kevin said.

"The church got no money for that kind of purchase, but Ver Dell told me he had some posts and wire up at his place we can have. Just got to go pick it up," Ginny Lee said.

"I can do that if you can tell me how to get there," Kevin said.

"Probably better if I showed you," Ginny Lee said. "It's easy to get lost in these hills."

They jumped in the car, Ginny Lee almost kicking over the box on the front floor.

"Whacha got here?" Ginny Lee said picking up the box.

Before Kevin could answer Ginny Lee answered her own question.

"I guess the Holy Spirit done grabbed you harder than I imagined. You went out and caught yourself a rattlesnake," Ginny Lee teased.

"Actually, two rattle snakes and I didn't catch them, I bought them," Kevin replied shyly.

Ginny Lee roared with laughter.

"Whaja plan on doin' with 'im?"

"I don't know. It was one of those impulse buys you make. You see them at the register on your way out of the store and you just have to have one or two," Kevin joked. "They get you every time."

"What should I do with them?" Kevin asked.

"Well the church does use them. Maybe you could ask Ver Dell about them," Ginny Lee suggested.

"Promise me you won't tell anybody about this, Ginny Lee. I'd be too embarrassed to ever show my face around here again," Kevin pleaded.

"We wouldn't want that to happen," Ginny Lee replied.

"I'll just tell Ver Dell someone dropped them off while you were straightening up this morning."

"Thanks," Kevin replied.

She set the box of snakes between her feet and they headed back into the woods up a dirt road behind the church.

"You really wouldn't want to go back in here without knowing someone. They don't take well to strangers," Ginny Lee explained.

Kevin and Ginny Lee passed several groups of men, some holding shotguns and some just staring, but they all seemed to relax a bit when they saw Ginny Lee.

"Ver Dell's place is just up and to the right across the creek. You can hear his wood chipper."

"Are you sure I can drive across that? It looks deep," Kevin said.

"I do it all the time," Ginny Lee replied.

Kevin turned and gunned his engine to make sure he made it across. His Nova bottomed out scraping noisily as he crossed.

"See I told you it was easy," Ginny Lee said.

As they exited the car and approached Ver Dell, Kevin did a double take at what he thought he had just seen. The wood chipper was blowing into the hog's feed bin and Kevin swore he saw Ver Dell shove a human leg into the chipper.

"Mornin' Ver Dell," Ginny Lee said, but Ver Dell didn't hear her over the whine of the chipper engine.

Ver Dell picked up a smaller dead pig from a wheelbarrow and tossed it into the chipper splattering blood and bone splinters onto his apron. He then switched the machine off.

"Mornin' Ver Dell," both Kevin and Ginny Lee said at the same time startling Ver Dell.

"Ya'll been hea long?" Ver Dell asked a bit suspiciously.

"No, we just now walked up," Ginny Lee replied. "We came to pick up those posts and wire you said you had."

"Yonder in the shed," Ver Dell replied. "I'll go fetch it."

Kevin waited till Ver Del was far enough away.

"What's he doing here?" Kevin asked.

"Just mixing a batch of slop for his hogs it looks like," Ginny Lee replied nonchalantly.

"He was grinding up another pig to feed his pigs and something else that looked like a leg," Kevin exclaimed.

"Probably was a leg. Horse's legs and cow's legs are used all the time as an additive for pig feed and for cow feed too," Ginny Lee explained. "That's the way things work even in the big feedlots."

"These 'ere should do 'er," Ver Dell said, handing a box to Kevin.

"Some folks dropped a couple of snakes off at the church this morning. Gave 'em to Kevin while he was straightenin' up. He wasn't sure what to do with them so I suggested he talk to you," Ginny Lee explained.

"Some folks you say," Ver Dell said eyeing Kevin. "Folks from the church?"

"I don't really know many of the church folk and they didn't give a name," Kevin replied.

"Seems a might peculiar to me," Ver Dell replied, "Folks just droppin' off snakes like that."

"Don't seem peculiar to me at all," Ginny Lee piped in. "Lots of new folks coming to the church filled with the Spirit and wantin' to do their part."

"Might be so." Ver Dell reluctantly agreed. "You look at 'em yet?"

"Not me, if I opened that box I wouldn't know how to get them back in," Kevin replied.

"Let's 'ave a look," Ver Dell said opening the box and pouring the two rattle snakes on the ground in front of him.

Kevin immediately jumped back.

"Coupla timber rattlers," Ver Dell said snatching one up in each hand then quickly slipping them back into the box.

"Aren't you afraid they'll bite you?" Kevin asked.

"I'm saved by the Holy Spirit, but I don't take stupid chances outside da church. Dem snakes hungry. Hungry snakes bite, so 'fore you bring um ta church make sure dey been fed. Da music in da church help bring forth the Holy Spirit. Also puts snakes in trance, but don't get me wrong it's da Holy Spirit dat protects us from dem serpents, the poisons, and da fire," Ver Dell asserted.

"You comin' down to the church for the lunch meeting?" Ginny Lee asked, changing the subject.

"I guess I betta," Ver Dell replied. "Ida said she bring long some corn bread."

"Tell her thanks," Ginny Lee replied. "We should get goin', Kevin."

"Don't forget your snakes," Ver Dell said to Kevin holding out the box for him to take. "Betta' find dem a coupla rats to eat 'fo long."

"I'll make sure I do," Kevin replied. "Thanks for the supplies and for your advice."

The car bottomed out again as they re-crossed the stream on their way out.

"I guess you got yourself a couple of rattle snakes," Ginny Lee laughed. "There's a feed store in town where we can pick up a couple of rats to feed them before tonight."

Several men were still standing near the trees by the side of the road with shot guns as they drove back down.

"Try not to look at them," Ginny Lee warned, "They've got a big distilling operation going on in the woods back over yonder and are a bit edgy about strangers."

Kevin kept his eyes straight ahead. "What do you mean feed them before tonight?"

"I thought you might get filled with the Spirit and want to handle your snakes tonight," Ginny Lee replied.

Kevin drove on quietly without responding. "I heard you tell Ver Dell about a lunch meeting today at the church. By the tone of your voice it sounded serious."

"Serious, but nothing we haven't had to deal with in the past," Ginny Lee replied. "You'll hear all about it 'cause I did promise you lunch, if you remember."

"And I did promise you a hard day's work so I need to get started," Kevin replied.

"Well, now that we have the supplies you can start by finishing the graveyard, fixin' the fence, pullin' the weeds, and seeing what you can do about that gate."

"Some paint would help," Kevin said.

"Paint we got plenty of in the storeroom. You should have no problem finding a color to match. Any tools you need you'll find there too. If you have any questions I'll be cookin' up at the house. I'll drop by now and again to see if'n you need anything," Ginny Lee said as they pulled back into the church lot.

Kevin wanted to bring up the newspaper story about the FBI's plan to exhume Emily Sue Whitman's remains, but decided to wait till after the lunch meeting in case that was part of the agenda.

The trip up into the hills to visit Ver Dell had spooked Kevin. He was sure that was no animal leg he had seen going into the wood chipper and those men standing around with shotguns brought back visions of some old movies he didn't want to think about and that even scared him more.

"So if the DNA they got off this chalice doesn't match Emily Sue Whitman's this New Orleans trip was a total waste of time," Jessica complained.

"Not a complete waste. Think of all the new necklaces you collected," Charlie laughed.

"Not funny!" Jessica replied sternly.

"We'll still make Jacksonville by mid-afternoon. That should give us plenty of time to start tracking down leads," Charlie said. "Why don't we take turns driving so we can both check with our people to see what they've come up with. I'm sure my people have located Emily Sue's relatives by now and have permission to exhume her remains."

"What if they deny permission?"

"We'll do it anyway because of the relevance to the ongoing investigation."

"What if they won't tell you where she is buried? I know the laws back in the 70's especially here in the South weren't too strict about recording internments. As far as you know she could have been cremated," Jessica exclaimed.

Charlie wanted to just say 'shut up bitch, I already know where her grave is', but he knew that would begin a terrible downward spiral that would not end pleasantly for anyone.

"Well, we can only hope that's not the case," he replied, trying to convey a positive attitude.

Jessica immediately sensed Charlie was not being straight with her and decided to start playing her own cards a little closer to her chest.

"It's beautiful isn't it?" The killer held the nearly finished chalice for Simon to see. "I have more inlay work to do and of course I want to polish it up much better than this, but doesn't it just take your breath away?"

Simon's swollen tongue had improved significantly but even if he could speak a little more clearly he refused to acknowledge the killer's sadistic pleasure.

"Come now, Simon, I know your tongue must be better by now, if not you better at least nod your head," the killer warned.

It took all of Simon's strength to force a half-hearted smile and nod his head in agreement with the killer's delight in his own handiwork.

"I bet you're hungry. I've gone and worked throughout the night again and it's already way past breakfast. I'll run upstairs and fix a little something for both of us," the killer said walking over to a large safe.

He turned the dial a few times and glanced over his shoulder at Simon. "Now don't peak at the combination," he giggled.

A moment later he pulled open the safe and Simon could see that the top half had been sectioned off with twelve velvet lined cubicles, four of which already held chalices similar to the one he now placed inside. There was also a considerable sum of money stacked in another section of the safe and what looked like several gold bars.

"I bet you're wondering where I got all my money," the man said. "At one time I did have powerful 'gifts of the Spirit', but I used them for my own purposes not God's. I became rich, wealthier than you can imagine, but that's in the past and we shall never talk about it again. I'll be right back with breakfast."

Simon listened as the man moved around upstairs preparing breakfast. He prayed that the FBI was close to breaking the case because he didn't know how much longer he could take this.

Suddenly, the calmness from the floor above was shattered by angry cursing and the throwing and breaking of what Simon believed to be his breakfast shake. Then for the first time since he had been held in the cage he heard a phone ring somewhere in the distance. Then came an uneasy silence and all Simon could do was wait.

CHAPTER TWENTY-SEVEN

It was almost an hour before Simon heard anymore movement coming from the floor above him. He heard the blender which he hoped meant the man was making him another shake. Moments later the door opened and the man came slowly down the stairs.

"I-I-I'm s-sorry I-I t-took s-so long," the killer stuttered. "I-I read s-some r-rather upsetting n-news in the p-paper."

He brought Simon his shake and took his own breakfast over to a table that faced Simon. He then went over to his stereo and turned on Lynyrd Skynyrd's *Freebird*.

"This s-s-song always relaxes m-me," he said. "I love the slide guitar in the beginning of the song and the solo at the end is just exquisite."

Simon just watched as the man seemed to lose himself in the music. His shoulders lowered and his breathing slowed and his overall demeanor brightened.

"It seems the FBI has been very busy in their investigation and has made more progress than I would have liked," the killer began.

Simon became acutely interested in the one-sided conversation.

"They have located my very first victim's skull and are seeking to exhume her remains to see if the DNA from the chalice matches the DNA from the remains. Tell me or shake your head, was it the chalice you were looking for at the Market Botanica in New Orleans when I captured you?" he asked.

Simon thought about lying but realized the futility of doing so and shook his head side-to-side signifying no.

"You were just following the trail of the snakes because of the venom in the victims, weren't you?"

Simon signaled yes.

"I'm afraid the FBI is getting a little too close for comfort with the direction their investigation is taking. I believe I'm going to have to derail it or send it off in a different direction. If not the timetable is out the window and that doesn't bode well for you I'm afraid," the killer explained.

"I'll be going away again for a few days so I'll make sure you have plenty of food and water. I'm afraid I'll have to chain your leg to the center of the cage again in case you get any wild ideas about trying to get away. Of course, if you prefer, I could put you in another one of those medical induced comas like we did before," the killer said.

Simon shook his head rapidly from side-to-side. He was groggy for days the last time the killer did that to him.

"I didn't think you'd want that, so I expect your best behavior," he demanded.

"As if I had any other choice," Simon thought. "At least the FBI has got him running scared and scared criminals tend to make mistakes."

"Step to the middle please," he said.

Simon did as he was told. The killer lifted his hand and the ankle chain opened, closed and locked around Simon's leg without being touched.

"Then again, this guy is no ordinary criminal," Simon thought. "I'm not even sure he's human."

Charlie and Jessica were just outside Tuscaloosa, Alabama when his cell phone began to ring. It was his turn to work so Jessica was driving. He saw it was the Birmingham bureau calling so he was able to answer on the first ring.

"Agent Daniels," he answered.

"Caressa, why the hell haven't you called me every day like I told you to and where the hell is Agent Bridges?"

"Sir, I've been working hard on this investigation and calling everyday just isn't always possible," Charlie began to explain.

"Well, from here on out you better make it possible or you'll be off the Apostle Serial Killer investigation and somebody capable of following directions will be in your place. You got that Agent Caressa? Now tell me where and what Bridges' is up to. His cell phone GPS hasn't moved from the National Guard Base where you two are staying but he sure as hell isn't there. I've already checked."

"Sir, I'm not in a position to discuss that matter at the moment," Charlie replied.

"Why the hell not?" Hannah insisted.

"That's something we should talk about when I get back to the Birmingham bureau," Charlie replied.

"And just when might that be?" Hannah asked.

Charlie looked over at Jessica whose driving had become very erratic.

"What is it you're not telling me Charlie?" she whispered angrily.

"I have some appointments in Jacksonville later this afternoon and this evening and didn't plan on returning to Birmingham until tomorrow," Charlie said to Hannah.

"Tomorrow, that's completely unacceptable. I want you here in an hour and a half," Hannah insisted.

"That's not possible sir," Charlie replied.

"It is according to your GPS location and the distance you are from Birmingham. An hour and a half will give you plenty of time to drive here and take care of your inconvenience that is keeping you from talking to me. You'd better have a damn good reason for that too, Caressa," Hannah raged. "I've heard you've allowed a reporter access to this investigation. That's a serious accusation that you're going to need to address."

"With all due respect Director Hannah, I believe I am handling this case with the utmost professionalism, have made great headway in the investigation, and am appalled at your lack of professionalism in blowing my cover at the Birmingham bureau not only endangering my life but possibly the lives of other agents and look forward to discussing these matters with you upon my return," Charlie fumed.

Charlie heard the phone being thrown down and Hannah snarling in the background.

Another voice came on the line. "Charlie, you still there?"

"Yes, I'm still here."

"I don't know what you said, but man was the director pissed off. Are you coming in?"

"I guess I have no choice. I'll be there within a couple of hours," Charlie replied

"Well, when you get here we got some interesting stuff on Chester Cunningham," the agent said.

"Thanks," Charlie answered and closed his phone.

"Did he say Chester Cunningham?" Jessica asked immediately.

"You could hear what was being said?" Charlie asked.

"Of course, but did he say Chester Cunningham?" Jessica repeated irately.

Charlie had had it with people talking to him in that manner. "If you could hear what was being said then why do you need to ask?" he replied flippantly.

"You've been going through my notes, haven't you?" Jessica accused.

"I haven't touched your notes."

"Then you've been on my computer."

"Jessica, I haven't touched your computer or your notes."

"Then how did you find out about Chester Cunningham?"

"His name came up as a suspect worth checking out. He's a medical doctor who came under suspicion," Charlie replied "Where did you come across his name?"

"That's none of your business," Jessica replied. "I think you need to take me back to my apartment."

"You're the one who's driving."

"So I guess it's Agent Bridges who is staying in the apartment next to you at the National Guard Base. Is he your partner, Agent Caressa," Jessica taunted.

"You know you can go to prison for interfering with an FBI undercover operation. And revealing the real names of the agents involved would be considered interference," Charlie warned.

"You'd have to prove intent to make it stick and that would be difficult. Those kind of things slip out all the time"

"Not when the Vasquez Cartel has a million dollar hit on the agent you're outing."

"I don't think it's me you should worry about. Your Director Hannah seems to be doing a pretty good job all by himself of outing his two undercover agents," Jessica responded. "That in itself would make a pretty good story."

"So should I call you later tonight when I know what my schedule is?" Charlie asked.

"No, I'll give you a call. I have a lot of work to do and I just may head on up to Jacksonville as planned," she replied.

"Whatever."

He could sense that the game was changing between him and Jessica and that he was about to be pulled for a new power hitter.

They rode the rest of the way to Birmingham in silence, but just before Jessica got out of the car she seemed to have second thoughts. "I'll call you tomorrow and we can compare notes on Chester. I found some things that link him to the rape in Jacksonville. And by the way, I knew from the very beginning that you were Carlo Caressa and I suspected Kevin Bridges was the other agent working the case." She gave him a deep kiss goodbye.

One thing Charlie now knew for sure was that he couldn't trust his senses when it came to women. Fifteen minutes ago he could have sworn this relationship had died.

"The graveyard looks great," Ginny Lee said when she came down to the church just before lunch.

Kevin had been expecting her to drop by much earlier and more often but those expectations never materialized. A bit of a blow to his ego.

"Actually, the graveyard didn't take that long. Ver Dell showed up, and we've repaired the guttering and rebuilt the wall over behind the shed. After lunch we were going to start painting the doors."

"That will look nice," Ginny Lee said her mind obviously elsewhere. "Hope you're hungry. I've been fixin' fried chicken all mornin'."

"That's what Ida said you were making. She told me you're famous for it. She's already inside with her cornbread and potato salad," Kevin replied.

"I told her not to tell you," Ginny Lee smiled.

"Chester's already inside, too," Kevin warned.

"I know, I saw his car. Did he bring his usual store bought apple pies?" Ginny Lee asked.

"I wouldn't know that, but I did see him carry in a bag full of something," Kevin replied.

As they were talking two other cars pulled into the parking lot.

"That's Billy and Sue Perkins. They've been with the church for over twenty years," Ginny Lee explained.

"I don't remember seeing him last Sunday," Kevin remarked as a surly looking man stepped out of a newer Cadillac Escalade.

"He wasn't here last Sunday," Ginny Lee replied. "That's Woland Kapkov, son of Russian immigrants who came to work the coal mines. He's been a member of this church ever since I can remember."

"What's he do for a living? He must have some money driving a car like that," Kevin assumed.

"I really don't know and he never has volunteered to say. He moved away from Sand Mountain more than twenty years ago, but still comes a couple of Sundays a month and an occasional Wednesday to church services," Ginny Lee said.

"How'd he hear about the lunch meeting?" Kevin asked.

"Someone must've called him," Ginny Lee replied. "I think we better get inside."

"I'll be right in. I need to wash up a bit," Kevin said, walking over to join Ver Dell at a sink back in the work shed.

"So how long have you been coming to the church here?" Kevin asked.

"Eva' since Ginny Lee's daddy started the church, back 'fo Ginny Lee was born," Ver Dell replied.

"So you know everyone buried in that graveyard," Kevin said.

"I pret' much buried er' one there," Ver Dell replied.

"I bet you pretty much built most of this church too," Kevin said.

"Reckon I did," Ver Dell replied, as they both headed inside.

Ver Dell had set up a large round table that comfortably seated ten people which was exactly how many that had showed up for lunch. Chester was sitting to the right of Ginny Lee but she made sure the space to her left was saved for Kevin. Luke and Emma Sunderland had arrived while Kevin was washing up and were seated next to Chester. Woland was seated next between the Sunderlands and the Perkins. Then Ida and Ver Dell who was next to Kevin.

"Chester would you please say grace," Ginny Lee asked.

Chester seemed a might put out but did as asked. "Lord, you are so great and wonderful. We ask you to bless this food, and ask you to guide us in our discussions and lead in the way you want your church to be led. We ask for your wisdom and your love, in your name we pray, Amen."

"Now I see no reason why we can't eat while we discuss our business," Ginny Lee said. "First off, I'd like you all to meet Kevin Jackson. Kevin is new to the church and was 'slain in the Spirit' last Sunday. He offered to help out around the church today and will be coming to the service tonight. I've already told him who you all are so you can make your personal acquaintances later."

"So I hear Peter Talbot came back making all kinds of threats," Woland said.

"That's why we're meeting," Ginny Lee said. "For those that may not remember Peter Talbot is one of the Evangelism Pastors from the National Headquarters of the Pentecostal Church up in Cleveland, Tennessee."

"Isn't he the one who came around here a couple years ago threatening to take our church away?" Sue Perkins asked.

"Yes and Ginny Lee told him the church was private property but he raised a ruckus until Ver Dell escorted him off the property with a shotgun," Chester added. "Not the most judicial way to resolve the problem."

"Wha' Chester say?" Ver Dell snapped.

"It was nothing," Kevin said placating Ver Dell's ire.

"Well he came back sayin' if we don't stop handlin' the snakes the National Pentecostal Church will revoke our fellowship to allow us to call ourselves a Holiness Church." Ginny Lee explained.

"So what? Then we'll just be an un-fellowshipped Holiness Church," Woland argued.

"If we do that don't we risk losing our Pentecostal affiliation as well?" Luke Sunderland asked.

"Does the church send part of their tithes to the national church?" Kevin asked.

"We call it monthly support and yes we do," Ginny replied. "It's not a whole lot, but it's been growing because our church has been growing so much lately."

"Then you have nothing to worry about. The national church is not going to cut off an income producing local church that is growing even if it doesn't completely agree with all of its doctrines," Kevin said.

"I just can't stand the thought of having the true scripture of Christ denied to me by some lackey of false religious authorities too afraid to live a truly Godly life both in Word and in Deed," Chester raged.

"Should one of us go talk to the National Church? It's only a couple of hours away," Sue suggested.

"I see no point yet. If we get a letter from them, maybe, but it just may be this Peter Talbot fellow is stirring up trouble on his own," Ginny Lee surmised.

"Then it's settled, we do nothing," Woland said. "Now I am troubled by something I read in the paper this morning."

It seemed obvious this was the real reason Woland had come to the meeting. Everyone stopped eating.

"What did you read," Ginny Lee asked.

"The FBI wants to exhume the remains of Emily Sue Whitman."

Several people at the table gasped.

"Why in heaven's name would they want to do that?" Ginny Lee asked.

"The FBI believes they have found her skull and want to do DNA testing on the remains to see if they match," Woland explained. "They are trying to locate next of kin."

Nobody spoke for several seconds.

"I don't think I want anyone digging up our graveyard," Ginny Lee finally said.

"Did the paper say where they found the skull?" Chester asked.

"In some Voodoo store down in New Orleans. It had been made into a chalice," Woland replied

"Whatsa chalice?" Ver Dell asked.

"It's like a drinking cup made from the skull," Kevin explained.

"Ain't right for the FBI to go a diggin' up 'er grave," Ver Dell said.

"I think we better be getting' home," the Sunderlands said.

"Us too," Sue Perkins said, as her and Billy left quickly with the Sunderlands.

"What was that all about," Kevin asked.

"I believe they thought this is more of a personal matter rather than a church matter," Chester replied. "They thought it best for only…"

"Chester, be quiet. Kevin has just as much right here as anybody else," Ginny Lee interrupted.

"The FBI will eventually track down any of Emily Sue Whitman's relatives who are still alive and ask for permission to exhume her remains," Chester said.

"They can dig her up without permission," Woland added, "because it relates to the Apostle Serial Killer case."

"You want me to dig 'er up an hide 'er?" Ver Dell offered.

"There's no reason to do that," Ginny Lee replied.

"I would think you would want her skull back with the rest of her bones," Kevin said.

Nobody responded.

"I kinda agree with Ver Dell," Ida said, "I tink that a can o' worms we don't wanna mess wit'."

"No, when they contact us we will cooperate. Kevin is right; the skull should be with the rest of Emily Sue's remains," Ginny Lee decided.

No one else at the table seemed to agree with Ginny Lee's decision which puzzled Kevin. He was definitely missing something. He just couldn't figure out what.

"I reckon we betta start on the doors," Ver Dell said to Kevin.

"I'll clean this mess up, Ginny Lee. I know you have a lot on your mind right now," Ida said.

"Thanks Ida, I do," Ginny Lee replied and hurried off towards her house without even speaking to Kevin or Chester.

"Let me give you a hand, Ida," Kevin volunteered.

"Thanks."

Kevin felt a little guilty. He only volunteered to help so he could collect the napkins used by the women who had attended the luncheon. He needed their DNA to compare with the DNA found on two of the Apostle Serial Killer victims.

"Chester could I have a word with you," Woland called as Chester was leaving.

"Can you meet me down at my office in Boaz? I have a 1:30 appointment but then I'm free until tonight's service," Chester explained.

"That'd be great. I have some ideas I'd like to talk to you about," Woland replied. "I'll see you a little after 2:00."

Kevin's first impression of Woland was worse than his first impression of Chester. For some reason the name seemed to ring a bell and it wasn't a very pleasant tone.

CHAPTER TWENTY-EIGHT

"Just what the hell have you and Bridges been doing down here Caressa?" Hannah screamed at Carlo in the private conference room at the Birmingham bureau.

"Sir, I hope you realize you have jeopardized this investigation by exposing both Kevin's and my real identities and put our lives at risk," Charlie responded.

"Do you realize who you're talking to son? I asked you a question about your investigation," Hannah repeated.

"Our investigation has been going extremely well. Agent Jackson has successfully infiltrated the church where Agent Caldwell believed the killer was associated. We have linked several of the victims to a rape that occurred in Jacksonville in 1970. We have found a skull we believe to be one of the Apostle Serial Killer's first victims. I think that is pretty damn impressive for only four days' work considering the FBI has been on this case for months," Carlo replied.

"What troubles me is you are sleeping with and sharing all this information with some news reporter," Hannah raged.

"I am controlling what information the media gets and also monitoring a previous leak in our organization. Almost everything she has printed came directly from the national file on this case given to her by the regional director out of Atlanta. She even knew the day we were coming, where we were staying and the cars being delivered for our use. I'm overseeing damage control with this lady," Carlo explained.

"And reaping the benefits in the process no doubt. What about those two private detectives? Did you get anything out of them?" Hannah asked.

"No, they were worthless. Whoever hired them was a pro."

"What do you mean pro?"

"NSA, CIA, or some other agency wanting to remain anonymous."

"Any thoughts on why they would be so interested in the case?" Hannah asked.

Carlo was surprised how Hannah had suddenly changed his attitude. "Somebody important has something to hide. They obviously knew about James Arnold being the Apostle Serial Killer's next victim so it would make sense they were in Jacksonville in 1970."

"Do you know when this rape occurred in 1970?" Hannah asked.

"According to the recording the two detectives made, Mr. Arnold said he had gone down to Jacksonville to watch a football game, so that would make it the fall of 1970."

"Well that's quite a relief," Hannah said. "I went to school at Jacksonville from 1968 to1972 but in the fall of 1970 I was studying abroad."

"That's a bit of a surprise," Carlo said.

"Maybe I can help you with the investigation in Jacksonville. I still have quite a few connections there," Hannah offered.

"That won't be necessary, sir, I know how busy you are," Carlo started to argue.

"No, I insist. I think I could be a big help and I'd like to meet your reporter friend," Hannah said. "We can head down there late tomorrow morning. I have some business I need to handle first. I see the bureau found an address for Emily Sue Whitman's mother. She's living in a home up in Scottsboro. Why don't you run up there and see if you can find out where her daughter's grave site is and get permission to dig it up?"

"Yes sir," Carlo replied, but before the words were out of his mouth Hannah was out the door.

"What a jerk," Charlie said.

"You got that right," the bureau's Supervising Agent Billings said coming through the door. "He comes by here a couple of times a month and just drives me crazy."

"He comes all the way down here twice a month?" Charlie said.

"He grew up in Birmingham. He's got one of those big old mansions near downtown. I think he commutes weekends from here to his office in Washington. The man is a real pain in the ass."

Charlie had told her he wouldn't call but he was sure Jessica wouldn't mind when she heard that FBI Assistant Director Peter Hannah wanted to meet her and join them in Jacksonville the next day.

And of course, he was right.

Charlie needed desperately to talk to Kevin but every time he tried the number Kevin had previously called from the recording said it was either out of range or currently not in service.

He knew the nursing home in Scottsboro was near Sand Mountain and decided to at least drive by in hopes that Kevin would see the car and turn on his phone. That is if he could find the church.

"It's at least worth a shot," Charlie said, as he pulled out of the bureau lot and headed for I-59.

"What say we take a break an feed dem snakes," Ver Dell said after about two hours of painting.

"I'd completely forgotten about them," Kevin said. His only thoughts that afternoon had been about what had occurred at the luncheon meeting and the reactions of everyone at the table.

"I'll drive," Kevin offered.

"If you want you can put your rattlers in the pit wit' the da others in da shed," Ver Dell offered.

"I didn't see any pit up in the shed," Kevin replied.

"Keep it covered," Ver Dell replied.

The feed store was just a mile down the road and had just about any size mouse or rat you could desire. Ver Dell bought several of the large mice.

"Rats for the big constrictors," he said, seeming to know what Kevin was thinking.

As they were climbing back into the car Kevin was startled to see Charlie's Trans Am slowly cruise by. They made eye contact and Kevin quickly turned away.

"Know 'im?" Ver Dell asked.

"No, I was just checking out that car," Kevin replied.

"He lookin' fo' you it seem," Ver Dell replied.

Kevin was becoming convinced that Ver Dell had to be some kind of mind reader. He was answering questions before Kevin even asked them and knew things that he couldn't possibly know.

Seeing Charlie wasn't a good sign. Charlie wouldn't risk looking for Kevin unless something really bad had happened. Somehow Kevin was going to have to find a way to call Charlie without anyone seeing him, especially Ver Dell.

"Did you know Emily Sue Whitman?" Kevin asked.

"No suh, neva' met the woman." Ver Dell replied. "And I don't wanna speak 'bout 'er."

"Tell me about Woland," Kevin said.

"Lord say not to gossip," Ver Dell replied.

Kevin could tell he was going to get no answers about anything or anyone out of Ver Dell.

"How many snakes do you use during tonight's service?" Kevin asked.

"'Pends on how many show up," Ver Dell replied, as they arrived back at the church. "You grab dem snakes. I'll git dem mice."

Kevin looked down the road as he headed for the shed but saw no sign of the Trans Am.

"I sure hope Charlie has a lot of patience," Kevin thought, "because this could take a while."

Charlie saw the church as he drove by but not seeing Kevin's car assumed it wasn't the right church. When he saw Kevin coming out of the feed store with the other man he stared out of surprise and initially slowed but immediately realized he would blow Kevin's cover so continued on, hopefully unnoticed.

Scottsboro was just a few miles up State Route 35 on the other side of the Tennessee River across the Comer Bridge. Charlie had called and the nursing home was expecting him, but had warned him Mrs. Turner did suffer from dementia and some days were better than others.

When Charlie arrived they had Mrs. Turner waiting for him in a sitting room area just inside the main entry.

"Ruth Ann, this is the man I told you about who wanted to talk to you. His name is Mr. Daniels," the nurse said as Charlie sat down facing Mrs. Turner.

"Hello Mrs. Turner. How are you feeling today?" Charlie asked.

"Fine, I'm feelin' jus' fine," she replied, rocking back and forth slightly.

"That's good to hear," Charlie replied. "Mrs. Turner, the reason I came here today was to ask you about your daughter Emily Sue."

"Ain't got no daughter named Emily Sue," she replied harshly.

"I know Emily Sue is no longer alive, what I meant was…"

"Ain't never had no daughter named Emily Sue," she interrupted, becoming extremely agitated.

"Before you married Pastor Turner weren't you married to Lloyd Whitman of Scrabble Creek, West Virginia?" Charlie asked.

"Nurse I want to go back to my room now," Ruth Ann insisted.

"Please Mrs. Turner, I just need to…"

"N-n-nurse," she screamed as her body began jerking.

"I'm sorry, Agent Daniels, perhaps you'd have better luck talking to her daughter," the nurse said, as an assistant helped Ruth Ann back to her room.

"Her daughter? She has another daughter?" Charlie asked.

"I don't know about another daughter, but I do know about her daughter Virginia Lee Turner who lives behind the Holiness Church cross the river near Macedonia," the nurse explained. "I'm sure she'll be able to help you."

"Thanks," Charlie replied.

He walked out to his car and sat on the hood to think.

"Now what do I do?" he said to himself.

CHAPTER TWENTY-NINE

Jessica was thrilled at the opportunity to move up the FBI food chain and wasn't going to let a chance like this slip away. She immediately got to work researching Peter Hannah to see what she could find out about him. Just like Charlie she was rather perplexed at his admission that he was in Jacksonville State at the time of the rape but allegedly spending his semester studying abroad. That was something she was for sure going to have her people check out and who would have thought he lived here in Birmingham.

She immediately called her A.E. back at the paper. "It's me Paige. Thanks for all the information on Chester Cunningham. Now I need a real big favor. I need everything you can get me on FBI Assistant Director Peter Hannah including his home phone number for his house in Birmingham, Alabama. I especially want to know about his college days at Jacksonville State in Alabama, what his major was, what fraternity he was in, when he did his semester of study abroad, who his roommates were, just about anything you can give me. And I need it fast. I'll take it in pieces I need it that quickly," Paige stressed. "I'm safe, the investigation is going well, there are some big and I mean big stories coming soon. Love you all."

"I think it's time for a nice bubble bath," Jessica said, "Lord knows I deserve it."

Peter Hannah had been busy before he arrived in Birmingham and now, he was really under the gun.

"Jenkins, this is Hannah. I appreciate your work on the various university records but now I need you to hack into the U.S. Department of State computer and alter passport records. It needs to show I was out of the country the fall of 1970 not 1971."

"Shouldn't be a problem sir. Would you like me to change the credit card records and flight records to match?" Jenkins offered.

"That's good thinking Agent Jenkins," Hannah commended.

"I'm here if you need anything else, sir," Jenkins replied.

"I appreciate that Son," Hannah replied and hung up. Agent Jenkins looked up at the man standing above him.

"Should I proceed as ordered, sir?"

The man sighed heavily. "Do it. Let's see how this game plays out."

"Ye got an itch in yir pants? Ye keep lookin' roun' like ye spectin trouble," Ver Dell said.

"Just getting hungry is all," Kevin replied.

"Dinna' be commin' shortly," Ver Dell replied. "Let's pick five 'r six snakes fer night's service."

They cleaned up their paint brushes and put their supplies away then headed back to the shed. Ver Dell moved a fifty-five gallon drum sitting on a piece of plywood then lifted up the plywood.

"Looks like yer two took well wit da others," Ver Dell said.

"I'm not even sure which two are mine," Kevin said.

Ver Dell grabbed a larger wooden box and a long stick with a hook on the end. He carefully lifted five of the snakes and placed them in the wooden box and shut the lid.

"Aren't you going to cover the pit?" Kevin asked.

"Not till we put 'em back," Ver Dell replied, shutting but not latching the shed.

They carried the box down to the church and sat it next to the stage. Most of the band had already arrived and had begun setting up their equipment. Chester was the only one noticeably absent and Casper didn't look pleased.

Kevin saw his chance and approached Casper.

"I just wanted to say I thought your band is one of the best I've ever heard. You are an excellent guitar player." Kevin praised, holding his hand out to shake Casper's.

"Thanks," Casper replied, taking Kevin's hand hesitantly.

Kevin was surprised how small Casper's hand felt but how long his fingers seemed.

"Ginny Lee says you are filled with the gifts of the Spirit," Kevin said.

"Ginny Lee is a sweet girl, but my gift is my music. The Lord has anointed my fingers to allow me to worship Him through my music."

"You certainly bring me closer to Him with your music and I thank you for that," Kevin said.

Casper just nodded and went back to work setting up for the night's worship.

"I've got sandwiches and salads for anyone who is hungry," Ginny Lee called out from the back of the church.

She had come in while Kevin was talking to Casper and he hadn't noticed her.

"The boy hea been wantin' food fo' past hour," Ver Dell said.

"Worked yourself up an appetite, huh?" Ginny Lee teased. "Well you better dig in before the musicians eat them all."

This was not a sit down meal like the luncheon had been. The church became a beehive of activity as people scampered around preparing for that night's service which looked to Kevin to be starting at any time. The Perkins and Sunderlands had already arrived as had several other people. Many were prostrate on the floor praying. Others were on their knees alone in corners while still others had gathered in groups.

"This is how it starts," Ginny Lee came over and explained to Kevin, "Many of our worshippers come early and begin praying for the Holy Spirit to come."

"I thought the Holy Spirit is always with you," Kevin replied.

"It's always with us. Some of us are on fire with the Spirit but sometimes others forget where they put it and have to go inside themselves, find it and sort of call it forth," Ginny Lee explained.

Kevin could hear several people beginning to speak in tongues and the hairs on the back of his neck and arms began to tingle.

Luke Sunderland stood up behind the pulpit and started reading from the book of Mark. Some people took their seats and listened while others continued their prayers.

As if on cue the band started playing. Kevin looked up and saw that Chester had just arrived and was rushing to set up his amplifier much to the displeasure of Casper.

As Kevin watched Casper's look of displeasure turned to an angry glare as Woland casually walked in the door that Chester had just entered.

"There's no love lost between those two," Kevin noted to himself.

Casper closed his eyes leaned his head back and suddenly the music grabbed the crowd and raised them to a higher level of inspiration and worship. Casper had single handedly filled the room with the Holy Spirit.

Kevin was drawn to the front like so many others in the church. People were thrashing and dancing seemingly uncontrollably around the floor in front of the stage. Several peoples' prayers in tongues had turned to shouts in tongues, but Kevin didn't notice. He was entranced by the power of the Holy Spirit.

"*Ho—ly, Ho—ly, is the Lord*," Kevin began to chant.

"*Ho—ly, Ho—ly, is the Lord*."

Ver Dell poured the box of rattle snakes onto the floor and picked up all five. Three in his right hand and two in his left.

Billy Perkins took the two from his left and Ida took one from his right. They held them above their heads and waved them all around their bodies.

"*Ho—ly, Ho—ly, is the Lord*," Kevin continued.

Ginny Lee took one of Billy's snakes and he threw the second into the air where Luke Sunderland grabbed it and began swirling it around.

"*Ho—ly, Ho—ly, is the Lord*," Kevin continued.

Another parishioner took the two snakes from Ver Dell and passed them around to several other people.

Ver Dell went to the stage and grabbed another box next to Chester's amp that contained two more rattle snakes and lifted them out of the box. One of these Woland took and the other he handed to Emma Sunderland.

"*Ho—ly, Ho—ly, is the Lord,*" Kevin continued.

The frenzy on the floor continued as snakes exchanged hands, people danced and flailed about wildly, and the band played furiously.

Kevin was startled from his prayer as Woland tossed him a rattlesnake. He had no choice but to catch it. He stared at it as he continued to sing.

"*Ho—ly, Ho—ly, is the Lord.*"

A power like he had never felt before rushed through his body. The Holy Spirit was protecting him.

Suddenly, Billy Perkins grabbed the snake out of Kevin's hand and almost instantly during the exchange the snake turned and sank its fangs into Billy's hand as it was side-by-side with Kevin's.

Ver Dell was the first to see what happened and immediately grabbed the snake and put it back in the box.

As several people rushed to Billy to pray over his wound, Kevin glanced at Woland who had a smug grin on his face. When he turned to Casper he could see a glare of hatred directed towards Woland, but Casper continued to play. Chester had stopped and was also staring back and forth between Billy and Woland.

"Ida, help Ver Dell collect the rest of the snakes," Ginny Lee asked.

"Kevin I need you over here," Ginny Lee demanded.

She grabbed Kevin's hand and placed it directly over the two puncture wounds.

"Now I need you to pray," Ginny Lee ordered.

"I'm not much at praying," Kevin replied.

"Kevin, you were 'slain in the Spirit' just three days ago which makes you 'filled with the Spirit' more than you can imagine, so just do as I say and pray," Ginny Lee repeated.

"Dear God, you are so," then suddenly a different language began to flow from Kevin,

"Park Kez Ter Hisus Kristos, Ammen.

Ter Astvats, orhnir ays tshvar mahkanatsuyin yev heratsru ays mahatsu aghetn ir kyankits. Bjshkir yev amboghjatsru nra marminn oo hogin. Yev togh vor nra kyankn, marimnn, oo mitkn park beri Ko Surb yev Orhnyal anvann oo gortsin. Togh vor ays tunavor portsutyunn aravel mot beri nran Ko parki Surb Chanaparin.

Mer Ter Hisus Kristosi Amenasurb anunov, Ammen.

The music seemed to crescendo and Kevin could hear several voices and feel numerous hands on his back and placed over his. Suddenly, his fingers began to burn and comforting warmth engulfed his entire body.

He opened his eyes slowly and saw Ginny Lee looking down at him.

"It happened again didn't it?" Kevin asked.

"If you're asking if you were again 'slain in the Spirit' then the answer is yes," Ginny Lee replied.

"I don't hear any music," he said.

"The band stopped about forty minutes ago," she replied.

"Thank you, thank you for your prayers," Billy Perkins said. "It's completely gone. God used you to make it completely disappear. It's a miracle."

"Billy and Sue have been waiting to thank you," Ginny Lee said.

"It's the Holy Spirit who did it," Kevin said.

"Yes sir, but he couldn't have done it without you. God bless you Son," Billy replied.

"I knew God sent you here for a reason. Good-night you all," Sue said, as they headed out the door.

"So what happened?" Kevin asked.

"You began praying. Your eyes rolled back and you started praying in tongues. Woland said it sounded like Armenian," Ginny Lee explained. "Suddenly, you got real warm, fell back and the fang marks were gone and you were out."

"How long have I been out?" Kevin asked.

"About an hour and a half," Ginny Lee said.

"That's not good," Kevin said.

"Maybe you needed the rest. Apparently God thought so," Ginny Lee replied.

"I need to use the restroom," Kevin said excusing himself.

He walked in and saw Casper at one of the urinals and walked up next to him.

"That was pretty impressive what you did for Billy tonight," Casper said.

"It's your worship music that allows me to do it," Kevin replied. "I've never heard anything better."

"Thanks," Casper replied and headed out the door.

Kevin washed his hands and rejoined Ginny Lee.

"I'd better get going," Kevin said.

"Are you sure you're feeling well enough to drive?" Ginny Lee asked. "I do have a guest room in my house."

"I'm feeling fine. I just had a great nap and you know how energized you get when the Spirit fills you up," Kevin said.

"That is true," Ginny admitted.

"Besides, I wouldn't want rumors to get started and people to start talking," Kevin said.

"This place could use a few good rumors now and again," Ginny Lee replied. "I talked to the church board; you have a job here if you want it. Part-time of course and you can set the hours."

"That's great, I'll give you a call and let you know when I can come up next," Kevin said.

"Don't wait too long," Ginny Lee said, writing down her number.

"I promise. You may even see me tomorrow or Friday. I'll call you in the morning to let you know. Take care," Kevin said as he got into his car.

Kevin was exhilarated as he started on his way back towards Birmingham. He was glowing in the Spirit thinking of his wondrous night when he decided to listen to some music.

He pushed the radio on and the song blaring from the speakers suddenly shocked him back to reality.

"Charlie, I've got to call Charlie," Kevin said with urgency.

The song was *The Devil Went Down to Georgia* by Charlie Daniels.

CHAPTER THIRTY

Kevin reached under his seat and found his throw away cell phone and turned it on.

"There's no way Charlie's still in the area," Kevin said.

Charlie picked up on the second ring.

"That took you long enough," Charlie replied.

"I'd have blown my cover if I would have called any earlier," Kevin said.

"I was afraid I'd blown it when I saw you with that hillbilly by the feed store. Who was that scary looking guy?" Charlie asked.

"His name is Ver Dell and I swear he is psychic. He seemed to know you were looking for me," Kevin explained.

"Well I was looking for you. You and Ruth Ann Turner," Charlie said.

"Ginny Lee Turner's mom? Kevin replied.

"If Ginny Lee is short for Virginia Lee and she lives behind the church over in Macedonia, then yeah," Charlie replied. "When the conversation went nowhere at the nursing home they said I should talk to Virginia Lee, but if I did that, I knew your cover would be blown so I headed back to Birmingham. I'll tell Hannah nobody was at the church."

"Tell Hannah, what's Hannah got to do with it?"

"That's why I was originally trying to contact you. Hannah's come to town raising holy hell. He's blown our cover at the Birmingham bureau, wants to participate in the investigation, and get this, he was going to school in Jacksonville when the rape occurred," Charlie said.

"What's he thinking?" Kevin replied. "He should know better than to get involved in an investigation that may involve him."

"He claims his connections in Jacksonville will help and when the rape occurred he was studying abroad that year."

"That seems easy enough to check out."

"And easy enough to hack into and alter," Charlie added.

"Do you think Hannah hired those two private detectives?" Kevin asked.

"It makes sense. He's an ambitious man and wants to protect his reputation at all costs. Did you know he grew up in Birmingham and still spends much of his time here? The local bureau chief says he practically commutes from his old family mansion to Washington every week."

"Wasn't Hannah a medic in the military?"

"What are you trying to say?"

"It's just a thought," Kevin replied. "You staying with Jessica tonight?"

"No, I'm at the base."

"Good, I'll be there in about an hour. I've got a lot to tell you and I have some samples for you to run DNA checks on. I hope you have something for me on Chester Cunningham," Kevin said.

"Plenty. See you in an hour."

Vasquez had an entire organization searching for Carlo and Kevin but had no success in tracking them down.

Samuelson knew that they were just looking in the wrong places.

He sat down at his computer and pulled up a map of Southern California.

"I know you're not here anymore, but you started from someplace around here. Let's figure out where." He said to himself.

Samuelson knew the FBI first got them out of their apartments and to a safe house.

"A true safe house is one that only a few people can access, like a private condo high rise," he thought, "No, too many people coming and going, not a good choice."

"Got it!" he said. "A police training facility or a military facility very controlled and limited access. The perfect solution. But which one?"

Samuelson poured himself another cup of strong coffee and leaned back to think.

"They would only have stayed there until they were reassigned somewhere else and then flown out. The airports are fairly well covered so chances are they stayed at a facility with an airport," Samuelson decided.

"Pt. Magu, that was easy," Samuelson said. "Now let's see if I was right."

Samuelson headed for the main hacienda and was stopped by two guards.

"What's this about?" Samuelson complained.

"Sinaloa Cartel took out several of our people. Vasquez is tightening security," the guard replied.

"I need to talk to Meathook," Samuelson said.

The guard headed inside.

"Yeah, what do you want?" Meathook growled.

"Who's our supplier up in Oxnard at the Air Base?" Samuelson asked.

"Why do you want to know?"

"I believe that's where the two FBI agents were being kept and were flown out of," Samuelson replied. "I want to know where they were flown."

"You got a date?" Meathook replied.

"No, but I got a general time frame and that will have to do," Samuelson replied.

"Give it to Jose and I'll take care of it," Meathook replied. "Anything else?"

"Just the sooner you get me the information the sooner Vasquez gets their heads."

Meathook just grunted.

"What happened between you and Jessica?" Kevin asked.

"First off, she knew all along who we both were even before Hannah blew our cover," Charlie said.

"That wasn't too hard to figure out," Kevin replied.

"I told Hannah that you've infiltrated the church. He's real upset that you're not carrying your phone."

"I imagine he is."

"Jessica and I were headed for Jacksonville when he called and told me to report to the Birmingham office. He put me on the spot with Jessica and things are a bit dicey."

"She won't blow our cover will she?"

"I don't think so, but we got into an argument over Chester Cunningham. Somehow she had come across his name and has her people working on it as well," Charlie said.

"How'd she do that?" Kevin asked.

"I'm not sure, but I'm guessing it has something to do with James Arnold's house."

"Send a team of criminologist back and have them tear that place apart," Kevin ordered.

"It might be too late."

"It's still worth the effort," Kevin said pulling out his computer.

"I think this Chester Cunningham could be our guy."

"I don't think so," Kevin replied, "but he may be worth watching."

"If he's not our guy why watch him?"

"Because I think he knows our guy," Kevin said.

Kevin 'Googled' the name Woland.

I thought I'd heard that name before," he said turning the screen towards Charlie.

"*The Master and Margarita*, I don't get it," Charlie said.

"It's a book by Mikhail Bulgakov. Woland is the main character who looks different to everybody who sees him. Woland is actually an old German word meaning devil. Woland Kapkov has been going to the Holiness Church for years and seems to have a lot of power over Chester," Kevin explained.

"Are you trying to tell me this Woland guy is the devil and he is making Chester do these killings?" Charlie asked with skepticism.

"I'm not trying to tell you anything. I'm just relating observations," Kevin replied. "Honestly, I'm having a hard time believing some of the things I've witnessed at that church myself."

"So you want me to have this Woland Kapkov checked out?"

"Both him and a guy named Peter Talbot out of Cleveland, Tennessee."

"Friday I'm going to have to head up to the church and talk to Virginia Lee about exhuming Emily Sue Whitman's grave," Charlie said.

"Why Ginny Lee?" Kevin asked

"From what I understand, Ginny Lee, as you call her, is Emily Sue's half-sister," Charlie replied.

"That explains why everybody acted so weird at lunch today when that subject came up," Kevin said. "Is there any way you can send an agent from the bureau up to do it? If Ver Dell is there he will recognize you and it will jeopardize my cover."

"I'll see what I can arrange," Charlie said. "If that's the case maybe I'll send him up tomorrow when Jessica, Hannah, and I go to Jacksonville."

"All three of you are going together?" Kevin laughed.

"It's not that funny."

"I hate to say it buddy, but Jessica is the type of woman that likes to move up the food chain," Kevin said.

"I've already thought of that."

"And?" Kevin probed.

"And what do you say we both have a beer," Charlie replied. "You get the beers and I'll call the agent on duty and arrange to have someone talk to Virginia Lee tomorrow. Who were those two you wanted checked out, Peter Talbot and Woland ...?"

"Kapkov, Woland Kapkov," Kevin replied. "The devil in disguise."

Simon was suddenly awakened by noise coming from above him.

"I thought he said he was going to be gone for several days," Simon thought.

"Maybe things aren't as serious as he led me to believe."

He waited for the killer to come down into the basement but he never came.

Simon thought he may have heard voices but it could have been the killer only talking on the phone.

He kept waiting but all was silent and the silence was beginning to get to him.

CHAPTER THIRTY-ONE

Peter Talbot was a man of God who had lost his way. Not that he wasn't still a man of God. It was just that he had let his own desire for authority override God's ultimate authority and he was blinded by the fact.

The Macedonia Holiness Church with Signs Following had snubbed him and he was helpless to do anything about it. He had insisted that their charter be canceled by the National Pentecostal Headquarters claiming that the handling of snakes, the drinking of poisons, and the handling of fire gave a bad name to all Pentecosts. But in its wisdom the national church recognized that the Macedonia Church kept its practices quiet, had a rapidly expanding congregation, and sent its fair share of monthly support to the national headquarters, which meant its fellowship was safe.

He had arrived just before dawn. He found the house on the East side of Cleveland. From the church website he knew Peter Talbot had a wife Elizabeth and two children Joshua and Mary.

There were two cars in the drive when he arrived, a white Ford SUV which the wife undoubtedly drove and a smaller and more economical Toyota Corolla used for Peter's work and travel.

He normally spent more time getting to know his target's routine, but circumstances dictated otherwise. It was a quiet street with no sidewalks which made it simple to slip in and flatten one of the Toyota's tires before the sun even hinted at the eastern edge of the skyline. Now all he had to do was wait.

"I was looking forward to seeing your head on the platter," Meathook said to Samuelson.
"Sounds like Pt. Magu was the right call," Samuelson replied.
"Lucky guess if you ask me," Meathook replied.
"So where did they go?" Samuelson asked.
"Our guy inside said a C-130 flew them out last Saturday to….," He paused to read the paper in his hand. "Here you read the damn thing *pendejo*."
"Says they were flown to the Birmingham-Shuttlesworth International Airport, the Alabama Army National Guard base that shares the airport. That makes sense, they're still being protected."
"Why'd they send 'em there?" Meathook asked.
"My guess would be they're helping out on that serial murder investigation. You know the one they call the Apostle Serial Killer," Samuelson explained.
"Yeah, I heard something about that. We could use a guy like that. Tell him he's got a job if he wants it when you go back there," Meathook laughed.
"I'll need five men and two cars" Samuelson said.
"Take whatever you need. Just get the job done," Meathook ordered.
Russia was looking better and better as an option to Samuelson.

Around seven-thirty Peter Talbot came out of the house to head to work and noticed his flat tire. He angrily slammed his briefcase on the hood of the Toyota and stormed back into the house. A minute later both kids ran out and looked at the car then ran back inside.

"Will he call a service or will he change it himself? That is the question," the man said.

Ten minutes later his question was answered when all four Talbots came back outside. Mrs. Talbot was dressed for work and hustled the two Talbot children into the Ford SUV. Peter Talbot had changed into work clothes which meant he intended to change his own tire.

"Wave goodbye to daddy," the man said.

"Oh, you should have kissed him goodbye. You're going to have a lot of guilt to deal with because of that choice."

He watched as the family drove away. He began to whisper as though praying then opened his door slightly.

Peter Talbot got right to work on changing the tire. In no time he had the spare out of the trunk and the lug nuts loosened and the car jacked into the air.

He was removing the lug nuts when a van pulled up across the street distracting him and causing him to drop one of the nuts. He reached under the car to grab it and a rattle snake sank its fangs deep into his wrist.

"Aaaah," Peter screamed falling backwards smashing the snake and his wrist into the undercarriage of the Toyota and then scrambling in a modified two legged-one-armed crab-crawl away from the car and the snake.

"Are you okay?" a voice said from behind him causing him to scream again from fright.

"A rattlesnake bit me. I need help," Peter cried.

"One like this?" the man said, pressing the fangs into Peter's throat.

As with most victims, Peter passed out from fright but the venom kept him out. The man collected the injured snake, snatched Peter quickly over his shoulder and hurried to his van.

Peter's wife would call several times and come home from work at noon to look for him.

She would see the droplets of blood in the driveway but wouldn't call the police until 6:00 p.m., almost the exact time her husband lost his head.

CHAPTER THIRTY-TWO

"I thought we were leaving early?" Jessica complained.

"So did I," Charlie answered, "but Assistant Director Hannah called the bureau and told them to let me know he is running late and wouldn't be available until at least 11:00 a.m. and I am not to go to Jacksonville without him."

"Well I'm not waiting," Jessica insisted.

"That's your choice, but I don't have a choice," Charlie replied.

"Suit yourself, call me when you get there," she said and hung up the phone.

"That went well," Charlie said, sitting down at a computer to see what information they had found about Woland and Peter.

"You sure he said he'd be here by 11:00 a.m.?" Charlie asked the agent in charge.

"Don't quote me on this, but you can't trust anything Hannah says. He was here until midnight last night questioning our involvement in the investigation. He even started researching those names you called in to have checked out," the agent said.

"That's just great. I just hope he doesn't head up to the church and blow Kevin's cover," Charlie moaned.

"I wouldn't count it out," the agent replied.

"You said you were going to call before you came." Ginny Lee said.

"I thought I'd surprise you and take you out to breakfast," Kevin said.

"I haven't even fixed my hair."

"It looks wonderful to me," Kevin replied.

"Yes, but the people around here know me and they would know I just got out of bed and wasn't it you who was concerned about rumors?" she joked. "It will just take me a few minutes. You can either wait here or down at the church."

"I'll wait at the church. You know how rumors get started." They both laughed.

Kevin walked down behind the church and wandered around the graveyard.

"So Ginny Lee had a half-sister. I wonder why she never mentioned it before." he thought. "Must be some skeleton in the closet nobody wants to talk about."

He heard a strange noise and looked up into the woods behind the grave yard. A mist clung to the ground but he swore he saw someone moving from tree to tree along the ridgeline.

"This place can be a little creepy," he thought, as a slight shiver ran up his spine.

He moved over towards the shed and found the door partially ajar and decided he better check it out. He walked inside and tried to switch on the light but nothing happened.

"The bulb must be burned out," he said nervously.

He had been in the shed a couple of times before and remembered that the bulb wasn't centered in the room but was off to the right. Even with the door open the sun didn't allow much light into the darkened interior of the shed.

Kevin started across to where he remembered the light was but tripped over the fifty-five gallon barrel turned on its side. The barrel normally sat on the plywood that covered the snake pit Kevin was tumbling towards. He began frantically thrashing his arms looking for anything to grasp onto and found the end of a sharpened hoe which he grabbed for dear life.

At that exact moment the light came on and he heard Ginny Lee calling his name.

"Kevin, are you in the shed?"

"A little help, please," Kevin yelled out.

Ginny Lee ran in and found Kevin lying precariously balanced on the edge of the pit gripping the sharpened hoe with bleeding fingers. Below him more than a dozen snakes were swirling tumultuously.

"You've hurt your hand," Ginny said, pulling Kevin away from the pit.

"It was the better of two options," Kevin explained. "Why is the pit uncovered anyway? And how did you get the light on?"

"The main power for the shed is turned on from a switch on the outside of the church. When I didn't see you and saw the shed door open I turned it on," Ginny Lee explained.

"Ver Dell said the pit is always covered but it wasn't," Kevin said.

"Sometimes some of the hill folk bring us snakes. Maybe one of them was delivering a snake or two when you came wandering down. They don't much like people they don't know so they probably left in a hurry and didn't want to make any noise closing up the pit. They figured they'd come do it once you were gone," Ginny Lee explained.

"I thought I saw someone through the mist up along the ridge," Kevin said. "That must be it."

"Now let me have a look at that hand," Ginny Lee said.

"I think I'm going to need some stitches," Kevin said. "Why do they keep they tools so sharp?"

"Well I could make a joke about not being the sharpest tool in the shed, but actually Ver Dell makes sure all our tools are kept razor sharp. Tools work much better when they are sharp and used properly."

"Are you inferring I wasn't using…"

"Just shush," she replied as she wrapped a towel around his hand and began to pray.

"You need to pray too," she admonished him.

"I'm afraid I'll pass out."

"Then we'd better go sit down inside," Ginny Lee said and led Kevin inside keeping pressure on the cuts.

"Maybe we should drive down to Boaz and have Chester take a look at my hand," Kevin suggested.

"You're joking right? You'd choose Chester over the Holy Spirit?"

"I've never seen the Holy Spirit stitch anyone up," Kevin replied.

"Apparently, you haven't seen Chester do it either," she laughed.

"Now pray with me," she said, squeezing the hand tightly.

Kevin did as Ginny Lee ordered and within minutes his fingers began to feel like they were on fire. His prayers came out in a language he didn't know but he did understand what he was saying. They'd prayed together for almost a half an hour before Ginny Lee finally let go of his hand.

"Take off the towel and let's have a look," she said.

The towel was soaked in blood but as Kevin unwrapped it he could tell the deep cuts were gone and in their place remained mean looking scars. Scars he knew would eventually heal and disappear.

"They're gone," he said.

"The Holy Spirit healed you," Ginny Lee said. "You have a strong gift for healing."

"As do you," he replied.

"No, I have a gift for seeing and focusing other people's gifts," Ginny Lee replied.

"I think I'm ready for that breakfast now," Kevin said.

"So am I," Ginny Lee replied, but as they prepared to get into Kevin's car a Ford Crown Victoria pulled into the parking lot.

"I wonder what he wants?" Ginny Lee said, walking over to talk to the man in the suit.

Kevin already knew what he was there for.

"Well it's 11:00 a.m. and still no Hannah," Charlie grumbled.

"And your surprised by this?" the agent said.

Just then Charlie's phone rang.

"Caressa, well the hell are you?" Hannah barked.

"Waiting for you at the bureau office as instructed, sir," Charlie replied. "And my name is Daniels, sir."

"Whatever. You're supposed to be here in Jacksonville. I told them to have you and the reporter meet me in Jacksonville," Hannah insisted.

"Apparently, there was some miscommunication, sir. I'll head up there immediately," Charlie said.

"Wait, the reporter lady, what's her name, Jessica, she's not coming with you?" he asked.

"No sir, when I told her I was ordered to wait for you she decided to head up to Jacksonville without me. She should already be there," Charlie said.

"Good, give me her number, I'll call her and make lunch arrangements for us. If you leave now you should make it in time for lunch," Hannah replied.

Charlie read off Jessica's number and Hannah hung up without further comment.

"He said his instructions to you were to have me meet him in Jacksonville," Charlie said.

"Bullshit," the agent replied.

"How far is it to Jacksonville?" Charlie asked

"About an hour and a half but if you drive Code 3 you can make it in about forty-five minutes," the agent suggested.

"Great, my Trans Am doesn't even have lights and a siren," Charlie replied.

"Yes they do," the Agent explained. "The light is under the dash. You just pull it out, put it through the window and stick it to the top of your car. The little switch under the steering column works both the siren and the light."

"Nobody ever mentioned it and I never bothered to look. Thanks," Charlie said and headed out.

"Are you Virginia Lee Turner?" the man asked.

"Folks around here call me, Ginny Lee," she replied, "and this is my friend Kevin Jackson."

"Ginny Lee, Mr. Jackson, I'm Agent Saunders with the Birmingham bureau of the FBI."

"What can I do for you Agent Saunders?" Ginny Lee replied, even though she knew what was coming.

"We tried to speak with your mother at the nursing home over in Scottsboro about Emily Sue Whitman," he began, hoping for a response but receiving none.

"She said she had no daughter named Emily Sue Whitman even though records say differently. The folks at the nursing home said we should contact you."

"Emily Sue Whitman was my half-sister who was murdered in 1975. My mother is suffering from dementia and has blocked that tragic memory from her mind," Ginny Lee replied. "And frankly, I'd rather not talk about it either."

"I'm afraid I have to insist we discuss it Ms. Turner. You see we've discovered a skull which we believe may be Emily Sue's. When her remains were discovered the skull was not with the body and it is important that we run a DNA test on the remains to see if they match the skull," Agent Saunders explained.

"Don't you need my permission to exhume her remains?" Ginny Lee asked.

"We would prefer your permission, but when it relates to an ongoing murder investigation it isn't necessary."

"When does it have to be done?" she asked.

"As soon as possible," Saunders replied.

"Will you take all the remains or just a few to test?"

"We would take the entire remains and hold onto them for no more than a week. If the DNA matches we would return the skull with the rest of the remains for reburial."

"What about the rest of the chalice?" Ginny Lee asked.

"Excuse me," Saunders said.

"What about the rest of the chalice? I read the papers. I know the skull was made into a chalice and they used other bones to make the stem of the chalice. I want the entire chalice put back in the coffin with the remains," Ginny Lee insisted.

"Umm…, I'm not sure…"

"Well you better make that clear to whoever is in charge or there will be one heck of a law suit the government will have to deal with," Ginny Lee assured him.

"I will let my supervisor know," Agent Saunders replied sheepishly.

"The body is buried in the graveyard out back. I will have two of my workers remove the coffin this afternoon, so have a means to transport it back to Birmingham by 5:00. I expect to have a guarantee in writing regarding the chalice and the fact that it will be returned by 5:00 p.m. next Thursday. Any questions?" Ginny said laying out her demands.

"I'll take care of it," Agent Saunders replied trying to regain some control of the situation.

"You do that. Now, if you'll excuse us, we're late for breakfast," Ginny Lee replied climbing into the Nova and slamming the door.

"Where to?" Kevin asked.

"Just drive."

They had gone about three blocks when Ginny Lee burst into tears.

Jessica had found nothing but dead ends in Jacksonville. She had come with such high hopes because of information her research team had found. They had learned that Peter Hannah had been a student at Jacksonville State at the time of the rape and was a member of one of the few fraternities active on campus at that time.

"No wonder the jerk is so interested in the investigation," she thought.

She found the fraternity he had belonged to and found Peter Hannah's individual picture on the big conglomerate yearly fraternity class photo, but of course there was no one around from thirty-five years ago and the fraternity historian explained how all the old crap was lost when they moved to the new frat house in 1998.

According to Charlie, Peter claimed to have been studying abroad the semester the rape occurred and university records seemed to confirm this. She stopped by the Study Abroad office to see if they kept past information, but 1970 was pre-computer and those records weren't saved. They did have some random pictures, one of which had the date Europe 1970 on it and Peter wasn't in the picture. That wasn't proof of anything, just a curiosity piece.

The local newspapers had no information nor did the campus police.

Jessica was about to check the library when her cell phone rang.

"Hello," she said cautiously not recognizing the number.

"Hi Jessica, this is Peter Hannah. I guess there was some sort of mix-up and Charlie is still back in Birmingham."

"I bet," Jessica thought.

"I was wondering if you would like to meet for lunch. I know Charlie is on his way and could probably be here in time to join us, depending on how soon we can get together."

"That sounds great," Jessica said, turning on her charm. "You know this city better than me, any suggestions?"

"How about Cooter Brown's Rib Shack up on Highway 204?" he suggested.

"I'm sure they'll have a salad," she replied. "Do you have an address?"

"Just head west from the Pete Matthews Coliseum at the university. It's about a mile so you can't miss it," he said.

"How about 12:30. It will give Charlie a chance to join us," Jessica suggested.

"It's only 11:15 and I am pretty hungry," Peter argued.

"Okay, 12:00 o'clock, but I may be a few minutes late," she warned.

"12:00 it is," he chirped, "see you there."

Jessica got the feeling she was being played and she would know because she made her living playing other people.

"Just what are you up to Assistant Director Peter Hannah?" Jessica wondered.

CHAPTER THIRTY-THREE

"I'm sorry you're so sad," Kevin said. "I wish they didn't have to do what they said they have to do."

"I never even knew my sister," Ginny Lee admitted. "And Momma refused to ever talk about her and made me promise to never talk about Emily Sue either."

"Why would she ask you to make such a promise?" Kevin asked.

"I don't know and I don't really care, but as long as Momma's alive I'm gonna honor the promise I made to her," Ginny Lee insisted.

"Where would you like to eat?"

"Just someplace away from here," Ginny Lee said. "Just away from here."

Kevin did as Ginny Lee requested and just drove. He went out to the Interstate-59 and headed north.

"You know I really think we should stop soon and eat," Kevin said finally breaking the silence.

"I know, there's a lot we need to get done at the church before the FBI comes back this afternoon," Ginny Lee replied.

"Any suggestions where I should stop?"

"There's a truck stop in just a few more miles. They usually have decent food and we can turn around there. Sorry I haven't been too friendly," Ginny Lee said.

"Hey, you got a lot on your mind. I'm here if you need to talk and I'm here if you just need to sit and think," Kevin replied.

"Thanks," she replied, slipping into silence.

Peter Hannah was waiting when Jessica arrived. Although she had never met the man she had seen his picture on the FBI website and had learned quite a bit about him from her research team. He, like her, wasn't afraid to bruise a few feelings to improve his lot in life and it appeared Peter Hannah had some pretty high career aspirations.

"So do I call you Jessica or Paige?" he said as he rose to greet her.

"Why Jessica, of course. I have no idea who this Paige person you mention might be," Jessica replied in her bimbo southern belle lilt.

"Well Jessica it's a pleasure to meet you. Charlie has told me so much about you," he said.

"Oh suh, I doubt that so very much, since Charlie and I have just barely become acquainted ourselves," she responded. "Speaking of Charlie, have you heard from him?"

"No, not since around 11:00 a.m. when I called to find out where he was," Hannah replied.

"Perhaps I should give him a call and let him know where we are."

"I'm sure he'll call when he gets close," Hannah said. "So tell me, what have you been up to this morning here in Jacksonville?"

"Trying to find any record of the rape of Emily Sue Whitman," she replied.

"And were you successful?" he asked.

"Not in the least," she replied, watching for a reaction from Hannah.

"Maybe when Charlie gets here the two of you may have more success," Peter speculated.

"I understand you went here at the time of the rape."

"I did, but by chance I was spending my year studying abroad when the rape occurred," Peter explained.

The rape was the fall of 1970 and you studied abroad the 1970-1971 school year?" she asked

"That's correct."

"Where abroad did you study?"

"Europe, my studies were in Europe."

"Europe's a big place. Where in Europe did you study? You had to be affiliated with a particular country and school. I read that at the Study Abroad office earlier today," Jessica said.

"Can I take your order?" a young woman said, saving Hannah from a desperate situation.

"Are you ready to order, Jessica?" Hannah asked.

"Perhaps we should call and see how close Charlie is."

Hannah immediately called Charlie and began talking to him while the waitress stood there impatiently.

"I think you should come back," Jessica finally told her.

"Three beers," Hannah called out as she was walking away.

"You would like a beer wouldn't you?"

"Sure," Jessica replied.

"Charlie's getting off the freeway now. He'll only be a few minutes," Peter said.

"What did you think of the skull chalice and all those snakes down at the Market Botanica in New Orleans?" Hannah asked.

"I thought the snakes were absolutely frightful, the skull chalice fascinating, and I find it puzzling that you're avoiding my question about what school and country you attended while studying abroad."

"Actually, when I went through the program you didn't have to be affiliated with a particular school or university. I designed my own program of study based on what I wanted to learn and where I wanted to go to learn it. I wrote papers and designed projects and sent them back to my professors here for my grades," Hannah explained.

Jessica listened but she wasn't buying it. That wasn't the way the program worked according to the people she had talked to in the office. But then again, this is 2005 and that was 1970. Things were very different back then.

"Here are your three beers," the waitress said.

"And here comes Charlie," Jessica said, as a black Trans Am came racing up the highway going much faster than the speed limit.

"He's going to pass the place," Hannah said.

But at just the precise moment Charlie hit his brakes hard locking them, cut his steering wheel hard, and drifted the car sideways onto the gravel parking lot of Cooters, just like Burt Reynolds would have done, generating several hoops, hollers and applause from the locals.

"Where did you learn to do that?" Jessica said laughing when Charlie entered.

"Driver's defensive training at the academy in Quantico," he replied. "First time I really ever tried it. I think I could get used to it."

"Don't even think about pulling a stunt like that again," Hannah demanded.

"So what have I missed?" Charlie asked.

"Jessica's been telling me about all the dead-ends she has encountered here in Jacksonville this morning," Hannah responded. "Isn't that so Jessica?"

"It hasn't been the most productive morning. 1970 was pre-computer and most information wasn't worth computerizing and was thrown out," Jessica lamented.

"I spoke to the local police station when I arrived. There isn't even anyone working there who was around in 1970. I asked about old files and was told they were all destroyed in a flood back in the 80's. So that's a dead-end too," Hannah said.

Jessica got a sense that Peter Hannah was not the type of person she wanted to be involved with. Yes, he was much higher up the food chain than Charlie but there was something about him. Not so much her woman's intuition but more of an unexpected fearfulness in her heart that told her leave this one alone.

"Let's eat, I have more work to do," Jessica insisted.

"Actually, I need to get back to Birmingham sooner than planned," Hannah said, "so I think I'll just finish my beer and leave lunch for you two."

"Am I missing something here?" Charlie said. "I feel like I'm getting the royal run-a-round."

"Relax Charlie, let's enjoy lunch and talk business," Jessica said.

"You two do that. Charlie, I'll be in touch with you later this evening. Tell Kevin I need to talk to him," Hannah said.

"I will if I see him, sir."

"Well make it a point to see him dammit, I want to know what he is up to," Hannah insisted, as he hurried out the door.

"What was that all about?" Charlie asked.

"I think he wanted to keep us both away from here while he did some last minute alteration of the facts," Jessica said.

"Alteration of what facts?" Charlie asked.

"I would bet my career that Peter Hannah was here during the rape of Emily Sue Whitman and with all the trouble he seems to be taking to make it look like he wasn't, I'm even more convinced," Jessica said.

"That's a damning accusation without a lot of proof," Charlie replied.

"If I keep looking I know I can find enough proof to make him very uncomfortable," Jessica replied.

"Or enough to make you very uncomfortable," Charlie replied.

"Are you suggesting Peter Hannah would do something to me?"

"I'm not suggesting anything, Jessica, because I know it could come back to bite me in the butt later. I'm just saying be careful when you're playing with fire because you sometimes get burned."

Jessica didn't care much for Charlie's answer, especially since she had her recorder going in her purse.

"So tell me what led you to Chester Cunningham?" Charlie asked.

"You first," Jessica said.

"Okay, Chester Cunningham is a doctor who belongs to a Holiness Church which as part of their religious practice handles poisonous snakes. The church came under suspicion very early in our investigation and he is somebody we are seriously looking at," Charlie replied. "Now your turn."

"I found his picture when I went back to James Arnold's house. He was a guitar player in a band that included three of your victims, James Arnold, Andrew Smith, and James Zeller. I think they came to Jacksonville not to see a football game but as the band for a fraternity party. The fraternity party where Emily Sue Whitman was raped," Jessica explained.

"Do you have the photograph?"

"Right here, but I want it back."

Charlie looked at the photo.

"Do you think this was taken at the fraternity party?"

"I'm not sure, I've been trying to figure that out, but it could've been a party anywhere," she replied.

"Were there anymore pictures?"

"I didn't take the time to look. We could go back and search later."

"No, I figured you had found something there so I sent back a criminologist team to tear the place apart," Charlie said.

"Well at least call them and tell them to look in the records by the stereo," she said. "That's where I found this."

"Did you figure out which fraternity Peter belonged to?" Charlie asked.

"Yes, but it was no help."

"Maybe we should go back and see if any of these faces in the background here show up in some fraternity picture," he suggested.

"Good idea, I didn't think of that," Jessica said. "I also had another idea. I wanted to check the archives at the library. I'm sure Director Hannah has the ability to change computerized records but I bet he forgot all about the archived newspapers at the library. Even if the rape was covered over the initial story will be there and may tell us something," Jessica said.

"Good thinking," Charlie said. "And I'll be happy to go there as soon as I finish these ribs."

"Big slabs of meat covered in sauce must be a man thing," Jessica said.

"Believe me, it is," Charlie smiled.

"You seem to not have much faith in Chester's skill as a doctor?" Kevin asked as they were just about back to the church after a quiet breakfast.

"I'm sure Chester is an excellent surgeon," Ginny Lee said.

"Surgeon, I thought he was a family practitioner," Kevin said.

"He's both. Chester's an extraordinarily bright person. It's just that God is a lot better healer than Chester could ever be wouldn't you say?" Ginny Lee said grabbing Kevin's hand and holding it up.

"I can't deny that. If there weren't so many doctors in the United States we'd see a lot more miracles of healing by the Holy Spirit," Kevin assured her.

"Would you help Ver Dell dig up Emily Sue's coffin this afternoon?" Ginny Lee asked. "I really don't want strangers stomping around in the graveyard."

"Of course I will," Kevin replied. "Should I head up to get Ver Dell?"

"No, he and Ida should be heading down anytime now. I'll let him know about my visit with the FBI."

Kevin decided now was not the time to ask about Woland or even push Ginny any further about Chester.

"If you want to get to know Chester a little better you should come to tonight's small group meeting," Ginny Lee suggested.

"What kind of small group?" Kevin asked.

"We won't be handling snakes and drinking poison if that's what you're worried about," she replied.

"I've never seen anybody here drink poison," Kevin replied.

"That's because you'd been 'slain in the Spirit' by the time we got around to the drinking of the poison and the holding of the fire."

"Do you drink the poison and hold fire?" Kevin asked.

"I do if the Spirit leads me to do so."

"Did he lead you either time I was here?"

Ginny Lee just smiled.

"You should come tonight. Chester leads us in worship and then we pray and discuss scripture. It would give you a chance to get to know him."

"Who else will be here?"

"I will be. Isn't that enough to make you want to come?" "How can I say no to an offer like that?"

CHAPTER THIRTY-FOUR

Samuelson and his crew took one of Vasquez's personal jets to Nuevo Laredo. Once there arrangements were made for his crew to cross the border as day laborers along with hundreds of others into Laredo, Texas. Samuelson's crossing would be a little more difficult but just a matter of a couple of phone calls and a little preparation. He could have walked across the border but he knew they had recently installed facial recognition software and there was a very good chance his face was at the top of the list of those being searched for. Therefore, it would be much easier to drive across but he would need to cross with other Caucasians in a vehicle registered in the United States.

One of Vazquez's Laredo distributors volunteered his *puta* girlfriend to provide the service. She was waiting at the airport for Samuelson when he arrived.

"Are you sure this car is clean?" Samuelson said as he entered the car.

"It's my mom's car, of course it's clean," she replied.

Even though he knew the guard at the border crossing was on the payroll and the girl and car looked innocent enough, Samuelson knew that the drug trade was becoming more and more competitive and it wouldn't take much for someone to sell out to the competition. Laredo wasn't exactly the Vazquez Cartel's home territory.

Samuelson threw his bag in her car and they headed for the border. He had fake identification but he hoped he wouldn't need to use it since the FBI had provided it for him.

"Just put on your sunglasses and relax," the girl told him. "You look nervous. That's a dead give-away."

He was nervous and he didn't need a drug dealer's girlfriend calling him on it.

"Just get me across the border."

He hadn't realized just how shot his nerves were. He had put himself in a hopeless situation with a very limited chance to get out.

"See nothing to worry about," she said as they breezed through the border crossing.

"Yeah, yeah," Samuelson replied, "Just drive to the rental car lot at the airport."

They rode the rest of the way in silence. When they arrived the rest of his crew was waiting. They had rented two Cadillac Escalades and began transferring an arsenal of weapons along with luggage into the two luxury SUVs.

"So where are you guys headed," the girl asked as Samuelson was getting out of the car.

"Do you really want to know?" he said.

"I suppose not," she replied meekly.

"A word of advice. Get out now before it's too late. You're getting in way over your head," he warned.

She glanced over as several machine pistols were placed in a nylon zippered bag and into one of the Escalades.

"Let's roll," Samuelson said, "It's a fifteen hour drive to Birmingham."

He hoped the girl thought about what he said.

Simon awoke to noises coming from the floor above. A light was constantly aglow in the basement so he had no real sense of day or night. He had no idea how long he had been asleep or how long his captor had been gone. He had actually lost all sense of time. He did know that the murder of James A had to come two months after that of Matthew and Andrew which had occurred in mid-June. He was captured in mid-July. James A was therefore killed in mid-August, which meant it was probably the end of August or early September Simon figured.

Suddenly the door to the basement burst open and the killer came stumbling down the stairs dragging a body behind him.

"How's the tongue Simon, can you speak yet?" the killer asked.

"A little," Simon whispered.

"Good, that's good," the killer replied, roughly tossing the body on the table. "I'm afraid the FBI has stirred things up a bit."

"It's about time," Simon thought.

"I bet you're happy as a clam about that aren't you?" the killer said.

Simon knew better than to respond.

"Well, I think I found the solution to slow them down at least for a while," the killer laughed. "It also gives me a chance to stick it to a couple of people who have been annoying me way too much lately. They should j-just leave me alone and l-let me b-be."

Simon could tell the killer was starting to get agitated by his stuttering.

"I know your curious, so let me introduce you to Peter Talbot," the killer said.

"Peter?" Simon whispered. "I thought…"

"I know what you're thinking. Peter isn't due to die for another two months. That's correct, but circumstances have forced the issue and I had to jump the schedule a bit," the killer explained.

Something wasn't right about this but Simon wasn't sure what it was.

"I'm even going to have to rush my usual decapitation," the killer explained. "Poor Peter here is already dead. He didn't react well to the rattlesnake venom."

The killer went to the stereo and turned on the Marshall Tucker Band Song *Can't You See* put on a gown and gloves came back to the table and began to surgically remove Peter Talbot's head.

"This isn't right," Simon wanted to shout out, "these are supposed to be ritualistic methodical serial killings."

The killer worked quickly but carefully, for he knew the decapitations had to look identical.

It took less the twenty minutes to complete the job.

"It's just not fun without the flair," he said to Simon, as he tossed Peter's head onto a pile of towels.

Simon didn't respond but continued to watch as the killer opened up a door at the far end of the basement that Simon hadn't noticed before. The killer went into another room and returned with a wooden cross which he laid on the floor next to the headless body.

"They always look so funny nailed to the cross without their heads." The killer commented, as he pulled Peter's body onto the cross.

"I know National Geographic did that special that said the nails through the palms could support the body's weight if the feet were nailed to the side. But don't you really think the Roman's drove the nails through the wrists?" the killer said, as he pounded the nails between the radius and ulna in Peter's wrists.

Once the body was firmly nailed to the cross the killer picked it up easily with one hand and set it next to the door at the back of the basement.

"If you'll excuse me Simon, I need to shower and freshen up. I'm expecting a guest this evening so I need you to be on your best behavior or you will suffer dearly for it. Do you understand?" the killer asked.

"I understand," Simon replied, but he understood less now than he had before and this concerned him.

CHAPTER THIRTY-FIVE

The Houston Cole Library at Jacksonville State University did have copies of the local paper, the *Jacksonville News* on microfiche dating back to 1936. After spending fifteen minutes reacquainting herself with how to use the reader Jessica was unable to find any mention of Emily Sue's rape.

"Jessica, I think I might have found something," Charlie said.

Charlie had accessed digitized issues of the Jacksonville State paper *The Chanticleer*.

"I found an article that talks about the rape of a nursing student at the Sigma Theta Fraternity. It doesn't mention any names but it calls for a clamp down on drinking and open parties at the fraternity houses," Charlie described.

"That's it?" Jessica said.

"Did you check Emily Sue Whitman's record? Did she ever graduate?" Charlie asked.

"She dropped out of school the semester the rape occurred and never returned."

"Any idea what happened to her between the rape and her murder?" Charlie asked.

"No, but I bet if we could find out where she was and what she was doing maybe it would give us a hint about the Apostle Serial Killer," Jessica suggested.

"Remember that James Arnold said Emily Sue was paid a ton of money to not press charges," Charlie said.

"I believe the term he used was 'shitload' of money," Jessica corrected.

"Whatever. If you just were given a 'shitload' of money and wanted to try and forget a bad experience what would you do?" Charlie asked.

"I'd move to Europe."

"Do you think Emily Sue Whitman was that sophisticated? I would have guessed the West Coast. 1970, the summer of love, California Dreamin'," Charlie replied.

"Run a check through the State Department, see if she left the country," Jessica said.

Charlie sent a series of messages through his laptop back to FBI headquarters. Ten minutes later he had the information he was looking for.

"According to the State Department, Emily Sue Whitman left New York in January of 1971 for Stockholm, Sweden. She returned from London, England in June 1975," Charlie said.

"And they believe she was murdered in July of 1975 here in Jacksonville?" Jessica asked.

"That's what I've been told."

"I wonder what she was doing all that time in Europe?" Jessica wondered.

"I hope enjoying herself."

"I think we've wasted enough time in Jacksonville today," Jessica said.

"There's nothing keeping me here," Charlie replied.

"Why don't you come over tonight," Jessica offered.

"I may be at the bureau late. Emily Sue Whitman's remains are being exhumed today and I'm having a rush put on the DNA results," Charlie said.

"Maybe I can join you for that," Jessica replied. "I'll drop my car at my apartment and grab a change of clothes. Follow me and pick me up there."

It was decided before Charlie had a say in it. The way things were going it was probably for the best. Knowing what Jessica was up to was always for the best.

Ida and Ver Dell showed up a little after noon just like Ginny Lee said they would. Ida brought sandwiches and ice tea and had extra for Kevin as if she expected him to be there.

Kevin waited outside while Ginny Lee talked with them and explained about the FBI coming later that afternoon. Kevin could hear them praying inside and considered joining them but decided against it. A few minutes later Ver Dell came outside.

"Shovels up in da shed. Git two. Meet me in da graveyard," he said and headed off towards his car.

Kevin turned the switch that sent power to the shed and collected the two shovels as Ver Dell instructed. He had never dug up a grave before and wasn't exactly cherishing the thought of desecrating Holy ground.

Ginny Lee walked up behind him as Kevin hesitated from entering the church graveyard.

"It's alright, Kevin," Ginny Lee reassured him. "It's something we gotta do. We've prayed about it and it's okay."

Ver Dell came around the corner carrying a block and tackle and a large four by six inch beam.

He carefully set it next to Emily Sue's grave and took one of the shovels from Kevin.

"Dig straight down," he explained, marking off the area to dig.

They moved to opposite sides and began to dig. The ground was harder than Kevin expected, but then again it hadn't been touched in thirty years.

Simon stared at the headless body nailed to the cross standing in the shadows across the expanse of the basement. The killer had left the victim's head lying atop the pile of bloody towels next to the glistening steel table.

"This doesn't make any sense," Simon whispered.

"This is a wasted killing. What is he planning?" Simon thought, as he heard the killer's voice talking rapidly above him.

Sleep wouldn't come. As hard as he tried, it continued to slip away from Samuelson as the two Escalades raced across Interstate-59 cutting across the southern portion of Texas towards Houston.

With each passing mile he saw his own life growing shorter and shorter. He began to formulate plans for escaping the task at hand, but escape from one nightmare to another was not a solution. He would have to finish this job for Vasquez and then, somehow, make his way to Russia. He was now convinced that that was his future.

The digging went slowly and even slower still when they neared the casket.

"Careful now," Ver Dell warned. "Let me finish 'er."

He had dug footholds in the sides of the dirt so he wouldn't stand directly on the coffin.

Ginny Lee had sensed that the job was nearing completion and came down from the house.

"Have some iced tea," she said to Kevin.

"Thanks," he replied, wanting to say more but realizing now wasn't the time.

"Thow me da' rope," Ver Dell called up.

Kevin handed the rope down to Ver Dell. After a couple of minutes Ver Dell popped out of the hole and sat the beam he had brought on two other head stones and attached the block and tackle.

"Git da sled outta da shed," Ver Dell said to Kevin. "Unda' da table"

Kevin wasn't sure what he meant but went to the shed to look. Underneath the table was what looked like a large wooden snow sled but with large skids. Instead of a rope it had a wooden handle like a wagon would have to pull it.

Kevin pulled it out into the graveyard and Ver Dell carefully positioned it.

"Help me pull," he said.

He and Kevin pulled the rope and with little effort the coffin came up and Ver Dell guided it perfectly onto the sled.

No sooner was it in place on the sled was Ida carefully brushing away the dirt and cleaning it off.

"Ida, you don't need to clean it," Ginny Lee said.

Ida nodded her head but continued with her cleaning.

"What time did they say they would be back?" Kevin asked.

"They didn't, but they have until five o'clock to bring me the guarantee and collect the coffin and I'm sure they will," Ginny Lee reminded him.

Kevin hadn't forgotten. He just hoped the local field office was organized enough to follow through on Ginny Lee's demands. He only wished he could call Charlie to make sure of it.

Charlie had ordered Agent Saunders to arrange for Emily Sue's coffin to be picked up and the guarantee to be drawn up, signed and delivered before five o'clock. He wanted her remains at the Birmingham lab no later than six so they could fast-track a preliminary DNA analysis. He wanted results that evening.

"Are we going to be spending the evening together?" Charlie asked, as they dropped off Jessica's car at her apartment.

"That all depends?" she replied.

"That all depends on what?" Charlie asked.

"On whatever I decide later this evening," she teased.

"Emily Sue Whitman's remains should be at the lab by now. I need to stop by my apartment to pick up a file and a change of clothes, just in case. Then we can get a quick dinner before we head to the lab."

Jessica just smiled and they continued their drive to the National Guard Base in silence.

As they pulled in front of the apartment, both Sergeants Boone and McClellan came out to see who it was.

"Good evening Miss, Agent Daniels," Sergeant McClellan said.

"It's Jessica," Jessica replied smiling.

"Oh I remember, from Banana Joe's," Boone said.

"I'm surprised any of us can remember much about that night," Jessica replied, "Especially you," she said specifically to McClellan who blushed and headed back inside.

"Everything alright?" Charlie asked Sergeant Boone.

"Yes, sir, it's just that our assignment to watch over you ends day after tomorrow and frankly were going to miss the vacation it's been for us," Boone said.

"Sorry it wasn't more exciting," Charlie replied.

"No sir, that was the best part. It wasn't exciting. Like I said it's been like a vacation."

"Maybe tomorrow we can return to Banana Joe's," Jessica suggested. "Your beard is really coming along and I'm sure the Charlie Daniels' thing would work again."

Sergeant McClellan walked back outside when he heard Jessica's suggestion.

"I knew that'd get your attention," she laughed.

"Let's see how things are going, but that's not a bad idea," Charlie remarked.

"Will you be staying here this evening, Agent Daniels?" Boone asked.

"We're not sure yet. I have some work to do at the lab and then we'll decide," Charlie replied.

"Have a good evening."

"You do the same, sergeants."

As they entered the apartment Charlie headed for the bedroom to grab a few things while Jessica waited. She noticed the door between the two apartments was open again and this time headed through without hesitation.

This apartment looked less lived in than Charlie's except for a big map of Alabama and surrounding states pinned to the wall.

"I know what this is," she said.

"You know what 'what' is?" Charlie said seeing the door open and coming into Kevin's apartment.

"Someone's been plotting where the bodies of the Apostle Serial Killer victims have been dumped," she said.

"Like that is some big secret?" Charlie replied.

"No, but predicting where the next one will be sure is," she said pointing to a red pin with a six written on it. I know this isn't your doing," Jessica said.

"Tyronza, Arkansas," Charlie read. "Why would the killer go that far away to drop off the next body?"

Jessica shuffled through some papers on the desk. "Because he is dropping the bodies in direct proportion to where the original Apostles were martyred," she explained. "That's how I knew James Arnold would be in Birmingham. Birmingham is the Apostle Serial Killer's Jerusalem. Apostle Peter was crucified in Rome which proportionately compared to the other locations where bodies were found means Peter will be found in Tyronza, Arkansas."

"I'm not sure about that."

"You're just trying to throw me off," Jessica accused him.

"No, I'm not, really. I think something would have been said to me if that was the case and this is the first I have heard of it," Charlie insisted.

"Whatever."

"Uh oh," Charlie thought, "so much for my evening."

Simon knew when the killer was in the shower because the giant water heater would kick on in the basement. He was curious as to if the killer actually meant a visitor was going to be visiting.

"Maybe this is my chance to escape," Simon thought.

His mind was frantically calculating the risk of trying to make contact with this mysterious visitor.

He heard Simon's voice, or what he believed to be Simon's voice coming from the floor above.

"Was the visitor here?" he wondered.

"Should I scream out?"

"What would be the risk?"

"Probably the loss of my tongue," he decided.

"But compared to certain death..."

His internal debate was interrupted when the killer opened the basement door and came down the steps.

The killer picked several items from the shelf including a box Simon knew contained snakes and placed them at the back of the basement near the crucified body. He then disappeared through the distant door.

"What's going on?" Simon tried to figure out.

He suddenly heard a familiar whirring noise.

"That's an electric garage door opening," Simon realized.

Then he heard a vehicle engine growing louder as it obviously pulled into the garage, but the electric door didn't close.

A moment later the distant basement door opened and for the first time since his capture Simon caught a glimpse of dim sunlight.

"It must be either dusk or dawn," Simon declared to himself as if he was suddenly victorious in a heated competition.

A small victory to be sure, but to Simon it was a victory. He had gained a minor sense of perspective in this ongoing nightmare and it empowered him.

The killer grabbed the cross and carried it back through the door.

"He must be loading it into a vehicle. My God he's got a partner in these killings," Simon suddenly realized.

Next the killer came back in and grabbed the items he had collected from the shelves including the box of snakes and took those out into what Simon now knew was a garage.

"Why would he be moving evidence?" Simon wondered.

"If he was worried about someone discovering it here, then there's a lot more incriminating evidence than what he just removed," Simon thought.

"Therefore, he plans on planting that evidence," Simon concluded. "That, along with the crucified body of Peter Talbot."

He heard the vehicle engine start back up and quickly grow silent.

Then he heard the whirr as the garage door slowly closed.

"Well Simon I bet that stirred up your curiosity," the killer said, coming back into the main part of the basement. "Any questions you'd like to ask?"

Simon had a million questions but wasn't about to ask one of them. He wanted the killer to wonder what clue if any, Simon might now have about his identity or the situation. Simon needed the advantage.

"I bet you're surprised that I'm not working alone," the killer said, trolling for some sort of response that he could use to break down Simon's new found hope.

"Well look at that," the killer said nudging Peter's decapitated head with his foot. "I almost forgot about it."

He filled a pot with warm water and sat it on a burner on his work bench.

"Do you remember what I showed you?" the killer asked.

Simon was suddenly confused. The killer picked up the head and carried it over to Simon's cage. With a wave of his hand the cage unlocked and the door opened. Simon felt a pressure push him back against the rear bars as the killer came in and sat the head on the table.

"I asked if you remember how I showed you to peel away the skin like you're peeling an orange?" the killer said.

Simon stood stunned, staring between the head on the table and the killer who now stood outside the locked cage.

"The important thing is not to scratch the skull with the knife blade," the killer said, as he floated a knife into the cage and onto the table next to the head.

"You can't be serious?" Simon gasped.

"Dead serious. You see, my schedule as to when the Apostles are to die is no longer an issue, thusly the order of death of the Apostles no longer is an issue. There is no reason Simon cannot be martyred before Thomas, Jude, and Matthias, although, I would prefer to maintain some sense of appropriateness," the killer waxed whimsically.

"The first cut will be the hardest, wait, isn't that a song? No, I guess the song is *The first cut is the deepest*, but don't make your cuts too deep. Scratches are difficult to fix and they make me angry and you know how I get when I'm angry. I'll come back in about a half an hour. That should give you plenty of time," the killer said.

Simon stared as the killer walked away humming to himself.

If he refused to do it would the killer murder him immediately?

Simon knew the answer to that question was a most definite yes.

"Am I ready to die?" Simon asked himself.

"Not quite yet," he thought.

He had considered trying to crush his own skull to make his body useless to the killer, but that would only mean another would have to die in his place. And his God would not allow him to take his own life.

"What would God say about me peeling away the face of Peter Talbot?" Simon thought.

"The man is undeniably dead but would I be committing a sin if I did what the killer has ordered me to do?"

Simon picked up the knife and turned it over in his hand contemplating it from every angle.

Then he turned and looked at the two eyes of Peter Talbot that stared blankly into the emptiness from the decapitated head sitting on the table before him.

"What evil has brought this forth before us?" Simon asked of the head.

He gently touched the cheek. It was cold. The elasticity of the skin had been replaced by a dry hardness. A slightly harder push left indentations as if the face was made of a memory foam material. Simon realized that was only because the underlying tissue still retained some body fluid moisture.

"Can you forgive me for what I'm about to do, Peter Talbot?" Simon asked.

"Can God forgive me for what I must do in order to survive?" Simon wondered.

Simon held the knife in his right hand and turned the face away from him with his left.

He placed the edge of the knife above Peter's right ear and slowly began to slice. The knife was razor sharp and the ear was off within a few seconds. Now that he had an opening to work with it would be much easier.

"Remember, it's just like peeling an orange," Simon said to himself as he peeled away Simon's right cheek and then vomited on the floor.

CHAPTER THIRTY-SIX

It was a somber mood at the church after the FBI left with Emily Sue's coffin. Kevin felt awkwardly out of place and would have gone back to Birmingham had he not promised Ginny Lee he would stay. It would give him a chance to get a better look at Chester who was looking more like a suspect in the serial killings. He also hoped Woland would attend the small group meeting. Little thought had been given to the possibility that it could be more than one person responsible for the Apostle Serial Killings. From what Kevin had seen at the church it wouldn't be hard to imagine an entire cult being behind the killings.

"I've got to talk to Charlie about these possibilities," Kevin thought.

The immediate problem was he and his clothes were filthy from the work he and Ver Dell had done all afternoon. Ver Dell went home to shower and change, but Kevin wasn't quite sure what to do about it.

"You're welcome to shower up at the house," Ginny Lee offered, "but I'm afraid there's not a lot I can do about your dirty clothes unless you have something else to put on in the car."

"I'm afraid I don't," Kevin replied.

"And me showering up at your house wouldn't be a very good idea," he said.

"S'pose you're right," she replied.

"But I'm going to have to do something, so I think I'll run down to Fort Payne and pick up some new clothes and find a cheap motel," Kevin said.

"There is a Wal-Mart right on Glenn Boulevard Southwest and a couple of motels just down the street from it," Ginny Lee remembered. "It's only about twenty minutes from here. You should be able to make it back in plenty of time for the small group."

"I'm looking forward to it," Kevin replied.

More than that, Kevin was looking forward to getting away from the church to call Charlie to see what information he had on Woland Kapkov and Peter Talbot. He was beginning to believe the strange Russian had a bigger part to play in the church than Ginny Lee was leading him to believe.

As soon as he was out of sight of the church he was on the phone.

Charlie answered on the second ring.

"So how was your day with Director Hannah?" Kevin joked.

There was just silence.

"Charlie are you there?"

"I'm here," Charlie bemoaned.

"That good, huh?" Kevin laughed.

"If I didn't know better I'd say he was working real hard at trying to hide something from us," Charlie replied.

"Don't be wishy-washy. You know damn well he's trying to hide something," Kevin replied. "The question is just how damning is the information he is trying to hide."

"Jessica thinks pretty damning."

"Jessica with you?"

"Yes, indeed," he replied.

"Can she hear everything I'm saying?"

"Probably," Charlie replied, as Jessica sat quietly grinning.

"Anything on any of those names I gave you?" Kevin asked.

"I haven't checked since I got back from Jacksonville, but we did learn something interesting. Emily Sue Whitman left the country for Sweden immediately after her rape and returned the month before her murder," Charlie explained.

"She spent almost five years in Sweden?" Kevin replied.

"It was four and a half years and we only know she initially went to Sweden. We don't if that's where she spent her entire time in Europe," Charlie said.

"Wasn't Peter Hannah in Europe at that time also?" Kevin asked.

"So he claims," Jessica answered.

"She can hear you just fine," Charlie added. "Jessica found out some interesting information about Chester Cunningham that may interest you."

"What's that?"

"Chester was a member of a band with James Arnold, Andrew Smith, and James Zeller that we are fairly sure played at the fraternity party the night Emily Sue Whitman was raped," Charlie explained.

"Three Apostle Serial Killer victims and Chester Cunningham. I remember no Apostles named Chester," Kevin said.

"Jessica copied the names of all the fraternity members who were active in the Sigma Theta Fraternity the year before, the year of, and the year after the rape."

"You really think this still has to do with revenge for the rape?"

"It's a good theory."

"It's a good theory if the victim wasn't murdered by the same killer. I've got a new theory," Kevin replied. "What if it wasn't just a single killer but two men working together or even a secret cult of several members performing these ritualistic murders? Maybe a group of religious fanatics who were in the fraternity at the time."

"None of the evidence points to more than one killer," Charlie replied.

"I think we've only considered the evidence in a mind frame of one person doing this. I'm just thinking maybe we should reexamine things from an alternate point of view," Kevin suggested.

"Would this have anything to do with the other names you gave me to check out?" Charlie replied.

"Possibly, but right now I have to shower and get cleaned up. So see if anything striking comes up on those names give me a call back before 7:45. That's when my phone gets shut down until late tonight," Kevin said.

"Will do, Charlie replied. "Are you going to be back at the apartment tonight?"

"No, I've got a room up in Fort Payne for the evening," Kevin replied. "I'm meeting with Chester tonight at the church."

"Let me know how that goes," Charlie replied.

"Take care," Kevin said and hung up.

"So you never told him about me finding his map," Jessica said.

"I guess I forgot," Charlie replied.

"What do you think about his multiple killer idea?" Jessica said.

"I think it's worth checking into," Charlie replied. "Why don't you get out that list of fraternity brothers and we'll start out by seeing how many are still living in the Birmingham area?"

"What about dinner?" Jessica said.

"We can order out. I'm sure one of the sergeants wouldn't mind helping us."

Sergeant Boone was more than happy to pick up Thai food for everyone and Charlie and Jessica set facing each other at the kitchen table with their laptops searching FBI data bases.

Charlie's phone rang and he answered on the first ring.

"Agent Daniels, this is Agent Taylor. I'm working the desk tonight at the office."

"What can I do for you?" Charlie said.

"Peter Talbot, you had us putting together a file on him. The Tennessee State Police just put a missing person report over the wire on him and called our office. Apparently, Peter Talbot disappeared this morning under mysterious circumstances. He was changing a flat tire in his driveway when his wife last saw him. When she returned home the tire was still in the process of being changed and there was some human blood and what looked like rattlesnake skin and rattlesnake blood on the driveway and undercarriage of his car."

"Sounds like a rattler bit him and he wandered off," Charlie replied.

"That's what the police figured but they searched everywhere and with Peter being the name for the Apostle Serial Killer's next victim and with a snake being involved they thought we'd want to know," Taylor said.

"It doesn't sound like a coincidence to me either," Charlie replied. "We may need to mobilize the team, but hold off for now; I'll get back to you shortly."

"Will do, sir," Taylor replied.

"Trouble?" Jessica asked.

"Maybe big trouble," Charlie replied, dialing Kevin's phone.

Charlie explained the situation to Kevin.

"It doesn't make sense. That would mean he's jumped his schedule ahead. Serial killer's don't do that unless they're desperate and believe they're close to being caught," Kevin replied.

"Maybe Chester is our man," Charlie surmised.

"Maybe Peter Hannah is our man," Jessica suggested. "He sure acted like a guilty man today."

"I think we need to find Chester Cunningham," Charlie said.

"That won't be hard. I'm on my way to see him right now," Kevin replied.

"We need to get a tail on him ASAP," Charlie said.

"He'll be at the church tonight. Send a team up now," Kevin ordered.

Charlie hung up and quickly dialed the bureau office.

"This is Daniels; I need a team sent now to the church up in Macedonia where we picked up Emily Sue Whitman's body today. Chester Cunningham is on his way there and I want him followed. He's now our prime suspect," Charlie ordered. "Have them call me when they get there."

"So what do we do now?" Jessica asked.

"Everything's on hold until we find out if Peter Talbot is the latest victim of the Apostle Serial Killer." Charlie said.

"What if it's not Chester? What if it is someone not even on the FBI radar? Shouldn't we head to Tyronza, Arkansas to see if we can catch him?" Jessica said.

"Arkansas is a long ways away," Charlie replied.

"Four hours and twenty-seven minutes, I just looked it up. If Kevin didn't think that was where the next body was being dumped why did he have it marked on the map?" Jessica asked.

"He never talked to me about it," Charlie replied.

"I don't believe you," Jessica spat back. "I think you're trying to keep me from the story."

"Jessica, I have no idea about Kevin's map, and even you should know that the timing is not right for the next Apostle Serial Killer to strike. Peter Talbot's name did come up as someone to look at but chances are it is merely a coincidence that he has turned up missing," Charlie replied, trying to calm her down.

"That's bullshit, and you know it, Charlie. Take me back to my apartment now," she demanded.

Charlie wasn't going to argue the point. Things were happening fast and it would be best if Jessica wasn't around for it.

"So what are you planning to do?" Charlie asked.

"File my story," she replied.

"I meant..." But he was interrupted.

"I know what you meant but until you're ready to be honest with me, I have nothing more to say to you, Charlie Daniels," Jessica snipped.

Not another word was spoken between them that evening, not even goodbye when he dropped her at her apartment.

"You surprise me Simon. I didn't think you had it in you," the killer smiled.

Simon glared at the killer. Droplets of vomit still hung from Simon's lips.

"I sense you didn't derive quite as much pleasure from the experience as I would."

Simon continued to stare, gripping the knife, wondering how he could peel away the killer's face.

"Set the knife back on the table, Simon," the killer ordered.

Simon turned the knife over and over in his hand.

"So I can see that your overwhelming desire is to kill me. You know I'm much too strong for that to ever happen," the killer explained.

Simon continued to turn the knife in his hand. Suddenly, it became very hot and he had no choice but to drop it on the table. Then his body was slammed against the back wall of his cage and pinned there.

"Simon, you make things so difficult for yourself." the killer said as he came in and collected the knife and Peter's peeled skull.

"I must be going away for a while again so instead of a warm maceration I've decided a cold maceration will have to do for our friend here. Of course, it will begin to smell somewhat and if you get hungry I'll leave the pieces you removed from the skull. I know the swelling in your tongue has gone down enough to allow you to chew."

"Why are you doing this to me?" Simon moaned.

"Just teaching you how depraved a person can become when they are given no other choice," the killer explained, as he turned off the flame and pretended to drop the head into the pot.

"Then maybe you'll begin to understand," the killer added as he headed up the stairs.

"I will never understand what makes you such a sick person," Simon whispered, "But I know God will see to it that you will suffer for your evil."

CHAPTER THIRTY-SEVEN

When Kevin arrived back at the church several cars and trucks were already there including Chester's white Dodge pick-up with a camper shell on it.

As he entered Chester was playing guitar and leading a worship song which had everyone singing along enthusiastically.

Ginny Lee saw Kevin enter and waved for him to come sit next to her. There were the usual core members of the church there who had been at the luncheon meeting and seven or eight others that looked familiar to Kevin but who he didn't know. Woland was conspicuously absent.

"Here, "Ginny Lee said, passing him some papers, "in case you don't know the words."

Kevin didn't have the best singing voice so he did his best to softly whisper the words trying not to attract attention. He spent most of his time watching Chester, using his skills as a trained psychiatrist to analyze every movement, every twitch, virtually every breath Chester took, trying to determine if he could actually be the Apostle Serial Killer.

Kevin listened politely to the reading and discussion of the scripture, responded appropriately to Ginny Lee and the others, and even engaged Chester into further clarifying some of his interpretation. But throughout it all, he continued his analysis of Chester's behavior and potential behaviors.

The meeting ended in prayer but Kevin hoped to get a chance to talk to Chester a little longer before he left. Both to find out about his background and to give the FBI team time to get into place.

"Ginny Lee tells me you are also a surgeon," Kevin said. "Do you have a specialty?"

"Not really, just a basic general surgeon, you know, fix a hernia, remove a growth, take out an appendix if I had to," Chester explained.

"Still, that requires a lot of extra schooling I would imagine," Kevin replied.

"It did, and believe I'm still paying for it," Chester joked. "Ginny Lee, the Sunderlands have invited us over for lunch again on Sunday after church."

"Not this week Chester," Ginny Lee replied. "I've had a lot to deal with this week and I don't want to make any commitments."

"It's only lunch," Chester replied.

"Not this week," she repeated.

"Kevin, it's been a pleasure to get to know you better. I'll look forward to seeing you in church Sunday."

"I'll see you here," Kevin replied, as he walked Chester out the door. "You need a hand with your guitar and amp?"

"No, I'm used to carrying it," he replied, "but thanks anyway."

Kevin looked around to see if he could spot the FBI team assigned to track Chester. He saw a Crown Vic parked down the road and knew the team was in place.

"Did you enjoy yourself tonight?" Ginny Lee said, grabbing Kevin's arm and startling him.

"I did, thanks for inviting me," Kevin replied.

"Did I scare you?" Ginny Lee asked.

"Just surprised me is all," Kevin replied.

"Would you like to come up to the house for a cup of coffee?" Ginny Lee offered.

"If I did, I'd be awake all night, and I'm really tired," Kevin replied. "Besides what would people think?"

"Sometimes I don't care what people think," Ginny Lee said.

"I should get back to the motel."

"Maybe another night," Ginny Lee said, obviously disappointed.

"I'll call you tomorrow, but I have to go back to Birmingham in the morning," Kevin said.

"But you will be here Sunday?" Ginny Lee asked.

"Sunday for sure," Kevin promised.

As much as he knew Ginny Lee wanted him to stay, Kevin had to know for sure if Chester was the man they've been searching for. He immediately called Charlie.

"What do you think?" Charlie asked. "You're the 'shrink', is Chester Cunningham a serial killer?"

"If he is, he's the most psychotic serial killer I've ever met. He showed absolutely no outwardly signs that would lead anyone to believe him capable of such atrocities," Kevin explained. "But having said all of that, you'd better have a damn good tail on him because I want to know everywhere he goes."

"I've got two teams on him. We're assuming he's headed back to his house in Birmingham, but both his offices are possibilities," Charlie said.

"Is Jessica still with you?" Kevin asked.

"No, she got all bent out of shape when I told her I knew nothing about the map on the wall of your apartment. She thinks I'm holding back information," Charlie explained.

"Well, you are aren't you?"

"Yeah, but not about the map. Do you really think the next victim will turn up in Tyronza, Arkansas?" Charlie asked.

"If the Apostle Serial Killer sticks to his pattern, then yes that is a good possibility, but not the only possibility. I left it there purposely to throw her off," Kevin replied.

"Well I don't know if you threw her off but you sure pissed her off," Charlie replied. "I wouldn't be surprised if she wasn't on her way there now."

"Hold on, I'm getting a call from one of the cars," Charlie said.

"Something's up. Chester's truck turned north on Interstate 59," Charlie reported.

"Let me pull out my map," Kevin said. "What's up that way that might interest him?"

"Peter Talbot disappeared from Cleveland, Tennessee. That's not much more than an hour up the road," Charlie offered.

"There's no way he would take that road if he was headed for Arkansas," Kevin decided. "I think I'll lay back and follow along."

"He just exited onto the 117 and is headed East," Charlie reported to Kevin.

"What's east on the 117? All I see is backwoods and hills. Rome! He's going to Rome," Kevin cried.

"Rome, Georgia? Why would he go there?" Charlie asked.

"He's not thinking Rome, Georgia; he's thinking Rome, Italy. The place where Apostle Peter was crucified," Kevin said, excitedly. "He must have Peter Talbot's body in the truck."

"That's pure speculation," Charlie replied, "If we pulled him over now without cause we could blow the entire case."

"I'm heading there," Kevin said, "If he dumps a body we've got him."

"Yes, but wait till he does something illegal or at least worthy of probable cause," Charlie pleaded.

"Nobody will make a move until a body comes out of that truck," Kevin promised. "Just make sure the other two cars know what I'm driving and who I am."

"Will do. By the way, the preliminary DNA results came back on the remains of Emily Sue Whitman. The skull does belong to the rest of the body. I think we need to twist our Voodoo friend's arm a little more," Charlie suggested.

"After tonight it may not be necessary," Kevin said.

"Unless we go with your theory of more than one person being involved in the murders," Charlie replied. "I think we're still a long ways from solving this case."

"We'll see after tonight," Kevin replied. "Keep me updated."

The two Escalades had reached and passed Houston, Texas. Samuelson couldn't have imagined a place bleaker than what they had driven through. Hour after hour of oil wells and flatness broken only by an occasional town on the verge of collapse. The miles of suburban

Houston sprawl was a refreshing respite that Samuelson missed since his exile to the Vasquez Cartel plantation.

Now that they were past Beaumont and into Louisiana the trees were a welcome relief.

"Some of the boys wanted to stop over in New Orleans," one of the soldiers told Samuelson.

"Once the job is done I think we can afford to spend a couple of days celebrating," he replied. "It will be my treat."

When the rest of the assassination team heard the news the morale increased significantly.

"How much further?" Samuelson asked.

"According to the GPS it's about six hours till we reach Birmingham."

"When we arrive we'll get rooms and rest up before we start our surveillance," Samuelson said. "If we're lucky we'll be in and out in a couple of days."

Samuelson was beginning to feel better about the job, but after the drive through Texas, even having your fingernails pulled out one by one would make you feel better.

It took Jessica less than a half an hour to regret her stubbornness for insisting that Charlie take her home. She had made her point but she was now cut off from access to any breaking information.

"They knew all along that Peter Talbot was the next victim and Charlie never once mentioned it to me," her ire rising.

"I bet they planned this entire thing," Jessica began to convince herself.

"Once I discovered the map they made everything else up about Chester so I wouldn't go to or write about Tyronza," she continued to weave the story together in her mind.

"Charlie knew I'd react like that and insist on him taking me home. They set me up from the beginning," her paranoiac mind raced.

"They used me," she cried, "and nobody uses Paige Eliot."

Jessica wrote a scathing report on the FBI's performance in the Apostle Serial Killer investigation. Hinted at cover-ups at the highest level of the bureau, named two agents working the case, one named Charlie and a second unnamed agent working undercover whose effectiveness comes into question since they both have million dollar hits placed on them by a major drug cartel. She mocked the shoddiness of the criminologists for their inability to find key evidence in James Arnold's house which she located within minutes, and touted several other of her coups-de-grâce over the FBI. She finished off with her prediction that the body of the sixth Apostle Serial Killer victim would be found that morning in Tyronza, Arkansas crucified upside down on a cross.

After she filed her story she arranged for a film crew to meet her in Tyronza and she grabbed a change of clothes and settled in for the four hour drive to Arkansas.

At the last minute she tried to call Charlie to see if he had any further comment on the story her paper was going to release in the morning, but his phone was constantly busy.

"Sorry, Charlie, but it's time to move on to bigger fish," Jessica laughed.

"Where are they now?" Kevin asked

"He crossed the Georgia border a few minutes ago and now is just crossing the 337 south of Menlo, Georgia," Charlie said.

"Do you have any idea what the big draw of Rome, Georgia is; do they have a big Court House, or a big War Memorial, maybe a famous town square?" Kevin asked.

"Let me 'Google' it real quick," Charlie replied. "I'll get back to you."

"Kevin, I got two possibilities. One looks a lot better than the other. They've got this old tower called the Tower Clock which you can supposedly see from anywhere in town, but the other is called the Capitoline Wolf. It's a sculpture in front of the Municipal Building of Romulus and Remus that was a gift from the Roman Governor by order of Mussolini in 1929. What better tie-in to Rome, Italy could you ask for?" Charlie relayed.

"Do you think Chester knows Rome, Georgia history that well? Where is he now?" Kevin asked.

"He's passing through Summerville. Should I alert the Georgia authorities?" Charlie asked.

"Like you said, we don't alert anybody unless we see a body on a cross on the ground," Kevin replied. "I believe I've caught up to one of our team cars."

"Flash your lights," Charlie instructed.

Kevin did as told.

"You've caught up," Charlie confirmed.

"I'd love to pass but Chester knows my car," Kevin explained, "but it does free one of our teams to jump ahead to the Municipal Building if you think that's our most likely target."

"If he's the one, catching him in the act would be best," Charlie agreed.

"Team One, pass him and move into place at the municipal building and watch and wait, but be ready to move if that's not the location," Charlie instructed.

"He could be headed to Atlanta as far as we know," Agent Taylor replied.

"If he's our killer, he's stopping in Rome," Charlie assured the men.

"He is stopping in Rome, isn't he Kevin?" Charlie asked to make sure.

"I guarantee it," Kevin replied.

CHAPTER THIRTY-EIGHT

Jessica was almost to Tupelo when she answered Charlie's call.

"Yes?"

"I saw you tried to call earlier but I've been real busy," Charlie explained.

"Are you ready to tell me the truth about Tyronza now?" she asked.

"I did tell you the truth. I knew nothing about it," Charlie replied.

A flush of doubt swept through Jessica's body. "I'm almost half way to Tyronza," she explained.

"I don't know what you expect to find there but I wish you luck," Charlie replied. "I thought I would fill you in on some information I've received. The preliminary DNA tests match between the skull and the remains."

"So the Apostle Serial Killer's first victim was Emily Sue Whitman. I guess revenge for the rape is no longer a motive for the killings unless she has an angry brother," Jessica said.

"Hold on a second," Charlie said.

"Kevin, Chester's car is just north of Rome right where the 27 turns into Georgia 1," Charlie reported. "Chase Car One is in place by the Municipal Building."

"Charlie, what's going on?" Jessica asked.

"It's the reason I called you. We think Chester Cunningham is the Apostle Serial Killer and is about to dump the body of Peter Talbot in Rome, Georgia. We have three cars tailing him now."

"Rome, Georgia! Why didn't you tell me this earlier?"

"Because we had no idea it was going to happen earlier. You were here when I heard about Peter and when we decided to watch Chester, but you insisted on leaving because of that map thing. I can't even remember the name." Charlie said.

"Tyronza, Arkansas," she moaned.

"Yeah, that's it. Then when we were following Chester's truck he headed for Georgia. Rome, Georgia." Charlie stressed the Rome.

"I get it, Rome is where Peter was crucified," Jessica said.

"It's a break from his pattern, but so is the timing," Charlie replied. "I've got to go, he's almost in town. I'll call you if and when it goes down."

"Damn! Damn, damn, damn, damn, damn," Jessica said pounding her steering wheel.

She cut her steering wheel hard to the right scattering traffic but making the off ramp while she called the newspaper.

She got her assistant editor's message machine. "I know it's late but you have to stop the story I put in earlier," she insisted. "I think the FBI is about to take the Apostle Serial Killer down within the hour in Rome, Georgia. His name is Chester Cunningham. The victim is the same, Peter Talbot. Call off the camera crew and stop that first story."

Unfortunately for Jessica, the first story had already gone to press and several thousand papers would be printed with the original story before it could be pulled.

Tomorrow was not going to be Jessica's best day.

"*Jefe*," one of the hired assassins called to Samuelson. "We got confirmation that the two FBI agents are staying in apartments at the National Guard Base at the airport in Birmingham."

"Is there any way we can access the base?" Samuelson asked.

"It would be *muy* difficult, but we also know what cars both the agents are driving so we can stake the place out and follow them," the man explained.

"Are you sure we can trust the information?" Samuelson said.

"Why would they lie to us if they know we would kill them for doing so?" the assassin replied.

"Because someone else will kill them if they don't lie to us," Samuelson replied. "but if you trust your sources, then that's what we'll do."

"*Jefe*, the boys wanted me to ask once more about stopping in New Orleans."

"I told them after the job is done," Samuelson replied impatiently.

"They're afraid New Orleans will be gone by then," he replied.

"What are you talking about?" Samuelson asked puzzled.

The assassin pulled out a copy of the newspaper he had picked up at their last stop.

"Katrina. Big hurricane. They say it's headed straight for New Orleans." He passed the paper to Samuelson who scanned through the article.

"Hell, they can never get these predictions right. Trust me, New Orleans isn't going anywhere. The bars will still be there for the boys after the job is done," Samuelson replied, tossing the paper on the seat next to him.

"If you say so *Jefe*," the assassin replied.

"Just what I need, a bunch of hung-over *pendejos* trying to take down two seasoned FBI agents," Samuelson bemoaned. "Just get our asses to Birmingham and let's take care of business."

"*Sì Jefe*, on to Birmingham."

Samuelson closed his eyes and lay back in his seat. The paper said it was going to be a huge storm but it wasn't due to hit until Monday.

"By Monday I should be on my way to Moscow," he thought, "or at least somewhere far away from Vasquez."

"Charlie, Chester just drove right by our position on Broad Street. It doesn't look like the Capitoline Wolf is his intended target," Team One reported.

"He's still headed down East 2nd Street," Team Two reported, following behind. "Wait he's turning left on East 2nd Avenue."

"Real creative with their street names here in Rome," Charlie said. "The Tower Clock is on East 2nd Avenue about three blocks ahead. Kevin are you there?"

"Still following Team Two," he replied.

"Team One hold your position," Charlie ordered.

"He's turning right into a parking lot by that big tower thing," Agent Davis of Team Two said. "Should we follow him in?"

"No hold your position on 2nd Avenue but one of you go on foot and see what he's doing. Don't let him see you." Charlie ordered.

"I'll go," Davis told his partner, "but if I yell you haul ass up here, you hear me?"

"I hear you," his partner replied.

"Charlie, I'm pulling down to the end of the block to see if there is another access into the park," Kevin said.

"Be careful," Charlie warned.

Chester's truck had driven up the gravel driveway to the parking lot for tourists and locals coming to visit the Tower Clock. However, instead of parking he drove over the shrubbery and up to the tower itself. As he climbed out of his truck he was muttering and stuttering a phrase over and over.

> "J-J-Jesus - can't take him
> 'the M-M-Master does not deserve the light,
> h-he deserves p-p-peace'."

> "J-Jesus - can't take him
> 'the M-M-Master does not deserve the light,
> he deserves p-peace'."

Chester opened the back of the truck and first pulled out the box of snakes and released them onto the ground. Then he pulled the cross with the decapitated body of Peter Talbot nailed to it and leaned it against the Tower.

> "J-J-Jesus - can't take him
> 'the M-M-Master does not deserve the light,
> h-he deserves p-p-peace'."

Agent Davis had moved slowly up through the bushes next to the gravel drive. He heard the engine of the truck still running but the truck wasn't in the parking area. He heard the radio blaring *Bound and Determined* by the Marshall Tucker Band.

"What the hell?" he said.

As he moved in closer he heard Chester muttering and caught a glimpse of him between the truck and the tower. It took him a moment to process the scene but when he realized what he was seeing he let a yell and started running towards Chester with his gun drawn.

"Don't move," he screamed. But no sooner had he said it did two timber rattlesnakes sink their fangs into his calf and inner thigh causing him to tumble down screaming in both pain and fear.

"Agent down," Kevin yelled into his phone as he saw Davis fall.

Kevin had parked near the corner of East 2nd Avenue and East 3rd Street where a wide set of stairs climbed up the hill towards the tower. He had made his way near the top to see Agent Davis running towards the tower, but could only glimpse the front end of Chester's truck behind the tower. However, he had no doubt what must be happening on the opposite side.

"Snakes everywhere," Davis yelled, "call 911."

Kevin slowed to relay the message to Charlie when Chester's truck came around the tower and straight towards him. Kevin barely had enough time to dive out of the way as the truck bounded down the staircase Kevin had just come up.

"Smith, stay with Davis, paramedics and police are on the way," Charlie relayed.

"Kevin where's Chester?" Charlie asked.

"Headed north on East 5th Avenue," Kevin said, "I'm getting in my car now."

"Team One head up to East 5th Avenue and stop him. Now we have probable cause," Charlie ordered.

"He just blew by us going fast," Agent Taylor replied.

"Watch out for Kevin," Charlie warned, "I'll notify Georgia State Patrol and Alabama State Troopers. He's probably headed back to Birmingham."

"We're in pursuit going Code three," Team One reported.

"Kevin turn your flashers on," Charlie instructed, "I know you don't have a light or siren."

"Turning left onto Turner McCall Boulevard," Taylor reported, "Still going fast. He's not planning on pulling over."

"Charlie, how's Davis?" Kevin asked, contemplating turning back to see if he could possibly heal Davis' snake bites.

"Paramedics are there, pumping him full of anti-venom but he's still in bad shape," Charlie replied.

"What about the snakes?"

"Two dead and at least two more in the bushes. Police are keeping an eye on the perimeter. Chester left a cross with a headless body leaning against the Tower Clock. No way to tell yet, but I'm guessing it's Peter Talbot," Charlie replied.

"Did he say anything to Davis?" Kevin asked.

"If he did Davis is in no condition to tell anyone about it," Charlie replied.

"Keep me posted, I'm staying behind Team One," Kevin said. "And contact the Atlanta Bureau. Tell them we need at least a half a dozen agents in Rome within the hour."

"Charlie, Turner McCall Boulevard has turned into Shorter Avenue," Team One reported, "and he still has no plans of pulling over."

"Shorter will turn into Georgia 20," Charlie said.

"Folks around here call it Alabama Highway," Agent Taylor joked, "because if you're on it you're heading for Alabama."

"Kevin, the Alabama State Troopers say they can throw up a roadblock around Cedar Bluff if we want it," Charlie relayed.

"I don't know if a roadblock is such a good idea," Kevin said. "Maybe a spike strip is a better idea."

"You're in the South boys. Down here we don't do spike strips we do road blocks," Agent Taylor said overhearing Charlie and Kevin's conversation.

"Tell them thank you, but no thank you, for now," Kevin replied. "Remind them that this is a federal pursuit."

"We're not going to let him get back to Birmingham are we?" Agent Taylor asked. "He's picking up speed and is going to hurt somebody if we get into traffic."

"Shouldn't be a whole lot of traffic this time of night," Charlie replied.

"You mean morning?" Taylor corrected.

"Taylor's right," Kevin said, "Call the Alabama State Troopers back and tell them we will take that roadblock. Tell them we want it at the opposite end of the causeway leading out of Cedar Bluff across Weiss Lake on Alabama 9.

Once he commits to the causeway we'll be behind him and the only place he can go is into the water."

"Apparently you didn't see *Vanishing Point*," Agent Taylor commented.

"Never even heard of it," Charlie replied.

"Doesn't matter," Taylor replied. "We're doing about ninety miles per hour just less than three miles from the Alabama border."

"Alabama State Troopers say they will have two cars in place in ten minutes at the end of the causeway," Charlie relayed.

"Remind them that two FBI cars are going to be coming right behind Chester's truck, so don't go getting trigger happy," Kevin said.

"Charlie, dammit get off the phone," Jessica yelled as she sped back towards Birmingham.

She had received the bad news from her assistant editor that several thousand papers went out with her original story in it. She also got word that the Alabama State Troopers were setting up a roadblock in cooperation with the FBI along Highway 9 south of Cedar Bluff to intercept a fleeing suspect believed to be the Apostle Serial Killer. Just about every news outlet in Alabama and Georgia had already sent crews there or to Rome, Georgia where it was rumored the latest victim of the serial killer was found.

"I'm a complete idiot," Jessica screamed. "What was I thinking?"

"That's the problem, I wasn't thinking, my ego was reacting. No wonder everybody hates me," she began to cry as she realized she was too late.

"J-J-Jesus - can't take him
'the M-M-Master does not deserve the light,
h-he deserves p-p-peace'."

Chester continued to mutter as he pressed the accelerator harder pushing the truck to that fine line where inertia is about to overtake friction.

"Charlie, we're passing the *Piggly Wiggly* in Cedar Bluff," Agent Taylor reported. "If I'm not mistaken the causeway across the lake begins just up around the bend."
"Alabama State Troopers are in position," Charlie replied. "It's show time boys."
As Chester's truck took the sweeping left turn onto the causeway inertia did overcome friction and his right side scraped the steel guard rail throwing sparks high into the air.
"What was that?" Kevin called out to Charlie.
"He's going too fast. He lost control and scraped the guard rail," Agent Taylor reported.
"Do those troopers have their lights on?" Kevin asked.
"I can see them in the distance," Taylor responded, bypassing Charlie.
"I got a bad feeling about this," Kevin said.
"Oh man, he's speeding up. Warn the Troopers that he may not stop," Taylor urged Charlie.
"They're pulling one car back and using just one car to block both lanes," Charlie advised.
"Hope it works," Kevin said.

The Troopers grabbed their shotguns and moved up the road behind some trees just in case Chester decided not to slow down.

"J-J-Jesus - can't take him
'the M-M-Master does not deserve the light,
h-he deserves p-p-peace'."

Chester still chanted as the troopers opened fire on his truck. His left front tire was blown out as he slammed into the Alabama State Trooper's car at nearly eighty miles an hour, pin wheeling his truck into and through the trees lining the lake front and into the lake.

"I saw several muzzle flashes and he hit the roadblock, he hit the roadblock," Taylor yelled into the phone.

Within seconds Team One and Kevin were both at the roadblock and running towards the water to find Chester.

The water wasn't deep but the truck was sinking in the mud and it was deep enough to cover the seats of the truck.

"The windows are blown out," Taylor called to Kevin who had just reached the scene.

"Is he alive?" Kevin asked.

"I haven't found him yet," Taylor replied, prompting Kevin to jump into the water. "The door is jammed."

Kevin climbed onto the crumpled hood and kicked away what remained of the windshield.

"I see him," Kevin said "I can reach him."

Kevin started to reach into the cab and jerked his hand back quickly.

"What is it?" Taylor called out.

"A water moccasin," Kevin replied, "hand me a stick."

Taylor handed Kevin a limb broken from the tree where the truck rammed through the brush.

Kevin carefully lifted the poisonous snake out and tossed it far out into the lake.

"How'd that get in there?"

"It was already in the cab," Kevin replied.

Kevin climbed halfway through the windshield and pulled Chester's shattered body from the truck.

"Is he alive?" Taylor asked, as Kevin laid Chester on the ground.

Kevin bent down to feel for a pulse when Chester suddenly sat bolt upright and spoke.

"J-J-Jesus - can't take him
'the M-M-Master does not deserve the light,
h-he deserves p-p-peace'."

Then just as suddenly he collapsed back to the ground and wheezed as what remained of his life escaped through his bloodied lips.

"What just happened?" Taylor asked. "I ain't never seen anything like that before."

"Watch out for more snakes." Kevin warned, as emergency crews began to secure the scene.

"Charlie, Chester is dead. Get a search warrant for his house and offices and I'll meet you at his house," Kevin ordered.

"I need this truck taken back to the forensics lab in Birmingham as soon as possible," Kevin ordered Taylor. "You take charge and make sure no evidence is left behind, but get it there quickly, and watch out for snakes."

"Kevin, it looks like Davis is going to pull through, but the Atlanta Bureau is trying to claim territorial rights to the crucified body of Peter Talbot," Charlie explained.

"That's a bunch of crap. Who's causing us the grief?" Kevin asked.

"Supervising Agent Hardin."

"Give me his number and I'll take care of it."

Kevin called the number.

"Supervising Agent Hardin."

"Agent Hardin, this is Agent Kevin Jackson. I've been put in charge of the Apostle Serial Killer investigation and have been given complete control of the investigation by Director Kaiser. I need the crucified body of Peter Talbot to be sent immediately to our forensics lab down in Birmingham," Kevin explained.

"I don't recall any Agent Jackson working in Birmingham," Hardin replied, "but I believe the labs in Atlanta are much better equipped to deal with this situation."

"Agent Hardin, normally I'm a patient man, but it has been a very trying day and evening and you know damn well who I am because it was your Assistant Supervising Agent who leaked the information to Paige Eliot about my under cover assignment, when I arrived in Birmingham, my real name, and even what vehicles I ordered for myself and partner assisting me on this case. So unless you want Director Kaiser and Assistant Director Hannah chewing your ass, you better rethink your position on sending the body to my lab ASAP. Am I clear on that?" Kevin said. "And just so there is no misunderstanding, I have two agents standing before me who witnessed this conversation."

"I'd call it more of a brow beating than a conversation, but you made it perfectly clear," Supervising Agent Hardin replied. "I will send the remains Code Three as soon as the criminology team gives the okay."

"You may want to encourage them to expedite their investigation," Kevin advised.

"I will advise them as such," Hardin replied. "A pleasure speaking with you Mr. Bridges."

Kevin immediately called Charlie back. "I took care of Hardin. I'm heading for Chester's in Birmingham."

"See you there," Charlie replied and started out the door when his phone rang again.

"This is Charlie."

"Charlie, it's Jessica."

CHAPTER THIRTY-NINE

Charlie explained to Jessica what had occurred but didn't invite her to join him and Kevin as they searched Chester's house. It did give her an opportunity to redeem herself somewhat by scooping many of the other reporters with details they couldn't possibly have found out. However, when Kevin and Charlie see her original story she knew things would change. She tried to explain what she'd done and Charlie seemed to understand, but she could tell he was too preoccupied to grasp the significance of her story and its ramifications.

"I'll call you tomorrow," Charlie promised. "Maybe we can go back to Banana Joe's."

"Sounds great," Jessica replied, but knew the chances of Charlie ever talking to her again were slim to none once he saw the morning paper.

Kevin was waiting at Chester's house in the Mountain Brook suburb of Birmingham.

"Taylor told me they call this area 'The Tiny Kingdom'," Charlie said, as he arrived.

"Why is that?" Kevin asked.

"It's where all the upper class and anyone with social aspirations live in Birmingham. It's like a different world compared to the rest of Birmingham. You don't break into the social scene there without an Alabama blue-blooded pedigree older than the Civil War," Charlie explained.

"Doesn't make sense Chester living here as the Apostle Serial Killer."

"Sure doesn't," Charlie agreed. "Although it's also pretty strange for a single man to be living in such a big mansion as this."

"It belonged to his father who was a surgeon," Kevin said. "His mother and father were killed in a car crash when he was in medical school. He was an only child and inherited the house and the fortune that went along with it."

"Why hasn't he married?"

"Believe me, he was working on it. She just wasn't interested."

The local police arrived and Kevin used the keys he'd taken from the truck to unlock the house.

"Where do we start?" Charlie asked.

"Let's start at the bottom and work our way to the top," Kevin suggested.

He asked the two police officers to cover the front and back of the house just in case someone else was inside and the search began.

"What's that smell?" Charlie asked. "Smells like burnt soup.

"Or something much worse," Kevin replied, as they cautiously headed towards the kitchen.

Simon had pushed the putrid pieces of skin as far from him as possible. He had decided he had taken all the abuse he could and would rather starve to death than be forced to eat Peter Talbot's human flesh that he had peeled from the skull. It had been several hours since the killer had left him but he felt empowered having glimpsed the rays of the setting sun through the open garage door. He now knew it was the middle of the night.

Simon heard the front door creak as it was opened and then footsteps moving deliberately across the floor above.

He began to sweat fearing the killer was back and would force him to eat the putrid skin and tissue. He sat quietly and waited.

"What is it?" Charlie asked, as Kevin turned off the flame under a large simmering pot on the stove.

Kevin scraped away a foamy gelatinous layer that had formed across the top of the pan with a wooden spoon he had found lying on the counter. As he did the skull bobbed to the top of the pot.

"It's Peter Talbot's head," Kevin replied. "Let's finish our search."

"This must be the door to the basement, I'll check it out," Charlie said.

Simon heard the door open at the top of the stairs and the light switch was turned on.

He looked up to see who was coming.

"Were you expecting someone?" the killer said, coming down the steps.

"I brought you something to eat. I knew you would rather die than eat human flesh," the killer said. "And it's not time for you to die yet."

"Thank you," Simon whispered. "Grateful that he was to be allowed to live for a while longer."

Charlie walked down the stairs into the basement but found nothing unusual. No hidden doors or passage ways, just a furnace, water heaters, old furniture, and a lot of boxes.

"The criminologists will have a field day going through all of this old stuff," he called up to Kevin.

They continued to search the house but found nothing else suspicious.

"Don't you think it's a little odd that we found the head in the pot but no surgical tools or operating table or anything else you would expect to find?" Kevin said.

"I'm sure we'll find all of that at his medical offices."

"Just doesn't make any sense to me," Kevin declared. "Something's not right."

"Maybe he's got another place we don't know about where he does the dirty work," Charlie suggested.

"Hopefully, you're right and somewhere in this house we'll find a clue as to where that place is."

The first two criminologists on loan from the police department had arrived and Kevin and Charlie were about to leave when a painting suddenly caught Kevin's attention.

"Does that painting look familiar to you?" Kevin asked.

"Not in the least."

The painting was a religious work depicting Christ washing the feet of his disciples.

"Remember the painting I told you to take pictures of at the Voodoo market?" Kevin said.

"Oh yeah, right," Charlie replied. "It does look to be painted in a similar style, but it's nothing like that painting."

"I know, but the face of Jesus looks the same to me. I'm almost sure the same artist painted both paintings," Kevin said.

"Seems possible since Chester was the Apostle Serial Killer and we know the Voodoo man had one of his skulls," Charlie said.

"You're getting ahead of yourself, Charlie. I'm not so sure Chester was the Apostle Serial Killer or at least not the only Apostle Serial Killer," Kevin replied. "The 'houngan' said..."

"The what?" Charlie asked.

"The 'houngan' that means Voodoo priest, said it was a woman who did the painting. Didn't the file say there was a woman's DNA on two of the victims?"

"Jeez, I forgot to tell you that there was also two female DNAs found on the chalice," Charlie said

"That just means a female probably used it to drink out of," Kevin replied.

"Well if she did she also was with two of the murder victim's because it was the same DNA that was found on them," Charlie replied.

"So maybe my idea of more than one Apostle Serial Killer is not as crazy as you once thought," Kevin replied.

Samuelson and his team of assassins rolled into Birmingham around 4:00 a.m. Friday. They drove straight to the airport and after driving the perimeter and finding the entrance to the National Guard Base returned to the public side of the airport and checked into the Holiday Inn right off of Airport Highway.

"I want two of you watching that gate at all times," Samuelson ordered. "Go rent two more cars from one of the airport lots. Each of you need to have a car. Remember we're looking for a 1989 Black Pontiac Trans Am or a blue 1980 Chevy Nova."

Samuelson passed out pictures of both Carlo and Kevin and of the two types of vehicles to look for.

"If you see either of those cars go in or out of that base you call me immediately. If they come out you call me and follow them. Is that understood?"

"*Sì Jefe*," one of the men replied for all the others. "We all understand and know what to do."

"I want no screw ups," Samuelson said. "We're going to have to coordinate this so they both get taken out at the same time if possible."

"We can handle it, *Jefe*."

"I'm here to make sure," Samuelson replied.

Preliminary searches of Chester's offices turned up nothing out of the ordinary. By the time Kevin and Charlie returned to the lab in Birmingham there was even more information to confuse the investigation.

"You ever seen one of these?" the doctor said holding up what looked like a piece of piano wire.

"No what is it?" Kevin asked.

"It's called a Gigli's Wire. It's used for sawing away portions of the skull. At least it used to be. These days everyone uses power tools. This one was used to turn Emily Sue Whitman's skull into a Chalice thirty years ago," the forensic doctor explained.

"You know that for sure?" Kevin asked.

"There is still evidence of the blade marks on the chalice and her DNA is still on the Gigli's Wire," he replied. "So yes, I'm sure."

"Any preliminary findings on what killed Chester?" Kevin asked.

"My guess is blunt trauma from the impact of the crash, but there are several shotgun pellet wounds on his upper left torso that may have done some serious damage inside. I'll have a better idea when I open him up this afternoon."

"Thanks doc, keep me informed," Kevin said.

"I've got some bad news, Kevin," Charlie said. "Peter Hannah has called a noon press conference to announce the death of the Apostle Serial Killer."

"Have you talked to him?"

"I tried, but he wouldn't listen to a word I had to say," Charlie explained. "It gets worse."

"What?"

"He's going to out us in the conference."

"He can't do that."

"He says he can because Paige Eliot already did in this morning's paper," Charlie replied, handing the paper to Kevin.

"What'd you do to piss her off so bad?" Kevin asked. "Never mind, I don't want to know. This is bad, but she didn't mention our names. We're a long way from finding the killer or killers so Hannah needs to keep his mouth shut about us. If he wants to make a fool of himself, so be it, but he's not dragging our names into it."

"What do you plan to do?" Charlie asked.

"I'll call Director Kaiser and explain the situation. Tell him to muzzle Hannah," Kevin said.

"Will he do it?"

"He damn well better," Kevin replied, placing the call to Washington.

It took several minutes for the connection to be made, but Kevin was finally put through to Director Kaiser and explained the situation. Kaiser understood completely and assured Kevin that he would censor Hannah's remarks at the press conference.

"Hannah's all taken care of," Kevin assured Charlie.

"So what do we do now?"

"I've got to head back up to the church and do some explaining," Kevin said.

"Shouldn't you get some sleep?"

"No, I'm going to run by the base to shower and get a change of clothes. I need to be there before that press conference," Kevin explained.

"I need to get some sleep," Charlie said.

"Call it a day, you've earned the break. I'll be back tomorrow afternoon and we can try to sort out the mess that Hannah creates for us at the press conference," Kevin encouraged. "Why don't you give Jessica a call? I'm sure she's feeling like a pariah about now."

"No doubt about that. I think her network ambitions took a big dive today," Charlie said.

CHAPTER FORTY

"Yeah," Samuelson barked, answering the phone.

"*Jefe*, both the Trans Am and the Nova just drove onto the base," one of the assassins reported.

"Were Bridges and Caressa by themselves?" Samuelson asked.

"*Sì, Jefe*, they were alone," the man replied.

"Good, we're heading over," Samuelson replied.

"Let's go boys, the hour of retribution grows near," Samuelson proclaimed. "Vasquez will have his revenge."

"What a surprise," Sergeant McClellan said as the two agents climbed out of their cars. "I thought you two would be out celebrating."

"So it's already all over the news I take it," Kevin said.

"Breaking news on just about every channel. You two going to be at the press conference when they reveal the Apostle Serial Killer?" the sergeant asked.

"I'll be in bed," Charlie replied.

"So any clues as to whom the killer is?" Boone asked, coming out to join the conversation.

"They haven't named anyone yet on the news? Charlie asked.

"Not yet, I guess you guys have kept it under wraps really well. They did name the latest victim; some guy from Tennessee named Peter Talbot. They found his body over in Rome, Georgia," Sergeant Boone said.

"I know, I was there," Kevin replied.

"So what tipped you off to this guy?" McClellan asked.

"Just a lot of circumstantial evidence," Charlie replied.

"I'd say it was more like a lot of circumstantial coincidence," Kevin reflected.

"You don't sound too confident in your killer's guilt," Boone noted.

"There's no doubt he dumped the body this morning and made a run for it, but to tell you the truth, I don't think he's the one we're looking for," Kevin exclaimed, "but that's not what you're going to hear at the press conference."

"Are you telling us that the Apostle Serial Killer is still out there?" McClellan asked.

"That's exactly what I'm telling you, but you better not repeat it. I'm positive the killer or killers are still out there and as soon as he or they drop off their next beheaded victim everyone else will know he's still out there too."

"Charlie, do you still have that list of fraternity members that Jessica collected?" Kevin asked.

"If I don't I'm sure she does."

"When you wake up later today start searching for a Peter on that list," Kevin said.

"Peter, he just killed Peter. Shouldn't we be searching for a Thomas?" Charlie replied.

"The murder was all wrong. Peter was crucified upside down. That's a mistake the Apostle Serial Killer wouldn't make, and dumping the body in Rome, Georgia is a joke," Kevin explained. "The real killer is toying with us."

"I think there were two Peters on that list of fraternity members and one was Peter Hannah," Charlie said. "Are you starting to think these murders are related to the rape of Emily Sue Whitman?"

"It's beginning to look that way to me," Kevin replied.

"Peter Hannah claims he was out of the country the year the rape occurred," Charlie said.

"Do you believe him?"

"Jessica doesn't, but I've seen no proof that says otherwise."

"It's not too difficult for someone in Hannah's position to have the means to access and change data bases," Kevin explained. "The FBI employs some of the best hackers around."

"I'll call Jessica when I get up and we'll see what we can find," Charlie said.

"Take the day off, let things settle down, and most importantly get some sleep. When I get back tomorrow we'll make a game plan," Kevin said.

"You're the boss. Sergeants, what do you say we have another run at Banana Joe's tonight? My beard is growing out and you have to admit I'm looking more and more like Charlie Daniels," Charlie said.

"What do you mean look like? You are Charlie Daniels," Sergeant McClellan laughed. "We'd love to be your bodyguards Mr. Daniels."

"Let me get some sleep and we'll make a night of it," Charlie replied.

"You going to join us Agent Jackson?" Sergeant Boone asked.

"No, I have some business to handle up in Macedonia that could get a little emotional, but thank you anyway," Kevin replied.

"Maybe next time," Boone replied.

"Maybe so, maybe so," Kevin said heading into shower.

"That man's got a heavy heart," Boone said.

"You would too if you had to tell someone that one of their best friends was a killer," Charlie replied.

Jessica hadn't thought it possible but when she arrived back at her apartment in Birmingham she sat down on the couch and was asleep before she knew it. Charlie's phone call had been encouraging but when the paper came out the next morning she knew her career was on thin ice and any hope of a network job was out of the question.

She awoke around ten-thirty and went out to pick up the paper and read the bad news. When she opened the door, someone had placed the paper neatly on her doorstep.

"Well somebody's still has that gentlemanly sense of southern hospitality," she said looking around to see who might be observing her.

She saw no one and picked up the paper, but as she did so an envelope slid out onto the ground.

"What have we here?" she said, hesitating momentarily then picking it up and turning it over.

There was a message written on this side of the envelope.

"Maybe this will help get things back on track. You're just ahead of your time."

Jessica opened the envelope and poured out its contents, a DVD and another hand written note.

The meddling of the FBI has forced me to alter my schedule and my pattern. I am much too powerful for you to stop. The Dominion of Darkness is coming soon and I deserve peace.

It is time to share the fear that the Dark Lord instills.

Jessica tried to call Charlie but his phone was either busy or turned off. She carefully laid the envelope and the letter on the table trying to touch them as little as possible. She knew she shouldn't but she couldn't keep herself from playing the DVD.

"I recognize that song," she said as the video started, but quickly lost any thought of trying to name it as the gruesomeness unfolded before her.

"Oh my God that's James Arnold," she said.

"Oh my God," she repeated over and over.

She was transfixed by the 51 minute spectacle and at the climax when the adrenaline rush jarred James Arnold wide awake and he witnessed his own head pop off his torso. Jessica lost it and puked all over the carpet.

"You sick son-of-a-bitch," she said, and burst into tears.

"Why'd I watch that? Why did I ever watch that? God forgive me," she prayed.

She tried calling Charlie several more times and even called the bureau but they didn't know where he was.

"I'm not giving this to anybody but Charlie."

"This proves the Apostle Serial Killer is still out there."

She quickly showered and dressed then texted Charlie that she was on her way to the airport.

"As she was dressing she had on the news and heard about Peter Hannah's press conference scheduled for noon. He was going to announce the solving of the Apostle Serial Killings.

"No, that's wrong. Charlie even knows that's wrong. Maybe I should head to the press conferences."

Now she wasn't sure what to do.

"Charlie, I'm keeping my phone with me so if anything happens I need to know about, call me immediately. If for some reason I can't answer I'll call you right back," Kevin explained.

"Are you going to be listening to the press conference?" Charlie asked.

"I'm not sure, it all depends on how my conversation goes this morning. I don't know if I want them to know that I'm FBI yet," Kevin explained. "If this case develops like I believe it might I will need to stay under cover at the church for a while longer."

"Is your phone on?" Kevin asked.

"It's always on," Charlie replied reaching for his phone and discovering it wasn't there. "It's always on, I just don't always know where it is."

He walked over to the Trans Am and picked up his phone from the seat.

"Jessica's been frantically trying to call me," he commented, looking at the phone. "She even sent me a text message."

"Is she trying to apologize," Sergeant Boone remarked.

"No, she says she's on her way here with a DVD left at her apartment by the Apostle Serial Killer sometime after 4:00 a.m." Charlie exclaimed.

"How soon will she be here?" Kevin asked.

"I'll call her and see," Charlie said.

"Charlie, thank goodness you called. I wasn't sure what to do. I was about to take it to Hannah at the press conference."

"No, come over here, I'll notify the guards at the gate to let you through."

"I watched the DVD Charlie. It's horrible. It made me throw up. I wish I hadn't seen it. I'll have nightmares about it for the rest of my life." Jessica was sobbing.

"Just drive safely," Charlie instructed her.

"I will," she replied shakily and hung up.

"She'll be here in about a half an hour. She's real scared. She watched the DVD."

"Probably not a good idea," Kevin said.

"Not at all," Charlie added.

"I can't wait, Charlie. I've got to be in Macedonia before that press conference. The real serial killer may be there or at least someone who knows who the real Apostle Serial Killer is," Kevin explained.

"You're not going to make it, Kevin," Charlie said. "It's already after eleven and Macedonia's two hours away."

"I know, but I have to try. Sergeants, are you willing to view the DVD when it arrives with Charlie so I can get three different opinions on it?" Kevin asked.

Boone hesitated but then agreed. McClellan was anxious to see what could have scared Jessica so badly.

"Even with the DVD I don't think we should do anything until tomorrow afternoon. We all need some rest and relaxation. In fact promise me you'll get some sleep before you watch it. Have Jessica spend the afternoon in my apartment running names through data bases. I think it best she stays around the base, especially since the killer knows where she lives. Sergeants you already agreed to accompany Charlie out this evening, I don't think Jessica would be much more of a burden. Just be sure you are armed," Kevin instructed them.

"And Charlie, I never thought I would be telling you to do this, but make sure you bring Jessica back here tonight."

.

CHAPTER FORTY-ONE

"Here comes the Chevy Nova," one of the assassins said.

"Hand me the binoculars," Samuelson ordered. "That's Bridges. He's the one I want. I want a driver with me in the Escalade and one man in the second car following him. You three stay here. Keep in contact. Let us know if Caressa leaves the base."

"Should we take him out if the opportunity is there, *Jefe*?" one of the men asked.

"If the opportunity arises you call me and I'll give the command if I think the time is right," Samuelson replied.

"*Sì, Jefe*," the assassin replied, although he didn't care for the response. He had been instructed by Meathook before he left Mexico that if he had the shot, take it, and not to wait for no *pinche gringo* to tell him what to do. Meathook had also given him other instructions for dealing with the *gringo* as well, but that was after the two agents were dead.

Peter Hannah loved to be in front of the camera. He had years of experience and knew exactly how to work it to his benefit. He was hoping this at last was the big break he needed to catch the President's attention for one of the more choice appointments he so desperately craved. Of course, Director Kaiser's call somewhat derailed his original plan but he none-the-less would announce the conclusion of the investigation with the death of the killer.

"Good afternoon ladies and gentleman, my name is Peter Hannah; I am the Assistant Director of the FBI out of Washington. I know you are all aware that a seventh victim of the Apostle Serial Killer, a Mr. Peter Talbot of Cleveland, Tennessee, was discovered last night below the Tower Clock in Rome, Georgia. What you may not know is our men were tailing the suspect who dropped off the body and who we believed killed Mr. Talbot and the other victims. Unfortunately, that suspect was killed when he tried to flee from our agents and crashed his truck into an Alabama State Trooper roadblock near Cedar Bluff. The deceased suspect is Doctor Chester Cunningham of Birmingham, Alabama. Further corroborating evidence has been found in Dr. Cunningham's home and in his vehicle which ties him to at least one other victim. This investigation is not, I repeat, not officially closed, but I believe all of Alabama and all of the South can sleep safer knowing Doctor Cunningham is no longer among us. I want to thank the Birmingham Bureau of the FBI for their diligent work on this case but cannot at this time single out the individuals who have worked so hard to bring this killing spree to an end. We still have much evidence to process before we can close this case and that could take several more weeks, but when the story is complete I guarantee you all will know the facts and who the heroes behind this investigation are. I will take just a few questions. You up front."

"You referred to Peter Talbot as the seventh victim of the Apostle Serial Killer. Isn't he just the sixth?"

"We have discovered during the investigation that the Apostle Serial Killer actually killed and beheaded his first victim, a Ms. Emily Sue Whitman, thirty years ago in 1975."

Now several hands shot up.

"Over on the left."

"We knew you were trying to tie a thirty year old murder to the Apostle Serial Killer but did the DNA prove it?"

"I'm afraid you'll have to wait for that information when the investigation concludes."

"Next question, yes?"

"What made you suspicious of Chester Cunningham?"

"His name was linked to three of the other victims. I won't say how at this time, but with his training as a surgeon and his belief in including snake-handling as part of his religious worship it made him a logical suspect."

"Can you tell us what church he attended?"

"No, I'm afraid I can't do that at this time," Peter replied.

"But you do know which church it was?"

"Of course we do."

"Is it the church in Macedonia by Sand Mountain?"

"No comment."

"Do you have agents who have infiltrated local churches looking for suspects?"

"I c-can't answer that question," Peter replied, growing nervous.

"Did they find Peter Talbot's head in Dr. Cunningham's house?"

"They did find the head but at this time I'm not releasing where we found it." Hannah replied.

"Do you think Chester Cunningham was working alone?"

"It is my belief that Chester Cunningham is the Apostle Serial Killer. However, the investigation is still ongoing."

"So you're saying not everyone believes he was doing this alone. Some of your agents believe there is possibly one or more killers still out there?"

"I d-didn't s-say that," Peter stuttered. "All I said is that the investigation is still ongoing. I want to thank you all for coming and we will update you if it becomes necessary."

"They ate Peter up," Jessica said, turning off the television.

"When news of this DVD gets out he's really going to look foolish," Charlie added.

"So are you sure we should sit on this DVD until tomorrow?" Jessica asked.

"That's what Kevin believes and he's in charge. I really don't see what good it would do releasing it today. Let's use the next twenty-four hours to see how we can use it to resurrect your career and take down the killer," Charlie suggested. "Right now I just want to take a nap before I view it and have nightmares for the next five years."

"Or more," Jessica added.

Sergeants, if you don't mind we're going to go catch up on some sleep. When we get up we'll have a look at the DVD and then head out to Banana Joe's," Charlie said. "My treat."

"We'd have gone even if it had to have been our treat," Boone laughed.

Kevin drove like a madman trying to get to Macedonia as quickly as possible. He even called the Alabama State Troopers and told them what he was doing and described his car so they wouldn't try to stop him.

"*Jefe*, he drives too fast," the assassin in the car called back to the Escalade.

"Don't lose him, but don't let him see you," Samuelson warned.

Samuelson had been listening to Peter Hannah's press conference on the radio.

"Man, that guy is still the world's biggest jerk," Samuelson said.

"Where's a map?" Samuelson said.

"I think we put them in the glove box," the driver replied.

Samuelson rummaged through a collection of maps they had brought until he found Alabama. He looked back and forth on the map for several moments and then wadded it into a ball and threw it out the window.

"I hate those damn things. Where's my computer?"

He reached over the seat and grabbed his laptop.

"MapQuest is easier," he said, as he opened the webpage and typed in Macedonia, Alabama.

"Shit!"

"What's wrong, *Jefe*?" the driver asked.

"There are six Macedonia's in Alabama," Samuelson replied.

"Which one is up I-59?" the driver asked.

"I don't know, let me look," Samuelson replied.

"It's got to be this one," he finally decided.

"*Jefe*, I've got to slow down, there's a State Trooper ahead," the other driver reported over the radio.

"Did the Nova slow down?" Samuelson asked.

"No way, he blew by the trooper going almost a hundred miles an hour. The trooper just waved," the driver said.

"Back off until it's safe to speed up again. I think we're looking for the Glenn Boulevard exit for Fort Payne. If you haven't caught him by then turn left on Glenn Boulevard and wait for us."

"*Sì, Jefe*," the driver replied.

"We'll just have to find the church on our own," Samuelson said.

Simon was perplexed as the killer carried a small television down into the basement and placed it on a chair near his cage.

"I thought you might be interested in this," the killer said.

"A friend of yours is about to hold a press conference. Wasn't it Assistant Director Hannah that assigned you to go undercover to find the Apostle Serial Killer?"

"Yes it was," Simon whispered.

"Well I guess your replacements must have been more successful. I think he's about to announce that the Apostle Serial Killer is no more." The killer began to laugh.

Both men sat quietly as the news conference progressed. An occasional gleeful laugh escaped from the killer.

"I must say I am disappointed," the killer said.

"I was sure Peter Hannah was going to announce that the investigation was closed and the killer was dead. It would have made everything that much more dramatic."

"What do you mean?" Simon said.

"You know exactly what I mean, Simon. Peter Talbot was just a diversion. He wasn't the real Peter."

"Had he been the real Peter you would have crucified him upside down," Simon said.

"Exactly! I knew you were paying attention."

"And these killings are about ritual and ceremony, neither of which took place with Peter Talbot."

"No, no they didn't," the killer replied, clapping his hands as if cheering Simon on.

"And dumping Talbot's body in Rome, Georgia was a joke," Simon continued. "But how did you get this Chester Cunningham to do it for you?"

The killer's demeanor suddenly turned sour.

"Chester was my friend," the killer said, "but he allowed the Deceiver to have too much influence in his life. I warned the Deceiver not to interfere but *glorybedaGoda* he just *shamnada hydakom* laughed."

The killer's body started to jerk violently. He lay prostrate on the floor praying in tongues while his body continued to jerk. Slowly the sudden motions eased.

"Are you alright?" Simon asked.

"I'll be fine, but circumstances are changing and my schedule has been pushed ahead. The Darkness is coming faster than I predicted so tonight I must kill again," the killer explained. "And tonight you will watch."

"What if I choose not to?" Simon said.

"I'm not offering you a choice. I'm telling you what you will do. Even if I have to cut your eyelids off, you will watch," the killer said.

"So tonight you are martyring another Peter?" Simon asked.

"No, tonight I am seeking retribution. Peter Hannah must die."

CHAPTER FORTY-TWO

"I thought you weren't coming back till Sunday?" Ginny Lee said when she saw Kevin pull into the church parking lot.

"I did say I would call today but I thought you might prefer the company," Kevin said.

"I guess you saw the news conference," Ginny Lee said.

"No, but I heard it on the radio and came as fast as I could," Kevin replied.

Ginny Lee looked at her watch and then at Kevin. "You had to already be on your way here if you heard it on the radio. Nobody can make the Birmingham drive that fast."

"I was actually on my way back to Birmingham when the news conference started. I slept in this morning and didn't even leave the Econo Lodge until almost eleven o'clock."

Kevin hated to have to lie to Ginny Lee, but he wasn't ready to confess that he was an FBI agent. Not the right time. Not the right place.

"I still don't believe Chester could have done it," she said. "He was a God loving man and no man of God could ever do such a thing."

"I guess we won't know for sure until they complete the investigation," Kevin said.

"Didn't you hear what that man said? They saw him drop off the body and they found the head in his house," Ginny Lee snapped back.

Peter Hannah hadn't actually said they found the head in the house but Kevin did find it there so it was pointless to argue with her.

"Was Chester close to anybody in the church?" Kevin asked.

Ginny Lee stared at Kevin.

"Sorry dumb question. I know he was close to you, but was he good friends or did he hang out with any of the men, like Woland for instance," Kevin said.

"You're sounding like a cop. Are you accusing Woland of being involved in these murders now, too?" she replied angrily.

"Look, I just came up to see if I could help. I'm not here to accuse anyone of anything. I'm trying to understand this just like you are," Kevin replied.

"If you want to understand it you can go inside and ask God to explain it to you," she quipped. "If you want to help, you can go out back and help Ver Dell dig Chester's grave."

Kevin knew now wasn't the right time to find out anything from Ginny Lee so he headed to the shed to grab a shovel and lend Ver Dell a hand. The light was on in the shed which was fortunate because the snake pit was wide open.

"Looks like somebody's been adding snakes," Kevin said as he peered in the pit.

A noise startled Kevin and he quickly turned in a defensive position.

"Hello Ida," Kevin said, letting down his guard.

"'Lo Kevin," she replied, grabbing a long handled scythe. "Gonna clean out some weeds."

"I thought I'd give Ver Dell a hand," Kevin replied.

Ida just nodded and headed out.

"Lord give me strength," Kevin prayed.

Peter Hannah wasn't happy at how his press conference had gone, but any media exposure is better than no media exposure was his mantra. If anyone was relieved to see the Apostle Serial Killer dead it was Peter. He had gone to great lengths to hide the fact that he was indeed involved in the rape of Emily Sue Whitman back in 1970. If there was ever a career killer, being involved in a gang rape was it.

As far as Chester Cunningham being the Apostle Serial Killer, it just all made sense. Chester was a member of the band that had been hired to play at the fraternity party. Emily Sue Whitman had gotten extremely drunk and passed out at the party. While the band was packing up one of his fraternity brothers found her lying in the bushes and brought her inside. From there things just seemed to get out of hand. Chester tried several times to stop the madness but was physically restrained by his own band mates who took their turns in the debauchery. Chester was at last pursuing his revenge on those involved. Unfortunately, Peter didn't remember Chester's name but tried to find it through James Arnold when he hired the two private detectives. That didn't work out but Agent Bridges and Paige Eliot managed to do the job for him. He had walked a thin line but the horror of that night thirty-five years ago was now behind him.

Peter Hannah lived in Redmont Park when he was in Birmingham. Like Chester Cunningham he had inherited his home from his parents when they passed away years ago. Redmont Park was in the Southside of Birmingham but stood atop a steep 350 foot ridge that overlooked Birmingham. The largest and grandest mansions in all of Birmingham were found here and Peter Hannah's was one of the grandest.

As Peter pulled up towards his gate he hit the automatic opener but the gate didn't move.

"What's going on?" he said.

He pulled his car up to the keypad and pressed in the code but still the gate remained motionless.

As he climbed out of his car he saw what looked like a city maintenance worker climbing out of a van.

"Is the power out? I can't get my gate to work," Peter called to the man.

"I wouldn't know, I'm just doing some painting at the Wyskop's," the man replied. "Maybe it's a short or something. Mind if I take a look?"

"I'm not getting in until I can get that gate to move, so go right ahead," Peter said.

The workman came over and fiddled around with the keypad for a moment. "It looks like a short. Let me grab a tool out of my van." He started to walk away when he suddenly turned back.

"Hey, I know you. I saw you on TV today. You caught that Apostle Serial Killer," the worker said.

"I didn't catch him. He pretty much killed himself," Peter replied, his ego boosted.

"Good job, anyway," the worker said, "Let me see if I can find that tool."

He walked to his van and started rummaging through it for several minutes. Peter Hannah was growing impatient.

"What tool are you looking for?" Peter called out, but the workman obviously didn't hear him.

"I've got some tools, maybe I have what you need," Peter called again, but still there was no response, so he walked over to the van's open door and stuck his head in.

"What tool…" but he was interrupted.

"This tool," the workman replied, grabbing Peter with his right hand pulling him into the van while burying the fangs of a timber rattlesnake in to Peter's neck with his left hand.

Within seconds Peter lay motionless on the van floor as the killer closed the door.

"So very convenient," the killer said as he drove only two blocks away and pulled his van into one of several garages in front of his mansion.

Simon heard a door open above him and recognized a familiar sound. The killer was dragging his latest victim across the floor towards the basement steps. Only this time he knew who the victim was, Peter Hannah, the man who had sent him to catch the killer that now held both of them.

"Simon, I've brought you a friend," the killer called in a sing-song voice.

"You are sick," Simon said to the killer.

"Dammit Simon! Don't go making me angry already," the killer snapped.

"What, you going to cut my tongue out, you sick bastard."

"I-I k-know what you're trying t-to do," the killer replied. "But it w-won't work." The killer's body began to jerk.

Suddenly, Simon's tongue felt as if it was being squeezed again, but then he felt he couldn't breathe. Within seconds he lost consciousness.

The killer removed Peter's body from the operating table and replaced it with Simon's.

"Let's see how you enjoy this," the killer said as he strapped Simon's body down and pulled out a scalpel.

CHAPTER FORTY-THREE

Samuelson and his crew had been searching side roads around the town of Section for almost an hour before they finally spotted Kevin's car parked in the church lot.

"We going to kill him in the church, *Jefe*?" one of the assassins asked.

"You got a problem with that?" Samuelson said.

"No just asking."

They watched the church for about a half an hour to see how many people were there.

"Bridges is out back digging in the graveyard with another man," one of his men reported.

"And there's a woman clearing weeds and another sweeping up," Samuelson said. "You think there are any more people inside?"

"Not on a Friday afternoon, *Jefe*. How fortunate Bridges is digging his own grave," the assassin laughed.

Samuelson called the other men watching for Carlo.

"Any sign of Caressa yet"

"None, *Jefe*," the assassin left in charge responded.

"We're going to take out Bridges and three witnesses. Keep me informed about Caressa."

"*Sì Jefe*."

"Okay, let's do this. Jose and I will get the two women inside. We'll have one of them call for Bridges to come in. When he comes in you take the old man out to the shed and take care of him. I'm going to make Bridges suffer a little before he dies," Samuelson explained.

The three men drove their cars into the church lot attracting Ginny Lee and Ida's attention.

"Afternoon ladies, I was wondering if I could have a word with you inside," Samuelson asked.

Ida turned and walked into the church along with one of Samuelson's men.

"What do you want to talk about?" Ginny Lee asked suspiciously.

"I need you to do me a favor," Samuelson said.

Ginny Lee fidgeted as she watched Samuelson's other man carefully work his way to the side of the church.

"What kind of favor?" she asked.

"I need you to call Mr. Bridges into the church," Samuelson said.

"Who's Mr. Bridges?" she asked.

"Kevin Bridges, he's digging in the graveyard out back," Samuelson replied.

"You talking about Kevin Jackson?" she said. "What do you need to see Kevin about?"

Samuelson was tiring of the conversation and pulled out his Glock. "I don't want to hurt you. Just step inside and do as you are told."

Ginny Lee wasn't going to argue with a gun pointed at her even though she wasn't scared of it. She was more afraid for Kevin.

When they went inside the other assassin had a machine pistol pointed at Ida's head.

"Now if you don't want your friend here to die needlessly, call Kevin inside," Samuelson ordered.

Ginny Lee walked to the back door.

"Kevin I need you in here right away," she yelled.

"Sure thing, Ginny Lee," Kevin replied, standing his shovel against a gravestone.

As Kevin headed for the church Ver Dell headed for the shed.

"Is everything …" Kevin didn't have a chance to finish his question as he was coming through the door. Samuelson smashed him in the temple with the Glock knocking Kevin to the ground dazed.

"Why'd you go and do that?" Ginny Lee said, kneeling down to comfort Kevin.

"I just wanted him to feel some pain before I kill him," Samuelson replied.

"Kill him? Why do you want to kill him? What did he do to you?" Ginny Lee asked.

"He did nothing to me personally. I was stupid enough to sell out my country and now as part of my punishment I have to kill him or I'll be killed," Samuelson explained.

"I don't understand?" Ginny Lee said.

"Kevin and I both work for the FBI. Or at least I used to before the Vasquez Drug Cartel bought me off. Kevin Bridges embarrassed Vasquez so he put out a million dollar hit on Agent Bridges or Jackson I guess was the name he gave you. He must have been working undercover here. Well it doesn't matter now, because you all will have to die," Samuelson explained.

The third assassin had followed Ver Dell as he headed into the shed.

"Hey, old man, I need to talk to you," the assassin called out but got no response.

He raised his pistol and slowly peered into the shed.

Ver Dell swung his shovel upward severely cutting the man's arm at the same moment the assassin pulled the trigger sending several silenced bullets through the roof of the shed. The shovel continued in a circular motion smashing into the assassin and knocking him into the snake pit where he began shrieking uncontrollably.

The screams distracted both Samuelson and the other assassin for a second as they both turned.

"That was Pa..." but the assassin's words were cut off in mid-sentence as was his head as Ida whipped the scythe though the air instantly decapitating Jose.

"Oh my God," Samuelson screamed as blood continued to squirt out of the still erect torso. He was too stunned to react.

When the body finally collapsed he lifted his Glock to fire at Ida before he too lost his head but the gun became so hot he had to drop it. He saw Ginny Lee's hand raised towards him as she prayed.

"Who are you people? Samuelson screamed.

By this time Kevin had somewhat come to his senses and gotten back to his feet. He was shocked at the sight of the decapitated head lying next to him on the ground and the torso pouring blood.

Ginny Lee seemed to be in a trance praying and Ida started towards Samuelson intent on taking his head as well.

Samuelson burst through the back door and saw Ver Dell grinning in the doorway of the shed. He had no car keys so his only escape was into the woods behind the church.

"Samuelson, give it up, you can't get away," Kevin called and began running after him.

Samuelson had a head start and Kevin was still woozy from his smash to the head. Samuelson was pulling away.

"Kevin, stop and come back now," Ginny Lee ordered, but Kevin staggered forward losing ground in the chase.

"Kevin, come back," she ordered.

As Kevin approached the ridge Samuelson had disappeared. Kevin was determined to keep going but suddenly a man holding a shotgun stepped out from behind a tree and blocked his way.

Kevin turned to go by him at an angle when another of the hill people seemed to appear from nowhere and stood before him.

Kevin was feeling dizzy and sat down on the ground. A moment later Ginny Lee was next to him.

"You shouldn't be here," she said.

"I need to catch Samuelson," he insisted.

"Samuelson or whoever he was no longer exists," she replied.

"You injured your head, you need rest," Ginny Lee said, helping him to his feet.

Kevin looked around; they were alone in the forest.

When they got back to the church Ida was busy cleaning the blood off the floor of the church.

"We need to call the police," Kevin said.

"Why?" Ginny Lee asked.

"Because of Samuelson and his assassins," Kevin replied.

"I told you Samuelson doesn't exist nor do his assassins," Ginny Lee replied.

"You can't just kill three men and pretend it didn't happen," Kevin said.

"God has a way of taking care of evil here at Sand Mountain," Ginny Lee explained.

"What did you do with the bodies?" Kevin demanded.

"Ver Dell took care of the bodies," Ida replied. "He'll take care of the cars too."

"I can't let you do that."

"Why, because you're the FBI? I knew you were with the FBI when you first came here, but I saw you 'slain in the Spirit', and I knew God had sent you for a purpose. You can claim that three men came here to kill you but I have three witnesses that say you took a shovel to the head and got knocked cold. None of us saw anything," Ginny Lee said.

"Is that how it's going to be?" Kevin asked.

"That's how it's always been. I think you need to rest. You took a pretty hard knock to the head."

Ginny Lee and Ida both laid their hands on Kevin and began to pray. Within minutes he was asleep.

CHAPTER FORTY-FOUR

Simon awoke with his eyes and tongue on fire. He tried to blink but there was nothing to blink.

He was strapped to a chair facing the operating table that now held Peter Hannah.

"I warned you that I would remove your eyelids if you didn't cooperate," the killer said.

Simon tried to speak but his tongue was again too swollen to allow him to do so.

"If you're wondering about your tongue, it's not swollen from my squeezing this time. It's swollen from the little operation I performed on it while you were out. I split it in two for you. It will take some getting used to but it should make for much more interesting conversations," the killer laughed.

"Why don't we wake Director Hannah so you two can say your goodbyes, well, at least he can say his goodbyes," the killer giggled.

He moved to one of the IVs attached to Hannah and adjusted its flow.

"Where am I, what's going on here?" A dazed Hannah whispered.

He was locked tightly in the apparatus and unable to move any part of his body.

The killer was walking near his head.

"Who's there? I know someone is there." Hannah said.

The killer released a lock and pulled a lever allowing the entire table to rotate and face Simon.

"Aagh," Hannah cried, revolted by the tortured face of Simon.

"Simon, Simon," Simon mouthed hoping Hannah would understand.

"Simon? Is that you Simon? Simon Caldwell?" Hannah asked.

Simon nodded his head.

"What has he done to you?" Hannah asked.

A stupid question Simon thought considering what the killer was about to do to Peter Hannah.

"Is this the Apostle Serial Killer?" Hannah asked.

Again Simon nodded his head.

"Am I about to die?"

Simon nodded once more.

"Okay, I think that's about enough reminiscing," the killer said, slamming the table back into position.

"Who are you?" Hannah demanded to know.

"I am your worst nightmare," the killer replied. "I'm what you've worried about for the past thirty-five years."

"That's impossible, Chester Cunningham is dead," Hannah screamed.

"And soon so shall you be," the killer said adjusting the IVs and putting Peter Hannah back to sleep. "It was kind of you to stay here in Jerusalem and await your death."

"I've heard tell that most of the field agents think Peter Hannah is a jerk," the killer said to Simon. "Do you think they would like to have a video of him witnessing his own beheading?"

Simon just stared at the killer. Both James Arnold and Peter Hannah seemed to be chosen to die not just for their names but for something they had done thirty-five years ago. There was something more to this that Simon was now beginning to understand.

"I rather think they'd enjoy it. I might even include you in this video as well," the killer said.

He took his camera and shot a few seconds of Simon sitting in his chair from several angles before placing it back in the apparatus designed to hold it for the filming of the decapitation.

Fifty-one minutes and fifteen seconds!

Three times seventeen minutes and five seconds, the length of the 60's psychedelic rock band Iron Butterfly's classic hit *In A Gadda Da Vida*.

Simon had heard it once before, but to witness it was more demented than he ever could have imagined. The scalpel danced in the killer's hand timed perfectly with the arpeggios and solos of the driving ostinato beat of the music, building and building until the third and final conclusion when Peter Hannah was shocked into consciousness long enough to witness his own decapitation.

The killer fell back into his chair.

"Wasn't that just marvelous?" he gloated.

"I'm sure you'd like to help out with the peeling of Peter's head, but this head I will be using so I can't risk unskilled hands wielding the knife. I hope you're not too disappointed?" the killer laughed.

The killer went out into what Simon now knew to be a garage off of the basement and brought in another crucifix. This one was different from the other and different from the one that had been used on Philip that Simon had seen while he was investigating the killings.

"I see you're confused by the shape of the crucifix. It is much longer at the top than the others. Do you know why?" the killer asked.

Simon nodded his head.

"Oh, you are a smart one, but if I recall we did discuss it earlier. Peter is to be crucified upside down so the top naturally needs to be longer," the killer said, dragging the torso to the cross and nailing it on.

He then lit the fire below the large pot on the stove.

"Remember we have to pull out the brains so they don't swell up and crack the cranium."

The killer stuck a wire up the nose and swished it around then pulled out globules of Peter Hannah's brains.

"Not a whole lot there," the killer laughed.

"How are your eyes? I bet they are really stinging about now."

He sat the head on the counter and grabbed a towel. He soaked it in water and pressed it against Simon's eyes.

"Does that feel better?"

Simon nodded.

"Let's get you back in your cage and you can rest your eyes for a while. Just hold that damp towel on them," he instructed.

The killer unfastened the bindings on the chair and told Simon to return to his cage. Simon knew the power the killer possessed and any attempt to attack or flee would only lead to more torture and pain, so he did as instructed.

Once inside the killer raised his hand and the cage locked.

Simon watched for a few more moments while the killer quickly removed the remaining brains and peeled the skin and tissue from Peter's head.

"I have a feeling tonight will be a busy night," the killer said. "I have much to do and I feel the need to paint. I will bring you some soup later and I expect you to remain quiet this evening," the killer instructed. "Do you understand?"

Simon nodded even though he knew he was through cooperating. He would rather die than continue the torture and suffering.

Charlie woke up a little before six. Jessica was sitting at the computer now searching a list of all the students who attended Jacksonville State University in 1970 who shared the name of one of the apostles not yet murdered. She had completed the list of fraternity members who still lived in the area and had come up with Peter Hannah along with three Johns and one Thomas.

"You didn't sleep?" Charlie asked.

"I couldn't. I kept thinking about that DVD," Jessica said.

"That bad, huh?"

"Worse than bad," she declared.

"You want to get something to eat?" Charlie asked.

"Maybe later. I thought you were going to watch the DVD with the sergeants?" she said.

"I am. I just thought you might want to eat something while we watch it," Charlie admitted.

"Trust me, after you watch it, you won't want to eat, just drink and forget about it," she replied.

"Okay, wait here. I'll go down to Boone's and I'll watch it with them."

"Don't say I didn't warn you."

Charlie picked up the DVD and headed out the door. When he looked back at Jessica, she was crying.

"Try calling *Jefe* again," the assassin said.

"I just tried ten minutes ago," the one in charge said. "Don't worry about it. *Jefe* put me in charge here. We'll wait for the FBI agent and if *Jefe* doesn't call we'll kill him on our own."

"*Jefe* won't like that."

"Meathook would like it less if we let the FBI *pendejo* get away," the leader explained.

Fifty-five minutes later Charlie walked back into the apartment ashen-faced.

"That is one sick bastard."

"Did you throw-up?" Jessica asked.

"Did I what?"

"Did you throw up at the end? I did, all over my carpet. I couldn't help it," she admitted.

"No, but I came pretty close. Honestly, I probably would have if Boone and McClellan hadn't been there."

"How did they take it?"

"About the same as me I guess. It's hard to tell how something like that affects a person," Charlie said.

"What are we going to do with it?"

"Kevin will want to see it tomorrow and then we'll probably take it and the notes to the lab to be analyzed to see if we can find a clue that may help find that sick son-of-a-bitch."

"So what do we do now?" she asked.

"You're right about not wanting food, but I sure could use a drink and I promised the sergeants another trip to Banana Joe's as Charlie Daniels and his entourage."

"Nothing like drinking the horrors away," Jessica replied.

"I'll let the sergeants know we're ready to go."

"No need Charlie. We're ready to rock and roll," Boone and McClellan said, standing outside Charlie's door.

"Let's take two cars, Jessica will ride with me and you two follow us," Charlie suggested.

"I don't know, I was thinking Jessica should maybe ride with me, you know for protection," Boone joked.

"Keep dreaming sergeant," Jessica replied.

"Yes ma'am."

"Tonight boys, and ma'am, let's drink to forget."

CHAPTER FORTY-FIVE

"That's the Trans Am," one of the assassins yelled excitedly. "What should we do?"

"*Pendejo*, I told you what we do. We follow it and kill the FBI agent as Vasquez ordered," the leader explained.

"But Samuelson said to call him before we did anything," the man insisted.

"Samuelson isn't answering his phone. He told us to follow Caressa and if the opportunity arises we will kill him with or without Samuelson's permission," the leader stated.

The three assassins started following with two in the Escalade and one in the Ford they had rented at the local airport. They hadn't noticed the two sergeants coming through the gate a few seconds behind the Trans Am and the Escalade cut them off to keep close tabs on the Trans Am.

"Hey, watch out," Boone yelled at the Escalade flipping it off.

However, the two men inside were too busy to even acknowledge what they had done.

"What's with those guys?" Boone said.

"A big black Escalade with Texas plates seem a little out of place to you?" McClellan asked Boone.

"Let's see if they follow Charlie."

As the Trans Am pulled onto the freeway four cars separated the sergeants from Charlie. The car directly behind Charlie passed him immediately once they hit the freeway. A Ford Taurus with a single male driver stayed behind Charlie but several car lengths back. The next car held a family and after a minute even they grew impatient and passed. The Escalade was now behind the Taurus and neither seemed in a hurry to get past the Trans Am.

"I got a bad feeling about this," Boone said. "Get in between the Taurus and Charlie and see what happens."

McClellan sped up shooting over into the fast lane pulling ahead of Charlie to disguise what he was doing and then slowed way down like he was trying to make his exit and pulled in front of the Taurus.

Almost immediately the Escalade shot past the Taurus and the sergeants and got back behind the Trans Am.

"I think that answers our question," Boone said.

A second later the Taurus sped by and crowded in behind the Escalade.

"Looks like there are three of them," Boone said.

"You got Charlie's cell number?"

"Nope!"

"Me neither. You did bring your gun didn't you?"

"I don't leave home without it."

"Should we call for back-up?" McClellan asked.

"Who do we call? We're not positive these guys are who we think they are," Boone said.

"Yeah, but if they are, you know they've got us out gunned," McClellan replied.

"But we got the element of surprise working for us. We know about them, but they don't know about us," Boone said.

"But Charlie doesn't know about them and if we try to warn him then they'll know about us," McClellan said.

"We're coming to the 8th Avenue South exit so this will tell us for sure," Boone said.

As the Trans Am pulled off the parade of cars followed close behind.

"We should try to beat them to Banana Joe's parking lot so we can be in place," Boone said.

"No, we got to stay close behind in case they make their move at a stop light on the way," McClellan reasoned.

"Good point. Stay up tight on the Escalade. Are you locked and loaded?" Boone asked.

"Locked and loaded and ready to roll," McClellan replied.

"When it goes down go for the guy in the Taurus first. He's the one I'm worried about," Boone said.

"I think they might be on to us. The passenger in the Escalade keeps checking us out and has been on the phone," McClellan said.

"Nothing we can do about it now. Just hang tight we're getting close," Boone said.

"I saw Charlie turn down the alley towards Banana Joe's parking lot. The Escalade is slowing down. He's purposely blocking us, pass him quick," Boone yelled.

McClellan tried to pass but the Escalade tried to run him into cars parked on the street.

"He's getting ready to fire," McClellan yelled, but Boone was already out the door and firing into the Escalade. His first shot blew away the passenger's head just as he was about to open fire.

"I'll get the Taurus," he yelled running towards the alley, but McClellan was too busy dodging bullets to hear him.

"You son-of-a-bitch," McClellan yelled and turned his car sharply into the Escalade firing his pistol through the windshield and pinning the Escalade up on two wheels against a corvette parked in front of the bar.

One of his bullets must have ruptured the gas tank of the Escalade because it burst into flames.

McClellan tried to open his door but it was stuck so he climbed through the blown out window before the fire engulfed his car along with the Escalade, Corvette, and two bodies.

The sound of machine gunfire from behind Banana Joe's jolted his shocked senses back to reality and he sprinted down the alley.

"Boone where you at?" he screamed as he rounded the corner to the parking lot ready to fire.

"It's over," Boone said, "The asshole shot Charlie. Charlie never had a chance."

Jessica was sitting on the ground next to Charlie sobbing. The assassin was lying next to Boone with multiple gunshot wounds crying in pain.

"Asshole," McClellan said, kicking the wounded man in the head.

"Is Charlie dead?" McClellan asked.

"Not yet, but it doesn't look good. The guy strafed him across the upper chest and his legs. Paramedics are on the way." Boone explained.

"We dropped the ball on this one partner," Boone said. "We knew they were coming and we couldn't stop it."

"What about Kevin?" Do you think they had a team follow him from the base when he left?" McClellan asked.

"I completely forgot about Kevin. If they didn't get him yet I'm sure they're trying. We've got to warn him."

"Grab Charlie's phone maybe the numbers on there," Boone suggested.

"Charlie doesn't have Kevin's number," Jessica said. "We'll have to wait for him to call us."

"Let's just pray to God that he does call," Boone said.

In the distance the sound of sirens grew louder.

"I guess one of us better call the FBI and tell them what happened," McClellan said.

"Drop your weapons," a police officer called from behind the door of his patrol car.

"Jessica, you keep Charlie's phone in case Kevin calls. I got a feeling it's going to be a long night for Sergeant Boone and myself," McClellan said, laying down his gun and raising his arms above his head.

CHAPTER FORTY-SIX

Kevin awoke with a start.
"What time is it?" he asked.
"It's almost ten o'clock," Ginny Lee answered.
"I've got to call Carlo. If they made an attempt at me, they will also try to kill Carlo," Kevin said.
"Who's Carlo?" Ginny Lee asked.
"Carlo's my friend and fellow FBI agent. The Vasquez Cartel also had a hit on him just like me."
"But we took care of those people," she reminded him.
"There will be others. I have to call him." Kevin stood up, and almost fell back down.
"You took quite a blow to the head so you need to move slowly," Ginny Lee cautioned.
"Can I use your phone?" Kevin asked.
"Of course."
Kevin called Carlo's number and Jessica answered.
"Jessica, this is Kevin, is Charlie there?"
"Oh, Kevin, they've shot Charlie. The doctor's don't think he's going to live through the night."
"Where is he? I'm coming there now."
"We're here at the UAB Hospital. Let me get the address. It's 1802 6th Avenue South. You need to hurry," Jessica said.
"I'm on my way."
"You're in no condition to drive anywhere," Ginny Lee said. "And I thought you said his name was Carlo"

"It is Carlo, but he was working undercover like me and using the name Charlie," Kevin explained.

"I'll drive you there," Ginny Lee said. "Kevin is really your name, right?"

"Right, but my last name is really Bridges not Jackson," he admitted.

"We better get going," she said.

Simon was holding the moist towel over his aching eyes when he thought he heard the electric whirr of the garage door opening on the other side of the far basement door.

He was sure of it when he heard the hum of a car engine echoing off the interior garage walls. A moment later the killer walked through the door.

"How are the eyes?" he asked.

"I'd keep that towel on them if I were you," he added.

He picked up the crucifix with one hand and carried it through the door. Simon heard what sounded like a sliding door of a van being opened and then slammed shut.

The killer walked back in smiling and walked over to the pot to check on the maceration process of Peter Hannah's head.

"Looks like it's almost clean as a whistle," he said. "I might even have time to work on it later tonight."

The killer walked over in front of the cage and stared in at Simon.

"I was joking when I said I split your tongue. I just nicked it so you would feel some pain and then dressed it like I had cut it up. I just wanted to make sure you stayed quiet when I performed my ritual on Peter Hannah," the killer explained. "Go ahead, take off the bandages."

Simon wasn't sure if he should believe him but did as he was told. There was nothing wrong with his tongue.

"You see, I'm not as evil as you thought," the killer laughed.

"No, you are much more evil than I ever imagined," Simon replied.

"And with each evil murder I grow stronger and stronger," the killer replied. "Darkness is upon us, you must accept it."

"Forces of darkness are always trying to push us down," Simon replied, "and I won't accept it."

"But you must accept it for I can be your savior, serve me," the killer demanded.

"I have but one Savior," Simon replied.

"Bah," the killer said, raising his hand and slamming Simon against the back of the cage.

"You will die like the rest of them," the killer said.

"Maybe, but unlike the others I wasn't part of the rape," Simon said, remembering James A's plea and knowing he was taking a chance with this comment.

"The r-rape has n-nothing t-to do with *glorybedaGoda alleluia* anything," the killer said beginning to jerk violently.

Simon believed that when the killer had these Tourette like attacks his powers seemed to diminish or at least he lacked control of them.

"Who was it that was raped so long ago that angered you so badly you feel you must kill so many to revenge that terrible crime?" Simon pushed.

"I-I *glorybedaGoda* d-don't... *shamnada hydakom* I d-don't," the killer's body was jerking so violently he couldn't even speak. He staggered to the staircase stumbling and falling but was able to drag himself up the steps and out of the basement.

"I'll probably pay dearly for that later, but I now have hope," Simon said smiling for the first time in weeks.

"How is he?" Kevin asked as he and Ginny Lee rushed into the hospital.

"He's still alive, but just barely according to the doctor," Jessica said.

"Ginny Lee this is Jessica. She's a newspaper reporter," Kevin said.

"Actually, my name is Paige Eliot, but I am a reporter like Kevin said," Paige corrected.

"Does everybody you know go by two names?" Ginny Lee gasped.

"Did the shooter's get away?" Kevin asked.

"No, Sergeants McClellan and Boone were there. They killed two of them at Banana Joe's and shot the other one up pretty bad, but I heard he died here at the hospital," Paige explained.

"Good, where are Boone and McClellan?"

"Dealing with the police still, I'm sure. It was quite a shootout in the middle of Birmingham. Their commanding officer showed up with the orders from the FBI about providing protection for you and Carlo so everything will be fine," Paige explained

"I'm going in to see Carlo," Kevin said.

"He's in ICU, they won't let you in," Paige said.

"Let them try to stop me," Kevin replied.

Kevin and Ginny Lee headed back to the ICU to first speak with the doctor to hear the prognosis.

"And just who are you?" the doctor on duty asked.

"I'm Dr. Kevin Bridges with the FBI," Kevin said, pulling out his credentials.

"You're a medical doctor and an FBI agent?" the doctor asked.

"Yes I am," Kevin replied, "So if you please, I'd like to hear about his injuries."

"He took two bullets to the lower legs, one passed through his left calf the second broke his right fibula. Neither are serious. One bullet went in and ricocheted off the right collar bone. A second lodged in his right shoulder, but the third is the problem. The third bullet passed through his neck and lodged in his spinal column very nearly severing it. We have a specialist coming in from John Hopkins in the morning to see if it's operable assuming he lives that long. Sorry to be the bearer of such bad news but those are the facts," the doctor explained.

"Mind if I see him?" Kevin asked.

"You are a licensed medical doctor, so I see no reason why not," he replied. "There are some extra scrubs over in that closet."

"Thanks," Kevin said.

"I'm coming with you," Ginny Lee insisted.

They both put on the gowns and entered the ICU. Carlo was hooked up to at least a dozen different monitors.

"Give me your hand," Ginny said.

"What?" Kevin replied.

"Give me your hand, we're going to pray," Ginny repeated. "That's the only thing that can save him."

Kevin took Ginny Lee's hand and Ginny Lee laid her hand on Carlo's arm and began to pray in tongues.

"You need to pray too," she stopped and ordered.

Kevin did as he was told, ignoring the looks of the passing nurses, but his prayers were in English. They had been praying for almost fifteen minutes when Ginny Lee suddenly stopped.

"We need to go," she said.

"Go? I can't leave Carlo. You said through God all can be healed. We are both filled with the Holy Spirit and with God's grace we can heal Carlo," Kevin pleaded with her.

"Yes, but there is another whose gifts are greater than ours. I must go and ask him to come," Ginny Lee said.

"I'll come with you," Kevin said.

"No, it would be better if I go alone."

Kevin wasn't going to argue. He knew the power of the Holy Spirit and if Ginny Lee said there was one filled with a greater spirit than either of them then he wanted that person too.

Woland Kapkov stood alone along a parapet surrounding the massive balcony outside of the bedroom of Peter Hannah's mansion overlooking the city of Birmingham.

It was a dark moonless night but the lights of the city glowed brightly.

"Night is coming," he spoke to the city. "Night is coming when no one can work."

The ultimate puppet master pulling all the right strings to feed the greed and fears of the skeptical unbelievers.

"Yes, the Darkness is upon you. Your fates are sealed just as Christ's fate was sealed on the crucifix. None of you deserve the Light, but I deserve the peace," Woland called to the night.

"I arranged it all thirty-five years ago. All of them by name, all of them to die. The storm is on the horizon and the time is near, I deserve the peace," he cried, "I deserve the peace."

"The Dominion of Darkness is at hand."

It was almost an hour later when Ginny Lee returned with Casper.

"That's right," Kevin recalled, speaking to Paige, "Ginny Lee had told me how Casper was filled with the Holy Spirit more than anyone she knew. I do know God has anointed his fingers musically. He is the greatest guitar player I think I've ever heard."

"Casper has agreed to help Carlo," Ginny Lee explained.

Thank you, Casper," Kevin said, "we should hurry."

Kevin led Casper, Ginny Lee, and Paige back to the ICU.

"Paige, you'll have to wait out here," Kevin explained. "Casper, there's some scrubs in the closet for you to put on."

"What's going on here?" the nurse said.

"I've brought in a specialist to look at Carlo," Kevin explained.

"A specialist, what kind of specialist? Does Dr. Dormann know about this?" she protested.

"Dr. Dormann knows my credentials, and my friend here is a specialist in miracles," Kevin replied.

"Well I need to notify Doctor Dormann," she insisted.

"You go ahead and do that," Kevin replied, "but we're still going in."

The nurse got on the phone as Kevin, Ginny Lee, and Casper entered the ICU. Casper immediately placed his hands on the bandages covering Carlo's neck.

"Both of you place your hands on mine," Casper whispered. It was awkward but Ginny Lee and Kevin shuffled around until they were able to do so without bumping any of the equipment or tubes attached to Carlo.

"Now we pray," Casper ordered.

Immediately, Casper and Ginny Lee began to pray in tongues. Kevin began to pray in English but to his surprise strange sounds were coming from his mouth and he too was praying in an unknown language yet he understood every word he was saying.

Kevin could feel heat coming from Carlo and he began to grow nervous when a soothing cool calmness came over the room reminiscent of the feelings he had when Charlotte would enter the room back at the Experimental Forest. Casper lifted his hands placing them over Kevin's then placed Kevin's hand directly over the neck wound. The words continued to pour from Kevin's mouth as from the others and the fervor seemed to grow. Suddenly, Kevin flinched as he felt something below the bandage under his hand. The vital sign monitor came to life almost as if it had been turned on. Bells started ringing and buzzers began to sound. Kevin stumbled backwards.

"Nurse, Nurse," Kevin called, "Something's going on here."

The nurse was already on her way in the door alerted by the monitors at the nurse's station.

"God's going on here," Ginny Lee replied.

The nurse pushed through the prayer warriors to see what was happening.

"That's impossible, these vital signs are almost normal," she exclaimed.

"Am I missing something," Carlo suddenly spoke.

"Doctor, doctor," the nurse screamed running from the room.

"Nice to have you back buddy," Kevin said. "I thought we lost you for a minute."

"That's impossible," the doctor said hurrying through the door.

Carlo started to sit up.

"For God's sake don't move. The bullet in your spine will kill you," the doctor screamed.

"Is that what I feel irritating my neck," Carlo replied.

The doctor looked at the bump in the bandage and carefully cut around it. A 9mm slug rolled onto the bed sheet. The doctor picked it up and compared it to the slug on the x-ray. There was little doubt that they were the same bullet.

"What is that?" Ginny Lee asked

"The bullet that was embedded in his spinal cord," Casper said softly.

"That's just impossible," the doctor insisted.

"Through God all can be healed," Ginny Lee replied. "For God nothing is impossible."

"Nurse get this patient back to x-ray. I want another picture of that bullet in his spinal cord," the doctor insisted.

The nurse finished removing the bandage from Carlo's neck.

"Doctor, there is no trace of the entrance wound," she said in disbelief.

"Just get me another x-ray," the doctor said. "What you're describing is impossible."

"No, it's a miracle," Kevin corrected.

Dr. Dormann turned and stormed out of the ICU.

"Carlo will be fine," Casper said softly, "However, he still has a broken leg and will be sore from those other bullet wounds."

"I feel fine," Carlo piped in, confused by everyone's concern.

"Yes, but he's alive," Kevin said, "and we have you to thank for that."

"It wasn't me who did that," Casper replied. "It was all of our prayers."

Casper turned and headed out of the ICU before the nurse wheeled Carlo towards x-ray.

"It truly is a miracle," the nurse said as she wheeled Carlo out.

"I ask again, am I missing something here?" Carlo said.

"I'll explain it all to you when you get back from x-ray," Kevin said.

"Just one more question," Carlo said, "Are Jessica and the sergeants okay?"

They're fine, but it's Paige, not Jessica. And I'm afraid you are no longer Charlie Daniels, but Carlo Caressa," Kevin said.

"That's too bad, I was starting to really like the beard," Carlo said.

Nobody wanted to tell him that half of the beard had already been shaved away by the emergency room nurses when he came into the trauma center.

CHAPTER FORTY-SEVEN

Tyronza, Arkansas was little more than a speed-trap disguising itself as a town in the southeastern corner of Arkansas. The killer knew this and had no intentions of entering the town directly. Peter Hannah's crucified body would be left at the Parkin Archeological State Park just south of Tyronza.

The killer arrived before dawn and was easily able to access the park grounds.

Along the banks of the St. Francis River a large platform mound still remained from an early American Indian village that occupied the area around 1000 A.D.

"This will be perfect for the crucifix," the killer said, pulling it out of the van and slamming it into the ground upside down, just as Apostle Peter had been crucified in Rome.

The killer didn't stay to admire his handiwork and quickly left the area for the long return trip home.

"Ginny Lee, it's too late for you to be driving home tonight and I'm still in no shape to drive you," Kevin said, turning to Paige. "I'll get you a hotel room..."

"That isn't necessary," Paige interrupted, "She can stay with me at my apartment tonight."

"I wouldn't want to impose," Ginny Lee said.

"Impose; you just saved Carlo's life. Having you stay in my apartment is the least I can do," Paige insisted.

"Do you have that DVD and those notes from the killer?" Kevin asked.

"They're right here," Paige said, reaching into her purse.

"Chester made a DVD?" Ginny Lee asked.

"Contrary to what you've heard, Chester is not the Apostle Serial Killer," Kevin told Ginny Lee.

"But I thought they caught Chester in the act?" Ginny Lee said.

"They caught him dropping off a body on a cross, but I believe he was either hypnotized, or brainwashed, or under the power of an evil spirit, or something at the time he did it," Kevin explained.

"The real killer left a recording of his decapitations of James Arnold," Paige explained. "I made the mistake of viewing it."

"I'll drop you two off at Paige's apartment and then take these things to the lab to see what they can come up with," Kevin explained. "After I check on Carlo in the morning, I'll drive you back to the church."

"I wouldn't mind checking in on Carlo before I go back," Ginny Lee said.

"You know I'm going to want to see how he's doing," Paige said.

"You and I need to go over what Carlo and you were working on," Kevin said. "We can do that when I get back tomorrow afternoon."

They waited for Carlo to get back from x-ray and to everyone's amazement he was awake, talking away and moving all his extremities just fine.

"So they tell me you guys prayed the bullet out of my spinal cord," Carlo said.

"Something like that," Kevin replied.

"Could you guys say a few prayers and fix my broken leg, I'd like to get out of here," Carlo complained.

"It doesn't work like that," Kevin said.

"Yes it does, "Ginny corrected. "You must have faith in God's ability to cure the sick."

"We'll see you in the morning," Kevin said, heading the two women out of the room.

When they arrived at Paige's apartment Kevin walked them to the door. It was fortunate he did, for taped onto Paige's door was another DVD.

"This is not good," Paige said.

"Don't touch it," Kevin said, "Get me a baggie and I'll try to get it off without disturbing any prints that might be there."

"Why do you think the killer left us another copy of the DVD?" Paige asked.

"Maybe he wasn't sure that you found the first one. He probably expected you to get it to the media outlets immediately, and when you didn't, he assumed you hadn't found it," Kevin surmised.

"Or else he's struck again," Ginny Lee said.

Her comment sent a shiver down Kevin and Paige's spine.

"Do you think it could be a video of a new victim?" Paige asked.

"I won't know till I get it to the lab, but I do know neither of you are staying here tonight. Paige, grab whatever you need for the next couple of nights until we find you a new place to live," Kevin ordered. "Tonight you two will stay at the Hampton Inn downtown. The FBI has an account there."

Neither of the women were going to argue after having found the new message from the Apostle Serial Killer. Once Kevin had them safely in their rooms he headed to the lab at the Birmingham Bureau.

"So you're the famous Dr. Kevin Bridges that's been working undercover on this investigation," Supervising Agent Billings said as Kevin walked in.

"Please, it's Agent Bridges, but call me Kevin," Kevin replied.

"Sorry to hear about Carlo Caressa. I know he was a good friend of yours," Agent Billings said.

"Agent Caressa has made a miraculous turn around," Kevin explained. "I wouldn't be surprised to see him back in the office in a day or two."

"That's impossible. I was at the hospital and I spoke to the doctor myself. He didn't expect him to make it through the night."

"The doctor underestimated Carlo's recuperative powers," Kevin said. "It's amazing what God and prayer can do."

"So what brings you to the lab?" Billings asked.

"I have some new evidence on the Apostle Serial Killer," Kevin explained.

"Hannah told us that case is closed," Billings replied.

"He did? Does that mean he found Simon Caldwell and where all the murders took place and the skulls or chalices of all the murdered victims?" Kevin replied.

"Of course we haven't found all of that yet, but we will," Billings replied.

"Chester Cunningham was not the Apostle Serial Killer," Kevin proclaimed. "Somehow he was drugged or hypnotized into doing what he did."

"Do you have any proof of that?"

"Let's watch a couple DVDs, shall we," Kevin said.

"I know this one is the killer's recording of his decapitation of James Arnold. It was left yesterday morning at Paige Eliot's apartment after Chester was dead," Kevin said.

"This DVD no one has seen. We found it a little over an hour ago taped to Paige's apartment door when I was taking her home from the hospital," Kevin said. "It's either a copy of the first, or the Apostle Serial Killer has struck again."

They set up a television and several agents came in to view the DVD.

"Just a word of warning; the four people who saw the first DVD swear they'll never be the same after what they saw," Kevin said.

Nobody left. Kevin started the DVD.

"That's Simon Caldwell," one of the agents called out. "What the hell have they done to him?"

"This must be a different recording," Kevin said, "Simon wasn't part of the first DVD."

The screen went blank for a second and then the face of Peter Hannah appeared strapped to the operating table.

"What the hell is that? Stop the DVD. That's Assistant Director Hannah," Billings yelled. "Somebody get Hannah on the phone."

"I don't think Hannah's going to be answering any phones," Kevin said.

"Send a car up to his house," Billings said, when they received no answer from his cell or home phone.

"Do you want to continue or not?" Kevin asked.

"Play the damn thing," Billings barked.

Forty-five minutes into the DVD the bureau got a call from the Arkansas State Police to tell them that a headless body had been found upside down on a cross in a park near Tyronza, Arkansas.

Six minutes and fifteen seconds later they knew for sure that the body belonged to Peter Hannah.

"Shit!" Supervising Agent Billings said, while two other agents watching vomited into trash cans.

"Now what do we do?" he said.

"We find the real Apostle Serial Killer," Kevin replied, "since now we have several more clues that may help us."

A team of agents was sent to Arkansas to search the crime scene and retrieve the body while the team sent to look for Peter Hannah was now told to secure the house as a crime scene.

"I'm running low on agents here," Billings complained.

"I'm here just to get some information and then I'm back undercover. I still believe the church up in Macedonia is our best lead," Kevin said.

"Good luck, I have to call Director Kaiser," Billings replied.

Kevin went down to the crime lab to see if Chester's truck produced any clues that might help.

"Remember that Gigli's Wire I showed you?" the doctor said.

"Yes," Kevin replied, "the antique Dremel tool."

"Right," the doctor, smiled. "Well we found a second set of DNA on the wire and it matches the DNA that was found on two of the killer's victims."

"I thought the DNA found on the victims' was from a female?" Kevin said.

"It was. So was the one found on the Gigli's Wire," the doctor replied.

"Are you inferring that the Apostle Serial Killer is a female?" Kevin said.

"I'm not inferring anything. I'm just stating facts. And here's a few more facts that will really confuse things. Remember those four female DNA samples you brought into us from the church?"

"Of course," Kevin said.

"One of them is a familial match to one of the DNAs on the Gigli's Wire," the doctor explained.

"Yeah, I expected that. Emily Sue Whitman's half-sister Ginny Lee was one of the samples," Kevin said.

"Yes, but it wasn't Emily Sue Whitman's remains that she matched. It was the other one. The same one found on the two other victims," the doctor explained.

"So the remains we took from the church and the chalice skull are not Emily Sue Whitman's?" Kevin gasped.

"Not if she was related to Ginny Lee Turner. It looks like Emily Sue Whitman might possibly be your Apostle Serial Killer," the doctor surmised.

Kevin was completely taken aback by the news. He didn't doubt that a woman was capable of such heinous and grotesque murders, but he knew of no woman who had the strength to lift Simon the way the person on the video had done. And it would take tremendous strength for a woman to nail a body to a cross and carry it around and place the crucifix into the ground. Yet the evidence is what it is.

"Could these be simply revenge killings for her rape thirty-five years ago?" Kevin asked himself.

"Agent Bridges," another agent called, as Kevin stood dumbfounded.

"We ran that name Charlie, I mean Carlo gave us, a Woland Kapkov, through every data base we could find and couldn't come up with anything. The man just doesn't exist according to records."

"I've met him, so he does exist, it just means Woland Kapkov isn't his real name," Kevin said.

Kevin knew what he had to do next and wasn't looking forward to it. He and Ginny Lee were going to have a long talk. Right now, however, the one thing he needed most was sleep and he wasn't going to get it at the lab.

CHAPTER FORTY-EIGHT

When Kevin arrived back at his apartment at the National Guard base the Trans Am was already there. Immediately Boone and McClellan came out to greet Kevin.

"Man we're glad you're alive. I guess we stopped them before they came for you," Boone said.

"Not quite, but it's a long story and I'm really tired," Kevin said.

"Really, a team tried to take you out, too?" McClellan asked.

Kevin knew he wasn't going to get any rest until he told his story and heard theirs so he listened and then retold what had happened at the church.

"I've heard about those hillbillies," Boone said. "It's like that movie *Deliverance*."

"Only for real," as Kevin described the wood chipper feeding of the hogs.

"I thought we'd lost Charlie, but I just talked to him at the hospital. He says it was a miracle," McClellan said.

"It was a miracle," Kevin affirmed, "but it wouldn't have been possible had you two not been there, thanks," Kevin said, man-hugging them both. "By the way we're back to our real names again."

"I guess that blows our free drinks at Banana Joe's," Boone joked.

"I need to get a couple of hours sleep. The Apostle Serial Killer struck again, so I've got a lot of work to do and no Carlo to help for a while. I'll talk to you two later," Kevin said heading inside.

Even with the visions of Peter Hannah's head popping off, Kevin knew he would fall asleep. And he was right.

Simon awoke when he heard the garage door begin to whirr just behind the far basement wall. A moment later the killer came rushing through the basement door with a bag in his hand.

"I bet you're hungry," the killer said. "I brought you a treat. I hope you like pancakes. I stopped by Hardees on my way back into town.

"Thank you," Simon said, removing the towel from his sore eyes.

"Actually, it was quicker than fixing us something. I have a busy day ahead. There's a storm coming. They say it will be one of the largest hurricane's to hit the South since Hurricane Andrew in 1992 and I have business to take care of before it hits New Orleans," the killer explained.

"Someone in New Orleans who must be punished?" Simon asked.

"That is precisely the problem. Someone you may even remember, Rastas Bartholomew Smith, the Voodoo priest and owner of the Market Botanica," the killer said.

"Oh yes, the supplier of poisonous snakes," Simon recalled. "Was he in Jacksonville thirty-five years ago as well?"

"I don't think you want to anger me since I no longer have a time table for my murders," the killer warned.

"If I recall Bartholomew is to be crucified upside down as well," Simon remarked.

"Yes, but only after I flay him while he is still alive, which unfortunately means he will probably not live long enough to watch his own head pop off. I will do my best to try to keep him alive for the experience," the killer explained.

"Thank you for breakfast," Simon said turning his back to the killer to pray and eat.

Simon had prayed every day since he had been taken captive for God to give him strength and to free him from the evil that kept him prisoner. Today as he prayed, he realized God had given him the strength he needed to prepare him for what was coming and for the first time since his capture, Simon felt a sense of peace.

When Kevin awoke, news of the Apostle Serial Killer's latest victim was on every news station across the country. Not only had he made a fool of the Assistant Director of the FBI's news conference declaring the case closed, he made the assistant director his next victim. Kevin knew that literally dozens of agents would now be coming to Birmingham to work the case and the killer would no doubt know it too. Ginny Lee, her mother, and the entire church would be hounded for weeks now with the FBI's latest DNA information.

Kevin called the hotel but neither Ginny Lee nor Paige were there. He called Paige's cell phone and discovered that they had already gone to the hospital to visit Carlo.

When Kevin arrived Ginny Lee was praying over Carlo's broken leg and even had Paige praying along with her.

"How's it going?" Kevin said softly to Carlo as he quietly entered the room.

Ginny Lee stopped her prayers and stepped back away from the bed.

"My leg feels all warm," Carlo said. "It feels much better."

"It is healing," Ginny Lee said, "but you still need to stay off of it for a few days."

"The sergeants were asking about you. They say you still owe them drinks at Banana Joe's," Kevin joked.

"Tell them tomorrow night I'll take them out," Carlo replied.

"You're not going any place for a least a week," Paige insisted.

"So did you see the news?" Carlo asked.

"Yes, and I also saw the new video," Kevin replied.

"New video?" Carlo asked.

"We found a new DVD at my apartment when we went there this morning," Paige explained.

"The good thing about it was that it showed Simon. He's still alive, but pretty messed up. It also showed Peter Hannah," Kevin said reluctantly.

"I'll never listen to Iron Butterfly again," Carlo said.

"Ginny Lee, I should get you back home before people start spreading rumors," Kevin joked.

"Macedonia could use a few good rumors about now," she replied.

Everyone said their goodbyes and Kevin and Ginny Lee headed back for the church.

"I didn't get a chance to really thank Casper for what he did for Carlo," Kevin said. "He seemed to have disappeared in all the confusion."

"Casper doesn't like the limelight. He likes to keep to himself," Ginny Lee said.

"Tell me about Emily Sue," Kevin said.

"Not a whole lot to tell. I never knew her. She was killed when I was just a five years old," Ginny Lee said.

"Did your mother and father ever talk about her?" Kevin asked.

"My mother denies ever even having another daughter," Ginny Lee said.

"Why is that?" Kevin asked.

"I don't know. I think it's just part of her dementia."

"She hasn't had dementia her entire life. Didn't she talk about her with your father when you were younger?" Kevin asked.

"I know Emily Sue dropped out of college and went away to Europe for several years. Maybe that might have had something to do with it," Ginny Lee said.

"Do you have any pictures of your sister?" Kevin asked.

"No, I don't have any pictures."

"Was she a big girl or a tiny girl?" Kevin asked.

"Why are you asking me all of these questions? You know how big she was. The FBI dug up her remains," Ginny Lee said annoyed.

"Ginny Lee, the remains that were buried in the church graveyard are not the remains of Emily Sue Whitman," Kevin said.

"What are you talking about? Of course they are," she insisted.

Kevin knew this wouldn't go well but he had hoped it would go better than it was so far.

"If it was Emily Sue, the DNA would have a partial match to your DNA since you have the same mother, and there is no such match," Kevin explained.

"Where did you get my DNA?" she demanded.

"Off of napkins I took when you invited me to lunch last Wednesday," Kevin admitted.

Ginny Lee sat quietly fuming. Kevin knew better than to speak.

"Well, maybe my mother adopted her, maybe she was right when she said she never had another daughter," Ginny Lee said.

"I thought of that and checked the birth records. Your mother and her first husband did have the one daughter Emily Sue Whitman," Kevin said.

"There must be some other explanation," Ginny Lee insisted.

"Would you like to know why Emily Sue dropped out of school and went to Europe?"

"You know that?"

"We're pretty sure. She was raped by several college boys in the fall of 1970. To avoid having her press charges the parents of one of the boys paid her a substantial sum of money. Enough to go to Europe for several years," Kevin explained.

"Okay, so if that's not Emily Sue who was buried in the graveyard and where is she?" Ginny Lee asked.

"That's where things get a bit stickier," Kevin said hesitantly. "What we believe to be Emily Sue's DNA has been found in four places. On the skull chalice, on two of the Apostle Serial Killer victims, and on a tool called a Gigli's Wire that is used to saw on skulls that we found in Chester's truck."

"Whoa, hold on," Ginny Lee said. "Are you implying that Emily Sue Whitman is the Apostle Serial Killer?"

"She's a suspect, if she's alive. The other thing I forgot to mention is that five of the six recent victims of the killer were all involved in the rape of Emily Sue Whitman back in 1970," Kevin added.

This was too much for Ginny Lee to comprehend all at once.

"I don't want to talk or listen for a while. I just need to think," Ginny Lee said.

"I understand," Kevin replied, as they drove on in silence.

CHAPTER FORTY-NINE

Ver Dell and Ida were cleaning up around the church when Kevin and Ginny Lee returned. It was more like they were waiting to see what was going to happen next.

"Yer friend okay?" Ver Dell asked.

"He is thanks to Ginny Lee and Casper," Kevin replied.

"It was real bad. We needed Casper's gifts to save Carlo's life," Ginny Lee said almost apologetically to Ver Dell and Ida.

"When's Chester comin' home?" Ida asked.

"Nobody's told me nothing yet," Ginny Lee said, looking to Kevin.

"I would guess they won't release the body till later in the week," Kevin said.

"Best cover da hole then wit' all da rain comin'," Ver Dell said, heading back towards the shed.

"We doin sumtin' special fer Chester tomorrow?" Ida asked.

"We better wait a week or two," Ginny Lee replied. "Let things sort themselves out a bit first."

"Chester didn't do it," Ida said, "Satan get his mind somehow."

"I know Ida. Kevin knows that too. The people who really matter will know Chester is innocent," Ginny Lee explained.

"Reckon they will," Ida said, moving back inside.

"Would you like some coffee and a little dinner before you head back? I figure it's safe for you to come up to the house now that we've spent the night together," Ginny Lee joked. "At least that's what the rumors will be."

"I'd love some coffee," Kevin replied.

As they entered the house Kevin saw a painting of a couple on the wall.

"Is that your parents?" Kevin asked.

"It is," she replied. "Isn't it beautiful?"

The picture had her parents standing in the Sistine Chapel at the Vatican surrounded by amazing replicas of some of the greatest artists ever.

"Someone actually painted exact replicates of the works in the chapel. This is an amazing piece of work," Kevin lauded.

"Casper painted it," Ginny Lee said.

"Casper, from last night? The guitar player in the band?" Kevin said amazed.

"I told you he had amazing gifts of the Spirit. The Holy Spirit has anointed his fingers," Ginny Lee said. "He makes a rather substantial income from his artwork."

"I've never met anyone with such talent," Kevin said.

"He has served God well and been rewarded," she confirmed. "He lives in one of those big mansions that overlook Birmingham in Redmont Park."

Kevin looked stunned.

"Tell me a little about Woland Kapkov. The FBI cannot find any record of him in any of their data bases or anybody else's data bases," Kevin said.

"That's odd," Ginny Lee replied. "He's been dragging that gimpy leg to church on and off since I can remember."

"Gimpy leg?" I don't remember him having a gimpy leg. He stood taller and looked stronger and more fit than Chester when they headed out after the meeting," Kevin described.

"Are we talking about the same person? The Woland I know limps badly, is shorter than Chester by at least six inches and has a rounded back," Ginny Lee said. "You must be thinking of someone else."

Kevin didn't know what to think. Maybe the stress was overwhelming her mind. The Woland he remembered looked nothing like who Ginny Lee just described. He recalled the Wikipedia reference to the character Woland in *The Master and Margarita* by some Russian author which seemed to mention something similar about appearing differently to different people. Maybe there was more truth than fiction in that Russian classic.

"Are you coming to church tomorrow?" Ginny Lee asked.

"Of course I am," Kevin said.

"You know, now that the Apostle Serial Killer has killed Peter Hannah the FBI is going to send dozens of agents here to work this investigation. They'll be looking into everything including what happened to those assassins from the Vasquez Drug Cartel," Kevin warned. "You might want to let Ver Dell and Ida know so they can prepare for them, as well as the hill people."

"It's going to get bad isn't it?" Ginny Lee said.

"I'm afraid it is."

"Is there nothing you can do?"

"I could find the Apostle Serial Killer and free Simon Caldwell before they arrive, but that's not too likely," Kevin admitted. "But I'm sure going to try."

"I'm sure God will show you a way," Ginny Lee replied. "You just need to have faith and pray for his Divine Intervention."

"I could use your prayers, too," Kevin said.

"You'll have all our prayers," she assured him. "Now have some dinner before it gets cold."

Ginny Lee prayed for their meal and Kevin prayed for Ginny Lee. She had already suffered enough.

Carlo was driving Paige nuts as he constantly complained about being stuck in the hospital while the investigation was taking off.

"Carlo, would you just be quiet for a while and count your blessings. The x-ray says your leg is healing ten times faster than it should. By all accounts you should be dead because of the bullet to the spine. Use the next few days to relax and recover like Kevin told you to do," Paige lectured.

"I can't just lay here watching television. I need to be helping on the investigation," Carlo complained.

"Then here," Paige said, tossing a laptop onto his legs making him grimace. "Search the 1970-1971 student records for Jacksonville State and make a list of names of possible future victims," she ordered.

At least it made him feel like he was doing something productive.

"That was a wonderful meal," Kevin said to Ginny Lee.

"Thank you, it took you long enough to come up here and let me fix it for you."

"Can I ask you a few more questions before I go?" Kevin asked.

"If you think it will help," she replied.

"Did Ver Dell or Ida know your sister?"

"I'm sure they did," Ginny Lee said "But I doubt they'll talk to you about her."

"Why is that?"

"They respected my mother and father too much. If Momma says Emily Sue isn't my daughter there had to be a reason and Ida and Ver Dell will honor that reason," Ginny Lee predicted.

"Could you ask them about it?" Kevin said.

"I will tonight when we pray and discuss what you warned me about," Ginny Lee said.

"I've also been thinking about a picture of my sister," Ginny Lee said.

"You have one?" Kevin asked.

"No, but I remember Momma and Daddy talking about a film crew who filmed a service back in Scrabble Creek, West Virginia where Daddy used to preach before he married Momma. I know my sister was in that video," Ginny Lee said.

"Do you know what it's called?" Kevin asked.

"*The Holy Ghost People*," Ginny Lee said.

"Did you ever watch it?"

"Momma wouldn't let me. She said there were too many bad memories there," Ginny Lee said.

"I'll see if I can find it," Kevin said. "I need to get back to Birmingham. Thank you for a wonderful meal."

"Thank you for being honest with me," Ginny Lee said. "I've got a lot to talk about with God."

"I'll see you in the morning," Kevin said.

As he was driving away he saw Ida and Ver Dell head up to Ginny Lee's house.

"I wonder how that conversation is going to go?" Kevin said, picking up his phone to check on Carlo.

CHAPTER FIFTY

"Hi Paige," Kevin said, when she answered Carlo's phone. "Haven't you had enough of Carlo's whining yet?"

"It's getting close," she said. "I finally put him to work doing some research."

"I have some more research for him to do. Put him on the speaker phone if you could please," Kevin asked.

"How'd it go up at the church?" Carlo asked.

"You knew what I had to tell her, how do you think it went?" Kevin replied.

"That bad huh?" Carlo said.

"Finding out your sister, who you thought has been dead for thirty years, might still be alive and is quite possibly the Apostle Serial Killer would be quite a shock to anyone, I'd imagine," Kevin replied. "But I think what troubles her more is knowing that she's about to be hounded by dozens of FBI agents now that Peter Hannah is dead and the DNA evidence is in."

"Yeah, it's going to get ugly," Carlo agreed. "So what is it you need me to look up?"

"Ginny Lee remembered that her sister was in a movie that was made back in the 60's about a snake handling church in Scrabble Creek, West Virginia called *Holy Ghost People*," Kevin said.

"I saw that in college," Carlo said. "In one of my classes."

He punched it into to 'Google'.

"It's available for free on line. Which one is she?" Carlo asked.

"I have no idea. Ginny Lee has never seen the movie, but I guess both her mother and father are also in it. I think it's worth checking out," Kevin said.

"By the way Supervising Agent Billings called looking for you. He thought you might want to have a look around Peter Hannah's house," Carlo said.

"Did he give a specific reason why?" Kevin asked.

"No, probably just to pique your curiosity to come see how the rich people lived. Peter Hannah lived in a big mansion up in an area called Redmont Park. It's supposed to be the where the old money of the South lived," Carlo explained.

"That's funny," Kevin said, "I just heard that name from Ginny Lee. Casper lives up in Redmont Park," Kevin said.

"Casper! The Casper who saved my life?" Carlo replied.

"The same Casper. Ginny Lee said he's made a fortune as an artist. I saw one of his paintings at her house. It was incredible," Kevin said.

"Didn't you tell me he was the best guitar players you'd ever heard?" Carlo asked.

"I did and I meant it. The guy is the most talented man I've ever met. As Ginny Lee puts it he has been anointed generously with the gifts of the Holy Spirit," Kevin said.

"You'll get no argument from me," Carlo replied.

"Who is this Woland I've heard you two talking about?" Paige asked.

"Woland is the mystery man it seems," Kevin said. "The FBI can find nothing in any data base about the guy."

"That doesn't seem possible," Paige said.

"No it doesn't. What is even more troubling, and I know this is going to sound a bit strange, but when I described Woland to Ginny Lee, her description of him was completely different. It was like we were talking about two totally opposite people," Kevin explained.

"Hey, that's just like in the book," Carlo remembered.

"I know, kind of freaky," Kevin said.

"What book?" Paige asked.

"*The Master and Margarita,*" Kevin said.

"By Mikhail Bulgakov, of course, I know that book. Woland is the name of the devil in the story. And if I recall Berlioz had his head severed by a woman in the book," Paige said, struggling to remember.

"That's rather coincidental, wouldn't you say?" Carlo quipped.

"How does it end?" Kevin asked.

"The Master and Margarita leave Moscow with the devil and for not losing their faith they are granted 'peace' but not 'the light' or salvation," Paige explained.

Carlo and Kevin both remained quiet for a moment.

"What was it Chester said right before he died?" Carlo asked.

"I believe he said '*Jesus - can't take him 'the Master does not deserve the light, he deserves peace'*," Kevin quoted.

"This Apostle Serial Case is starting to become a little too supernatural for my tastes," Carlo said.

"It's been a spiritual war from the beginning," Kevin said. "Charlotte warned me about what was coming and told me to prepare for it."

"And are you prepared?" Paige asked.

"I wish I could answer that," Kevin said. "I'll see you two tomorrow. I'm going to stop by Peter Hannah's house and then get some sleep. I promised Ginny Lee I would come to church in the morning but I'll be back in the early afternoon. Paige, don't let Carlo out of bed."

"I won't, even if I have to climb in there and hold him down myself," she laughed.

"And I'll make sure she does," Carlo added.

"I don't want to hear it," Kevin replied, "You two behave yourselves."

It was dark when Kevin arrived at Peter Hannah's mansion in Redmont Park but there were still three police cars and two FBI cars parked out front. There were several trees making it difficult to see any of the neighboring mansions.

"Agent Bridges, nice of you to stop by," Agent Taylor said. "Here on business or just curious?"

"A little of both I guess," Kevin replied.

"You wonder why a single man would live in a place so big," Taylor said. "This house has eight bedrooms and ten bathrooms."

"Mind if I wander on my own?" Kevin asked.

"No problem. We figure the killer snatched him from the driveway. His car was in front of the gate. Probably never entered the house," Taylor said.

Kevin wandered through the upstairs bedrooms admiring the view of downtown Birmingham. He could see why this was the prime location to live. As he headed into the basement he felt an odd sensation. He looked around but nothing seemed familiar.

"Maybe the smell reminds me of my childhood," he thought.

He had always enjoyed playing in his basement when he was a kid growing up in the mid-west. When he moved to California basements were something houses just didn't have.

"Thanks for the tour," he said to Taylor on his way out.

"Anytime," Taylor replied, grumping. "I'm here all night."

Kevin drove the streets of Redmont Park trying to decide which mansion belonged to Casper, but most were hidden by trees or walls and without an address it was a waste of time.

"Maybe tomorrow,' Kevin said, heading back towards the airport. "Let's see what tomorrow may bring."

CHAPTER FIFTY-ONE

When Kevin arrived at the Macedonia Holiness Church with Signs Following, the parking lot was more crowded than he had seen it. Of course, this was only his second Sunday at the church and Ginny Lee had said more and more people were coming as they sensed the coming Darkness.

"Looks like a lot of folks today," Kevin said when Ginny Lee greeted him at the door.

"Lots of new folks," Ginny Lee said. "I think the storm has them scared."

Kevin had heard about the hurricane that was approaching but had paid little attention to it. Predictions were that it would strike sometime early Monday near New Orleans.

"Katrina is the name they've given it, right?" Kevin asked.

"That's right; they say it's going to be the worst hurricane we've seen in years. I know it's the work of Satan. Part of the coming Darkness," Ginny Lee insisted. "It doubled in size yesterday."

Kevin had heard it would be bad especially since most people were refusing to leave lower ground and the coastal areas for safer locations inland.

The band was already playing a worship song and Casper was performing at an awe inspiring level. His fingers seemed to fly across the strings and the fret board effortlessly. Where Chester normally sat was an empty chair holding only his guitar.

"It's a bit of a tribute," Ginny said, noticing where Kevin was looking. "I don't think we're going to mention it."

The Holiness Church didn't attract a lot of onlookers and everyone there was quickly caught up in the fervor of the worship music and prayer.

Kevin felt the pull of the Holy Spirit calling him to prayer but he kept watching for Woland and wondering if any of these women could be Ginny Lee's half-sister Emily Sue.

Scriptures were read and bodies gyrated to the entrancing rhythms and grooves laid down by Casper and his fellow band mates.

Kevin had joined the fray alongside Ginny Lee and prayed. He didn't know what Ginny Lee prayed for but he guessed it wasn't too different from his own prayers, nor from the prayers of the others that had come to worship that day. He needed God to intercede and help him bring an end to these horrific killings and turn the tide on the coming Darkness. People could feel the Dominion of Darkness rising.

Ver Dell grabbed a box sitting on the stage and reached in pulling out several timber rattlesnakes and began passing them out to those moved by the Holy Spirit. He laid one in Kevin's outstretched hands.

Kevin continued to pray.

"As long as it is day we must do the work of him who sent me. Night is coming when no one can work," a man's voice said in Kevin's ear.

Kevin turned but only Ginny Lee stood beside him still praying, but also holding a snake.

He looked around the room and saw that Woland had entered the back of the hall. He looked at Casper whose hands moved effortlessly across the guitar, but Casper's eyes were like daggers aimed at Woland.

Kevin began to swoon as visions began to swirl in his head. The swirling turned into a vision of a hurricane that grew stronger with each passing moment. He heard a demented laugh and turned to see a vision of unimaginable evil against the swirling blackness.

"I will not pass out," he ordered himself.

In his raised right hand the snake swayed. Ver Dell touched his shoulder and suddenly in Kevin's left hand flames burst forward.

"The glory of the Lord looked like a consuming fire," Ginny Lee hailed as in her hand a fire also burst forth.

Kevin began praying in tongues as visions swirled in his mind. Visions of the artwork he had seen at the Market Botanica and at Ginny Lee's house and even the painting he and Carlo had seen at Chester's house. They all seemed to blend together as one. Then he felt the same sensation he had had when he entered Peter Hannah's basement and recalled the background of the basement in the DVD the Apostle Serial Killer had left at Paige's door. Then he saw the fingers of the killer effortlessly slicing away at Peter Hannah's neck as he prepared for the decapitation accompanied by the driving guitar solo of the *Inna Gadda Da Vida*, and then flashed to the hands of Casper's incredible playing at that very moment. Suddenly, it all seemed perfectly clear yet it wasn't.

The music grew to a fever pitch and once again the Holy Spirit overcame Kevin and he fell back into the arms of the waiting Ver Dell.

When he opened his eyes all was quiet and he was alone on a cot in the back of the church. He sat up slowly and saw Ginny Lee and several others still praying in the front.

He looked around anxiously for Casper having remembered the vision he had right before he blacked out, but Casper along with the rest of the band was gone.

"How are you feeling?" Ginny Lee asked, coming back once she saw him sit up.

"I feel great," Kevin replied, "It's just that I don't like the part where I have to pass out to feel this way."

"The Holy Spirit works in mysterious ways. You were really moved by the Holy Spirit today. I've never seen you hold the fire before," Ginny Lee said. "You know every time you are 'slain in the Spirit' it is said you gain another gift or your gifts grow more powerful."

"I'd prefer to stay conscious with the gifts I already have," Kevin said.

"Were your prayers answered today?" Ginny Lee said.

"Why do you ask?" Kevin said.

"Because that's what I prayed for today. I prayed that God would show you the way to end this evil that is upon us. He revealed to me and to the others that you were sent as the warrior to stave off the coming Darkness. That is why we were still praying. I think your time at the Holiness Church has come to an end. I'm going to miss you, Kevin, but it is God's will," Ginny Lee said. She took his hands in hers and kissed them. "One day we will meet again." Ginny Lee turned and walked out the door.

Kevin sat there dumbfounded.

"What just happened?" he said to himself. Then he remembered his visions.

Everything seemed to point to Casper as the killer but Kevin knew first hand from a previous trip to an adjoining urinal that Casper was a male and he was positive the killer was Emily Sue Whitman, whoever and where ever she may be. Which led back to the multiple killer theory once again with Woland behind it.

As he was going through this in his head Ver Dell walked up.

"Woland da devil," Ver Dell said, "Devil jus tempt dem who weak. Neva' catch da devil." Ver Dell placed his hand on Kevin's head and said a prayer then picked up his box of snakes and headed out to the shed.

There had been several other people praying in the front but all of them except Ida had gone out through the front door. Ida was still praying. Kevin knew she too had something to say to him.

Kevin started to walk up to say goodbye to her but she hurriedly came back towards him.

"Sit back down," she said, 'Gots to tell ya sometin."

Kevin did as she asked.

"Ver Dell and I know it weren't Emily Sue buried out back. We promised Ginny Lee's momma neva to tell Ginny Lee what happened to Emily Sue."

"What did happen to Emily Sue? Kevin asked.

"Afta' da rape she all messed up. Her momma and daddy tried to talk her out of it but she went ta Sweden an' had a operation."

"What kind of operation?"

"Kind to make er a man. She had da 'gifts of da Spirit' but da devil gave er a 'deeds of da flesh' too," Ida said.

"So Casper Zemsta is Emily Sue Whitman?" Kevin said.

"Doncha eva' tell Ginny Lee," Ida warned.

"I promise," Kevin said.

"Butcha be careful. Casper got very pow'ful gifts and deeds that can hurtcha," Ida warned.

"I will be. And thanks," Kevin said, hugging Ida.

CHAPTER FIFTY-TWO

As Kevin headed back to Birmingham he knew he had to face Casper by himself. It was meant to be that way from the beginning. Casper could easily kill any of the agents or police sent to capture or kill him.

"Maybe if they blew up his house with him in it or had a dozen machine guns firing at once perhaps there was a chance, but such actions would be completely out of the question," Kevin said, in his usual discussions with himself when he was deeply troubled.

"I don't even know if I should tell Carlo," he said.

"No, I do need to let Carlo know what I'm doing, but he must guarantee not to send in the troops for at least an hour."

"The key thing is to get Simon safely out of there."

"Or is the key thing destroying Casper?" Kevin pondered.

His thoughts were interrupted by the ringing of his cell phone.

"Hey Kevin, Carlo wants to know if you're on your way back yet?" Paige asked.

"Hi Paige, is anybody else in the room?"

"No."

"Good, then put me on speaker phone. How are you feeling Carlo?" Kevin asked.

"Like I'm ready to leave this place," Carlo replied. "We came up with an interesting tidbit of information. Remember the Voodoo priest, Rastas Bartholomew Smith?"

"Of course, Kevin replied.

"He was at Jacksonville State the same year Emily Sue was raped," Paige said.

"We were thinking he might be the next victim," Carlo said, "and with the chance of New Orleans being wiped off the map tomorrow morning, we thought tonight might just be the time the Apostle Serial Killer would strike."

"You might be right about that," Kevin said, hesitantly.

"What is it you're not telling us? I've known you way to long and can tell when something big is on your mind. What is it?" Carlo asked.

"I've found Emily Sue Whitman," Kevin said.

"Alive?" Paige asked.

"Very much alive and I believe very much the Apostle Serial Killer," Kevin replied.

"Where is she?" Paige asked.

"Right here in Birmingham, but she is now a he. The years spent in Sweden were for a sex change operation. You can change the parts, but you can't change the DNA," Kevin said.

"Well who is she or he?" Carlo asked.

"The man who saved your life, Casper Zemsta," Kevin replied.

"I don't believe it," Paige said. "How do you know for sure?"

"Actually, several things. I recognized the hands from the DVD as the same hands that held mine on Carlo's neck. The same hands I watched move flawlessly across the guitar at church. Then there were the paintings. The one at the Market Botanica, at Chester's house, and one I saw yesterday at Ginny Lee's house. All incredible works that I knew were done by the same master painter. As it turns out, that painter was Casper. Ginny Lee said he became wealthy selling his art and lives in a mansion in Redmont Park. That's the same area that Peter Hannah lived in. When I went to Peter's house last night I felt like I had seen the basement before and today realized it was very similar to the basement in the DVD," Kevin explained.

"Wow! That's some amazing investigative work," Paige said.

"Don't be too impressed because ten minutes after I had this vision and put it all together, Ida, one of the old women at the church, came and told me the story about Emily Sue's sex change operation," Kevin admitted.

"It doesn't matter how we found out, what matters is now we can send up agents and have him arrested and the killing spree will be over," Carlo said.

"Not quite yet," Kevin stated.

"What do you mean? Why not?" Paige and Carlo both asked.

"Paige, you saw what Casper did for Carlo. Do you think that was normal?" Kevin asked.

"Not in the least, it was miraculous, beyond human capabilities," she replied.

"Exactly! And Carlo, you saw the video of the person moving objects with the flick of their hand and knocking down people by raising their hand. Can a normal human being do that?" Kevin reminded him.

"No they can't," Carlo admitted.

"And somehow Casper had the power to cloud Chester's mind so badly he was willing to dump Peter Talbot's body, possibly even kill Peter Talbot, and then kill himself by driving into the State Trooper roadblock. Is a normal human capable of such powers?" Kevin asked them both again.

"So Casper has these superhuman powers?" Carlo asked.

"They are called 'gifts of the Spirit' when given by God and the Holy Spirit and cannot be taken away. He also has been given 'deeds of the flesh' which are also very powerful gifts not from God, but from Satan," Kevin explained.

"You're really starting to scare me," Paige said.

"It should scare you. Evil is a very scary proposition. The Devil does exist and really does want your soul," Kevin warned.

"So I know you've got a plan or you wouldn't be telling us all this," Carlo said.

"I do," Kevin replied. "If you remember before we left Los Angeles we visited with Charlotte at the Experimental Forest. She forewarned me about a spiritual battle I was soon going to fight and she said I would be prepared for that battle."

"And have you been?" Carlo asked.

"Ginny Lee seems to think so. I've been 'slain in the Spirit' three times this week and received 'Gifts of the Holy Spirit' each time. At least that is what I've been told," Kevin explained.

"What are these gifts?" Paige asked.

"I know I've been given the gift of speaking in tongues and the gift of healing," Kevin said. "I pray I have been given the gift of miracles and miraculous powers because I'm going to have to face Casper by myself."

"You can't do that," Carlo yelled.

"No, I have to do that," Kevin replied sharply, "and you need to understand that."

"What do you want me to do?" Carlo said.

"I could use all the prayer you can manage, but I think Ginny Lee has that covered, so I'm going to need you to wait one hour after I enter the house and I mean one hour not a second sooner, and then send every FBI agent, Alabama State Trooper, and Birmingham Police officer you can to that house. I don't even mind if you climb out of bed and hobble there," Kevin exclaimed. "Any questions?"

"I'll do exactly what you said to do," Carlo replied.

"I'll call you right before I enter the house. That's when you start the clock. Promise me you'll do nothing stupid."

"I promise," Carlo said.

Paige, I expect you to make him keep that promise," Kevin added.

"I will," Paige replied. "Good luck."

CHAPTER FIFTY-THREE

Having the address and daylight made finding Casper's house much simpler than his random wanderings the previous evening. Kevin had decided the best approach was to walk right up to the house and start up a conversation and see where it led.

He pushed redial on his phone as he pulled into the driveway.

"Start the clock, I'm heading in," he said and quickly hung up before Carlo could give him any advice or try to talk him out of it.

Kevin tried to park his car to block Casper's van from leaving but the size of the driveway made it impossible.

He climbed out of the car and headed for the door.

"I should be back by tomorrow evening," Casper explained to Simon.

"Aren't you taking your table? How will you delight in his horror without your table?" Simon sneered.

"Like I said before, I doubt he will survive the flaying," Casper replied.

Casper carried a medical bag and boom box through the back basement door and into the garage area. Simon could hear him loading what sounded like another wooden cross into the vehicle, but this time he didn't hear the familiar sliding doors but the sound of two doors closing.

"Not taking your van this trip?" Simon said.

"I see you've taken an interest in my vehicles. I have several you know," Casper replied.

"It's just I didn't hear you pull…"

They were interrupted by a pounding on the door above them and then the ringing of a doorbell.

A worried look crossed Casper's face.

"Expecting company?" Simon smiled.

"Y-you h-hold your t-tongue, or y-you c-can b-be sure I will," Casper stuttered and began to twitch.

Simon wanted to press him knowing the surprise visitor had made him nervous, but pushing him too soon would limit his ability to scream later if the opportunity arose.

Casper hurried to the stairs then paused contemplating not even answering, but then the pounding started again.

"Anybody home?" a voice must have boomed, but was barely heard in the confines of the basement.

"Oh my," Casper said, and scurried up the steps.

Simon could sense his prayers were being answered.

"Where do you think you're going?" Paige said to Carlo as he climbed out of bed and began to dress.

"To go help Kevin of course," he replied.

"You heard what he said. Under no circumstances are you to get involved…"

"You can save your breath," Carlo interrupted, "Kevin's my partner and there is no way I would let him face the Apostle Serial Killer alone."

"Then I'm coming too," Paige insisted.

"Of course you are, you have to drive, but you're not going anywhere near the house. You have to call for back-up at exactly one hour as Kevin ordered," Carlo explained.

"And where will you be?" Paige asked.

"Covering Kevin's back God willing," Carlo replied. "Let's go."

"Easy on the leg, it may be healed but it's still very weak," Paige reminded him.

Kevin pounded on the door once again and put his ear near the door. He could hear faint footsteps approaching.

"Yes what is it?" a gruff voiced Casper asked.

"Hello Casper," Kevin said. "I've come to have a word with you."

"I'm really busy right now, perhaps you could come back at another time," Casper replied.

"No, that's not possible. I saw one of your paintings at Ginny Lee's house. It was a portrait of her mother and father standing inside the Sistine Chapel. You're as great a painter as you are a guitar player, truly gifted."

"Thank you, but I presume you didn't come here to discuss my artistic talents," Casper replied.

"No I didn't," Kevin replied. "May I come in?"

"Are you sure you want to?" Casper said.

"I have no choice," Kevin replied.

"Then by all means please come in."

As he opened the door for Kevin he scanned his property making sure no others were approaching. He saw no humans but saw glimmers coming from within the greenery of several of the trees scattered throughout his property.

Below in the basement Simon could hear the muttering of voices and then two sets of footsteps on the floor above. He wasn't sure what to make of this. The knocking had caught the killer by surprise yet the killer had allowed the guest into the house. Simon was afraid that would not bode well for whoever had just interrupted the killer's plan.

"Tell me about Woland." Kevin asked, catching Casper by surprise.
"Woland? Why do you want to know about Woland?" Casper replied.
"I could see in your eyes that you have a hatred for him, yet you seem beholden to him at the same time. I guess my question is which one of you is the Master?" Kevin challenged.
"I-I d-don't know what you m-mean," Casper replied, beginning to twitch.
"Casper, I know all you really want is peace. Peace from the awful memory of what happened to you thirty-five years ago. Peace from your parents turning against you for your choice. Peace from the temptations Woland lured you with. You knew all along he planned it from the beginning," Kevin challenged.
"Sh-shut up, Sh- *glorybedaGoda* shut *shamnada hydakom* sh-shut up," Casper screamed, his body now jerking violently.

Suddenly, a buzz filled the air and Kevin turned to listen. He realized it wasn't a buzz but the sound of voices praying in tongues.

Kevin peered through the open door at the dozens if not hundreds of worshipers who were on their knees in the front yard all with their hands raised praying to the Holy Spirit and to God.

"No!" Casper screamed and raised his hand to slam the front door, but Kevin raised his to stop it.

"You're to w-weak," Casper cried, and the door shut but not with the force he anticipated. A shocked look came over his face.

"I may be weak but with every prayer I grow stronger," Kevin replied, "and waved his hand opening the door.

"The Darkness has grown too strong," Casper screamed, recovering from his violent jerks. He pushed his hand towards Kevin, knocking him down and back into the wall. Kevin, using every bit of energy he could manage, stood against the powerful force pushing against him.

"Enough of this," Casper spat and cupped his hand as he had so often done before causing Kevin to feel an extreme choking grip on his throat.

As the others had done before him Kevin's hand shot to his own throat trying to stop the crushing before it was too late.

"Time to die," Casper said, but suddenly the prayers seemed to grow louder. Kevin began to peel the imaginary fingers off of his throat one at a time. As he did so Casper's fingers would shoot out straight as if suddenly shocked.

Casper knew he had to get away from the house. The prayer warriors weakened him and strengthened Kevin. Just before Kevin could pull the last two fingers from his neck, Casper used his remaining power and hurled a giant antique oak cabinet across the room smashing it into Kevin.

When Kevin went down Casper ran to the basement stairs locking the door from the inside and hurried down.

The prayers of the warriors seemed to resonate even louder in the basement.

"Sounds to me like God's shown up for the battle," Simon said. "There must be hundreds of them outside. I guess you're reign of terror is over."

"Not quite yet," Casper replied, "How about a little more terror for you."

Casper grabbed the box holding the snakes from the shelf and threw it hard against the side of Simon's cage shattering the box and throwing four timber rattlesnakes into the cage with Simon. Immediately he was bitten twice.

"Till we meet again," Casper said and hurried through the back door into the garage.

Almost immediately Kevin burst through the locked door and hurried down the stairs.

"Help me," Simon wheezed as a third rattlesnake sank its fangs deep in his leg.

Kevin heard the whirr of a garage door opening and the rumble as a large V-8 engine powered up. He knew he would be too late to stop Casper, but he still had time to save Simon.

He grabbed another wooden box and hurried over to the cage raising his own hand and opening the cage the same way Casper had done so often. Without hesitation he picked up each of the snakes, knowing the Holy Spirit would protect him and placed the snakes in the wooden box and sat it outside the cage.

Simon had lost consciousness but Kevin lifted him in his arms and carried him out of the cage and up into the living room. He knew it would take a lot of prayer to save Simon.

"What's going on?" Paige said as they came to a sudden stop over five blocks from Casper's house. "What are all these cars doing here?"

Someone else must have had the same concern at all the cars sitting empty blocking the streets for a police car pulled up behind Carlo and Paige.

"I don't know but it looks like we're walking from here," Carlo said, pulling out his emergency light and sitting it atop the car.

"What's going on? The policeman asked.

"I'm not sure but I'll go find out." Carlo told the officer as he flashed his FBI credentials.

"You stay here," Carlo ordered Paige. "Twenty more minutes."

"Are you sure?" Paige asked.

"That's what he said," Carlo replied heading up the road.

An ambulance pulled up a side road behind the police car and seeing all the traffic turned and headed back towards downtown.

The empty cars clogged the road all the way to Casper's and as Carlo approached he saw the reason. Hundreds of people were gathered on Casper's front lawn praying. The door was ajar and he rushed into the house gun drawn.

Kevin was standing in the living room holding the limp body of Simon praying in a language Carlo had never heard.

"Shang di, ni sh wei da quan neng de wo ba Ximeng Xiong di jiao tuo gei ni, zai tax u yao de she hou.
Ta zai wie e zhi ren de shou zhong shou le ji da de ku chu,
Xian zai ypu zao shou du de yao shang.
Wo qing qiu ni shi yong wo lai jin xing zhe shen qi de liao zhi.
Wo yi ni shen sheng de ming dao gao.
A men

As Kevin prayed he touched the three separate bite marks left by the rattlesnakes. Carlo could see he was growing weak and stood next to Kevin supporting both Kevin and Simon. Carlo recognized the word Amen and lifted Simon's body from Kevin and laid it on the couch as Kevin seemed to collapse back against the wall.

"Kevin are you okay?" Carlo called out.

"I will be," Kevin replied. "Call in the troops. Casper got away."

Carlo called Paige and told her to contact the FBI only and request an ambulance for Simon.

"Thank you, thank you," a weak but recovering Simon wheezed softly. He waved Kevin to come to him.

"Are you the one God sent?" Simon whispered.

"I am," Kevin replied softly gently stroking Simon's head.

"Kevin, you're Kevin Bridges. The Lord has sent a worthy warrior. He's headed to New Orleans," Simon said.

"I know, but don't tell the others. There is nothing they can do. This is a battle only I can fight."

Simon squeezed his hand knowingly.

"The chalices are in the safe in the basement," Simon said. "He must not get a hold of them."

"We won't let that happen," Carlo said coming over to see how Simon was doing.

"Carlo Caressa, thank you," Simon said, recognizing another agent.

"I've got to get those people to move their cars," Carlo said. "There's no way for an ambulance to get up here."

Carlo headed out the door but was surprised to see only a few of the hundreds who had come to pray still remained and they were climbing in the closer cars waiting as the traffic was quickly clearing away. Paige was even pulling into the driveway in the Trans Am.

"Who were all those people?" Paige asked.

"Prayer warriors," Kevin replied.

"Where'd they come from?"

"All over the area I guess," Kevin replied.

"How'd they know to come here at this exact time?" Carlo asked.

"That's one of those questions only God can answer," Kevin replied.

"What happened to Casper?" Paige asked.

"He got away. It was either chase after him or save Simon. He had a car waiting and took off out the back," Kevin said.

"What kind of car? We can get everybody looking for it," Carlo stated.

"That's not a good idea," Kevin said.

"I had all these people praying for me and I still was barely able to keep him from killing me and trust me, the Holy Spirit has been very generous with me as far as gifts are concerned," Kevin explained.

"I can vouch for that," Simon whispered, "Kevin just brought me back from the brink of death."

"Healing the sick is one thing, fighting a killer with supernatural powers is another," Carlo said.

"I'm the only one who can," Kevin replied.

"Not alone, not this time," Carlo said.

Kevin raised his hand and used his gift to gently push Carlo back against the far wall then up the wall.

"That's not funny, Kevin. You could reinjure his leg," Paige cried.

"Just trying to prove a point," Kevin said, slowly lowering Carlo to the floor. "Now do you believe me that I'm the only one who can do this?"

"I'm not quite sure what to believe anymore. How did you do that?" Carlo gasped.

"I didn't. It was the power of the Holy Spirit running through me. I need your car before any of the other agents get here," Kevin said.

"Do you know where Casper went?" Paige asked.

"I do, but I won't tell you," Kevin replied. "I need to do this alone."

Paige handed him the keys.

"Stay here and supervise the scene. Make sure Simon is safe and protect the chalices," Kevin asked.

"What do we tell them about you?" Carlo asked.

"Tell them I went after Casper."

They'll have Casper's picture to every agency in the South within the hour and if you don't call in they'll have an all points on your car," Carlo warned.

"Katrina has everyone too busy to be looking for Casper," Kevin replied, "and just don't let them know I took your car."

"You know they'll eventually figure it out," Carlo said.

"I know, but that's why I need you to stay in charge here for as long as you can to give me some time," Kevin replied.

"How much time?" Carlo asked.

Kevin looked at this watch. It was almost five o'clock.

"See if you can hold them back till midnight," Kevin asked, "That should give me more than enough time."

"I'll see what I can do," Carlo said, as the wailing of sirens could be heard in the distance.

"Thanks," Kevin said, and hurried out the door."

"Are you ready for that exclusive I promised you," Carlo said.

"Exclusives just don't seem to matter that much anymore," Paige replied, getting a moist towel for Simon's exposed eyes.

CHAPTER FIFTY-FOUR

Just as Casper expected, nobody paid attention to an ambulance hurrying down the freeway towards New Orleans. Nor was he stopped at any of the roadblocks steering traffic away from the coastal communities.

"What fools," Casper gloated. New Orleans was destined to be the marrow of the evil one's coming Darkness and yet they had only now begun to evacuate the city. Far too little, far too late, but they have brought it upon themselves. Evil had long had a foothold and the Darkness had grown strong and now it was Satan's time to reign.

Casper knew he could never go back, but he had known that from the beginning. Anger and revenge, two emotions exploited by Satan, had entrapped Emily Sue Whitman into a hellish spiral that had led her to become a him and now to this.

It is so ironic that one so devout and so gifted was the one so vulnerable to Satan's attacks and temptations.

Casper was driven to continue his scourge. Bartholomew must be sacrificed before the storm rips him from Casper's grip. It was Satan's way of letting Casper know that he was still in charge.

Five more still had to pay for what they had done to Emily Sue. Satan's perverse plan of having her raped by boys who shared their names with the Apostles seemed ludicrous, but Casper knew that once the chalices were complete, a greater evil awaited.

It was close to ten o'clock when Casper approached the outskirts of New Orleans. Only twelve hours earlier Mayor Ray Nagin had ordered the mandatory evacuation of the city and now the freeways were jammed with those trying to escape the impending devastation. Casper knew Bartholomew would not be among those to flee. He had invested too much into Market Botanica to allow the looters to take what he had worked so many years to create. As a prominent Voodoo houngan, his presence alone would be enough to deter most anyone bent on plunder.

The going was very slow and even with the siren people didn't move out of Casper's way. Fear had gripped the city and those that could were struggling to leave before it was too late.

When Casper did finally arrive at the Market Botanica on Reynes Street in the Lower Ninth Ward he was not surprised to find it still open. Several people were rushing to get the juju they needed to help protect them and their families from Katrina. Mr. Bart, as he called himself, was more than happy to sell it to them, even at this late hour.

Casper entered the store and it was as if an evil dark pall had covered the market. Almost simultaneously everyone looked up as if a death toll had sounded in the distance. Several customers dropped what they were looking at and rushed out of the market. Bartholomew hurried through the curtain from the back room fearful of what he was about to face.

"Hello Bartholomew," Casper softly greeted.

"C-Casper, what brings you here in such troubled times?" Bartholomew asked.

"I came for my chalice," Casper replied.

"I-I no longer have it. It was taken from me by the FBI. Didn't you read about it in the paper?" Bartholomew asked.

As they talked, the remaining customers still in the store all hurried out the door. These were the real practitioners of Voodoo, all finely attuned to the darker side of the occult and all well aware when true evil was present. Evil in which none of them wished to confront.

"Did you tell them where you got it?" Casper asked.

"Of course not," Bartholomew answered, beginning to sweat.

None of this really mattered to Casper; he was just giving the customers time to leave.

"Let's go to your house and talk," Casper said.

"I can't leave my store," Bartholomew pleaded.

Casper raised his hand and Bartholomew began to choke.

"I just want to go to your house and talk, don't make me kill you," Casper said, lifting Bartholomew off the ground and dropping him with just the movement of his hand.

Casper heard several gasps and turned to the door as several of the customers who had left the store but stayed near the doorway now ran for their lives in abject fear.

Bartholomew resolutely picked himself up off the floor and headed for the door.

"I'll drive," Casper said. "It's the ambulance parked right in front."

The rain was relentless as Kevin barreled down Interstate-59 through Mississippi as was the stream of vehicles heading away from the coast.

"Thank God I ordered Carlo the Trans Am," Kevin said, "the Nova couldn't have made this trip."

The emergency light and siren were also a big help in speeding Kevin along his way.

Kevin knew he would be arriving in New Orleans only hours before Katrina was due to hit the city, or at least near the city. No one was really sure where it would actually make landfall, but it was so large it wouldn't make much difference. The devastation would be horrendous regardless.

Kevin's concern was not for the impending apocalypse of Katrina but the even more foreboding evil that awaited him at either Market Botanica or Bartholomew's house. He knew Satan's servant Casper was at this very moment growing stronger as he prepared to sacrifice another victim in his string of Apostle serial killings.

Kevin knew these were more than simple revenge killings for Emily Sue Whitman's rape. This was an orchestrated scheme developed over the past fifty years by Satan beginning with the birth and naming of the victims. It wasn't by chance that they all ended up at that fraternity on that one night when Emily Sue Whitman was there. All of them were brought together for one purpose.

"Just what is that purpose?" Kevin pondered.

"Woland has overseen this for all of these years, why would he let it fall apart now?" Kevin asked himself.

Then he realized Woland hadn't let it fall apart. He had done all he could to try to save it.

"It is the Holy Spirit that has shattered Satan's plan," Kevin realized.

"It is all the prayer warriors and all the true believers who have come to fight the coming Darkness who have disrupted Satan's plan," Kevin said.

"And it's me," he suddenly realized. "Charlotte told me God has glorious plans for me and even Ginny Lee said I was the warrior sent to stave off the coming Darkness."

With renewed confidence Kevin pushed the gas pedal to the floor.

"With God on my side, who can stand against me?"

"Agent Caressa, what happened to Agent Bridges?" Supervising Agent Billings asked.

"He is investigating where he believed the Apostle Serial Killer may have escaped to," Carlo replied.

"By himself?" Billings replied.

"I believe that's why he works undercover," Carlo replied, "in order to not draw attention to what he is doing."

"Well from what I've heard happened here, several hundred people seemed to be drawn to what he was up to," Billings replied harshly.

"They were here to help him," Simon wheezed as the paramedics prepared to remove him.

"What are you talking about?" Billings said.

"The Apostle Serial Killer is not a normal human being. He is a servant of Satan and has extraordinary powers," Simon replied.

"Take him out of here," Billings ordered. "He's delirious."

"This case has had its share of supernatural occurrences and miracles," Carlo added. "If you recall two days ago I was given up for dead until our alleged killer removed the bullet from my spinal cord with prayer and his fingers."

"And then that church lady healed his broken leg in a matter of minutes," Paige added.

"I got a call from the doctor about that. He wanted to know what secret medical breakthroughs the government was keeping from the public. He started making all sorts of threats. I had to have him brought in and sign a declaration of secrecy to shut the guy up. I still don't know what all he was raving about," Billings complained.

"You saw the initial video when Simon was captured and the power the killer had then," Carlo said. "Well it's grown substantially."

"This whole case just doesn't make any sense to me," Billings declared.

"Trust me, this is a case that only Kevin can solve and I'm confident he will," Carlo replied.

"He damn well better," Billings replied, storming out of the house.

"That went well," Paige joked.

"I just pray that Kevin knows what he's doing," Carlo replied.

"Aren't you going to help him?" Paige asked.

"Not this time. I wouldn't know where to go or what to do when I got there," Carlo replied.

"We know he went to New Orleans," Paige said. "We should head there."

"Not with Katrina about to hit the city. If you want to help Kevin you should think about praying," Carlo said.

"Last week I would have laughed at you for telling me that," Paige replied. "Today I think I'll pray."

Kevin knew he couldn't be far behind when he reached Slidell, Louisiana. Casper couldn't have driven as fast as Kevin and Casper had less than an hour head start. What Kevin didn't like was the roadblock set up across all lanes of the I-10 in front of him.

"I'm in a big hurry officer," Kevin said, holding up his credentials, "I really need to get to New Orleans."

"You won't be doing it on this freeway," the officer replied. "We just shut her down."

"It's an emergency. I have to get through," Kevin repeated.

"That won't be possible sir. Katrina has taken out several sections of the bridge. Nobody's going this way for a long time."

"Did any cars get through in the past hour?" Kevin asked.

"No sir, it's been closed. Only emergency vehicles have been allowed on it since around seven," the officer replied.

"Have you been here the entire time?" Kevin asked.

"Yes sir."

"Did anything unusual come through here?" Kevin asked.

"Sir, there's been all sorts of unusual vehicles coming through here. Buses, ambulances, heavy equipment, boats, you name it, it's headed for New Orleans."

"Thanks," Kevin said, "Any suggestions on how I can get into the city?"

"They're still allowing emergency vehicles to use the Lake Pontchartrain Causeway," the officer replied. "It's about forty minutes up the I-12 in this weather and traffic."

"Thanks," Kevin said.

"I think I'm going to be late," Kevin said, wondering just what it was he was going to be late for.

CHAPTER FIFTY-FIVE

The rain had been coming down steadily for several hours and the wind had begun to howl. The streets were already flooded as were the yards of many of the houses in the Lower Ninth Ward including Bartholomew's on Tennessee Avenue. There was nowhere for the water to go since New Orleans was below the water level of the lakes, rivers, and canals that surrounded the city.

Casper pulled the ambulance into the driveway up near the garage. The many trees and bushes that surrounded the house hid the ambulance from view.

"You carry the cross," Casper ordered Bartholomew. "After all, Christ had to carry his own, it's the least you can do."

Bartholomew was too dazed to complain or fight. He could still feel the pressure of that choking grip still stinging his neck. Any ideas of fleeing were soon dismissed when Casper opened the doors with just a flick of his hand and then tossed a large broken limb out of their path with a flick of a finger. Even a Voodoo priest as powerful as Bartholomew knew that a greater evil than he had ever known was now present and in control.

"We must hurry," Casper said, "I must be away from here by the morning."

The forty minutes Kevin expected turned into an hour and twenty minutes just to reach the causeway. Once there he had to wait in line while several dozen emergency vehicles in front of him were cleared to cross over into

New Orleans. Once on the causeway it was slow going as the wind raged and the water whipped across the road before him.

"This is going to take forever," Kevin said, as the pace grew ever slower as the winds grew stronger.

It was 4:00 a.m. by the time Kevin reached the I-10 freeway once again. Even at this early hour the freeway was crowded as people still were trying to flee the city. Kevin thought trying to navigate the surface streets would prove even more difficult so he decided to stick with the I-10 until he had to exit.

He finally exited at Elysian Fields which he knew would take him to Florida Avenue. From there it would be a straight shot over to the Lower Ninth Ward and the Market Botanica.

"Uh-oh," Kevin said as he turned East onto Florida Avenue.

Water was starting to creep over the roadway.

"That's more than just rain accumulation," Kevin said. "The canals must be starting to leak."

In fact the rising water in the Industrial Canal had begun leaking into neighborhoods along both sides of the canal, but it was only the beginning.

The water lapped at the bridge as Kevin crossed the canal into the Lower Ninth Ward. Water filled the streets here as well but Kevin knew it was only a matter of time before things became much worse.

When he reached the Market Botanica the door was open and looters were helping themselves to anything and everything in the store. Kevin was not looking for a confrontation with the looters but did have to search the store. The flashing light on his car didn't exactly promise him a warm welcome.

Several people hurried away when they saw him arrive but several others took a defiant stand.

"Whatchu want mon?" a dreadlocked man said stepping up in front of a small group of looters.

"Just looking for Mr. Bart," Kevin said.

"Mr. Bart not here, he put me in charge." Several in the group laughed.

"I'll just have a look for myself if you don't mind," Kevin said headed for the door.

"We kina do mind, mon," the leader replied. "You got a problem with that?"

Kevin raised his arm and using his gifts swept the entire group of men off their feet and into the street.

"Ayibobo," several of the men screamed, calling to their Voodoo god, "It is the devil himself."

The men wanted no part of who they perceived as the devil and scrambled over each other trying to escape.

Others who had witnessed the interaction decided looting could wait and disappeared quickly into the raging storm.

It didn't take Kevin long to realize Bartholomew wasn't in the market. As he searched the basement he saw the empty space where the chalice had sat for so many years. He checked the snake pit which was quickly filling with water and saw that there was one rattlesnake still inside.

"I can't leave you here to die," Kevin said pulling a box from the shelf and lifting the snake from the pit with the hook and placing it in the box.

When Kevin returned upstairs, so had some of the looters.

"Desperate times require desperate measures," he thought as he saw several mothers with young children grabbing powdered milk and water.

"God help them," Kevin said, as he hurried out to his car.

When Kevin turned onto Tennessee Street he saw the same dreadlocked man that had challenged him at the market. Kevin pulled up in front of him and waved him over to the car.

"Come here, I won't hurt you," Kevin assured him. "I remember you. You're the same drug-dealing punk that tried to run me out of here last week."

"Sorry mon," the kid held his head down not wanting to make eye contact.

"Which house is Mr. Bart's?" Kevin asked, unable to remember or even read addresses in the howling storm.

"Dat one der mon, da one wit all da trees," he replied.

"Get out of here before the storm gets any worse," Kevin advised.

The man turned and ran down the street wanting nothing more to do with the white devil.

Kevin pulled in the drive and almost ran into the back of the ambulance.

"So that's how he got through all the road blocks," Kevin said.

The yard was already flooded and water was starting to seep into the first floor of Bartholomew's two story house.

Kevin climbed out of the car bringing the snake with him.

"I imagine Casper will be expecting me," Kevin said, "but I see no need to go announcing my arrival."

He entered the house slowly and was immediately met with a macabre scene. A gurney was positioned in the middle of the living room and pinned to the wall was the just flayed skin of Bartholomew. It had come off in pieces. As to the order, Kevin couldn't tell. It appeared to have been constructed from the feet up, with each extremity carefully peeled of the outer epidermis. The torso was in one giant piece precisely sliced away from the dermis never even close to approaching the subcutaneous layer.

The head was done somewhat differently. Bartholomew had not survived the flaying of the lower portion of his body. At least Kevin prayed he had not, for Casper had diligently peeled the head as close to the bone as possible including Bartholomew's full scalp. It was a truly sickening sight crucified upon the wall.

Kevin knew even more horrific sights waited for him elsewhere in the house.

On the stove sat an empty pot that once held Bartholomew's skull. Casper had chosen a hot water maceration to rid the skull of any unwanted tissue and to rush his ritual. He too knew the fury of the Darkness that was upon the land and knew he must be gone before the brunt of its ferocity struck.

With snake in hand Kevin headed to the second floor but found it empty. A staircase led to the roof and the door was open beckoning Kevin upward.

The rain had stopped and when Kevin reached the roof he found Casper sitting serenely next to the headless, flayed bloody mass that once was Bartholomew now crucified upside down on the roof of his own home. On a table in front of him sat a chalice already constructed from Bartholomew's skull.

"Isn't it wonderful," Casper rejoiced as the Darkness swirled and howled around them.

"The dawn is on the horizon," Kevin replied.

"Yes, but this dawn will bring unimaginable terror," Casper crowed.

"But your reign of terror is over," Kevin replied.

"No, my reign of terror has only just begun," Casper stated.

"I'm here to end that reign," Kevin declared.

"You must realize by now I'm much stronger than you even with your legion of prayer warriors. By the way where are they, were they afraid of a little storm?" Casper joked.

"I no longer need them," Kevin replied.

"Oh I see you came to fight me with a snake. As you can see I have several slithering around the roof already," Casper noted.

"Don't you see you are just a slave to the puppet master Woland? He arranged all of this before you were born," Kevin challenged.

"Then it is my destiny," Casper replied.

"Evil is never a man's destiny," Kevin declared. "You make that choice. Our Lord Jesus Christ will forgive you for all of your sins no matter how heinous they may be. All you have to do is accept him as your savior."

"Yes but man will not forgive and I don't choose to spend the rest of my life in prison," Casper replied.

"So you'd rather spend eternity in Hell?" Kevin asked.

"Who's to say your God will always be the one making the decisions? Your God revealed his plan through his apostles and prophets and now my Lord Satan prepares to reveal himself through his apostles," Casper said pointing to the chalice. "Like you said, he has planned this for many years."

"And now it is time to end it," Kevin said raising the snake above his head.

As he did so the snake turned into a glistening white sword. With one swift movement he cleaved the Chalice made from Bartholomew's skull cleanly in two.

"No," Casper screamed, grabbing a snake which also turned into a sword and striking Kevin in the arm opening a deep gash.

"What have you done?" Casper swung again smashing the sword from Kevin's hand then swung around slicing Kevin's calf. Kevin was hobbled but managed to duck the next few swings. The Darkness sensed it had been attacked and hail began to pelt the ground. Lightning flashed and the wind grew even stronger. Branches began to rip from trees and roof tops peeled away flying through the air.

"You've ruined everything," Casper cried. "The ritual cannot be completed."

He swung again smashing his sword into Kevin's shoulder. Fortunately, the broad side of the blade hit first separating this shoulder rather than shearing it from his torso.

Kevin was helpless when a scripture came to him and he shouted it out, *"The LORD will cause men to hear* his majestic voice and will make them see his arm coming down with raging anger and consuming fire, with cloudburst, thunderstorm and hail."

Casper raised his sword for the killing blow when a bolt of lightning struck his sword just like the scripture said. Casper burst into flames in God's all-consuming fire of raging anger.

Kevin stared in disbelief as Casper screamed," *J-J-Jesus - can't take me, 'the M-M-Master does not deserve the light, h-he deserves p-p-peace'.*" His body began to jerk and twitch as it continued to blaze.

Kevin wasn't about to take any chances and picked up his sword and ran it into Casper's side then fell back exhausted as Casper's body collapsed to the rooftop. The hail had turned to rain but the body continued to burn as Kevin sat exhausted bleeding and watching. The clouds had lightened meaning somewhere behind the Darkness the sun was shining, but the storm was only beginning to rage.

As the flames that had consumed Casper's body began to flicker out, Kevin knew he needed to leave quickly. The loss of blood was beginning to take its toll and the Holy Spirit told him he must leave immediately.

The wind had increased as had the rain. Kevin picked up the sword and ran down the stairs to his Trans Am. He stumbled as he approached the car growing light-headed from his loss of blood.

As he climbed in his car he looked at his dashboard clock. Seven forty-three. He headed South on Tennessee Avenue only because that was the direction he was facing when he backed out of the driveway. He had barely gone four blocks when the clock turned to seven forty-five and two of the floodwall sections on the eastside of the Industrial Canal failed, releasing walls of water tearing through the Lower Ninth Ward tossing cars and houses off their foundations as if they were toys.

In his rear view mirror Kevin saw the oncoming onslaught and floored the gas pedal reaching the Claiborne Avenue bridge just as debris rushed past his rear bumper.

Bartholomew's house and those of all of his neighbors had disappeared, but Kevin had no time to consider what was occurring for his strength was quickly ebbing as the blood continued to flow from the wounds Casper had inflicted.

Kevin drove on through the howling winds guided by the Holy Spirit until he found himself at the St. Louis Cathedral at Jackson Square.

He staggered from his car, sword in hand and pounded upon the massive doors until someone finally opened them.

"I'm sorry, but you must seek shelter ..." The resident reverend began to say.

"Please, I need prayer," Kevin whispered.

"You're injured," the reverend said.

"I've been in a spiritual battle and need prayer," Kevin repeated.

"You need to a doctor."

"No, I need prayer," Kevin insisted. "Please pray with me."

The reverend grabbed Kevin's arm and lifted him up causing the sword to fall to the ground. He jumped back almost dropping Kevin.

"Do not be afraid," Kevin said, laying his hand on the reverend's head.

Suddenly, the reverend felt a total sense of peace.

"Now, I understand," he replied, picking up the sword and helping Kevin inside.

"Lay your hands on my wounds," Kevin instructed and pray with me.

The reverend did as Kevin said and as they prayed the wounds seemed to heal before him. Tears filled his eyes.

"I've never seen God work such miracles before in my presence. I've always believed but now I know," the reverend said as he continued to weep.

"Who are you?" he asked.

"I am just one of God's many warriors seeking spiritual healing," Kevin replied. "I need to rest."

The resident reverend helped Kevin to a room that had a small cot in it and Kevin lay down. He slept for two days.

CHAPTER FIFTY-SIX

Casper's house was one of stark contrast. Upstairs were rooms filled with museum quality artwork which undoubtedly would bring a fortune on the open market, while downstairs was his chamber of horrors.

No one from the Birmingham office was able to open Casper's massive safe nor were there any local qualified safecrackers up to the task so an expert was being sent in from Washington D.C. to handle that duty.

Katrina had made landfall and now Birmingham was inundated by heavy rain and winds.

For the next two days Carlo supervised the search of Casper's house, but the entire time his attention waned as he constantly wondered where and what Kevin was up too.

"New Orleans is in shambles right now," Paige reminded him, "I'm sure Kevin will contact you as soon as he is able." But even Paige doubted Kevin had succeeded in stopping Casper.

By Wednesday morning Carlo was on the verge of commandeering a helicopter and personally searching New Orleans when he received a most unusual phone call.

"Good day, I am Father Oder. I work for the Doctrinal Office at the Vatican. Is this Agent Carlo Caressa with the FBI?" Father Oder asked.

"Yes it is, how can I help you Father?" Carlo replied.

"It seems one of your agents has been under our care at the St. Louis Cathedral in New Orleans for the past two days."

"Kevin Bridges is with you? Is he safe?" Carlo asked excitedly.

"Not with me personally. I'm in Rome, but he is safe with several members of our staff there," he explained. "I do know he was seriously injured when he first arrived but his injuries seemed to miraculously heal themselves when he and the reverend began to pray. That is part of the reason I called. Is this self-healing something he does often?"

"No, Kevin just recently has received Gifts from the Holy Spirit. One of those gifts is healing. He has some other powerful gifts as well," Carlo replied.

"Why did the Holy Spirit grant him such Gifts?" Father Oder asked.

"Kevin was chosen to lead a spiritual battle against one of Satan's most powerful demons here in Alabama. They called him the Apostle Serial Killer," Carlo replied.

"I read about this man," the Father replied.

"Believe me, he was more than a man. He had unimaginable powers given to him by Satan. I witnessed them firsthand," Carlo said.

"And you say Kevin Bridges was God's spiritual warrior sent to battle him?" Father Oder asked.

"That's how I understand it," Carlo replied, "but I'm not a religious man, or at least I wasn't. However, with the miracles I have seen I am now a firm believer in Jesus Christ."

"Can you tell me where he got the sword?" Father Oder asked.

"I don't know of any sword," Carlo replied. "When he left here Sunday afternoon for New Orleans he had no sword."

"When he arrived at the St. Louis Cathedral he was carrying a Templar Knight's sword we believe was from the 12th century," Father Oder replied.

"Did he say if he defeated Casper?" Carlo asked.

"He claims to have not only defeated Satan's agent but ended Satan's hideous plot by destroying the chalice," Father Oder said.

"Did he say when he would be returning?" Carlo asked.

"I'm sure you will be hearing from him shortly. He has been asleep for two days recovering from his ordeal. I spoke with him just before I called you. Thank you for the information and I am happy that you have come to your Savior Jesus Christ, Mr. Caressa. I look forward to someday meeting you," Father Oder said.

"Thank you Father, goodbye," Carlo replied hanging up the phone.

"Do you know who that was?" Paige asked.

"Yeah, he said he was Father Oder from the Vatican," Carlo said.

"I just 'Googled' him. He is the Vatican's chief investigator of miracles," Paige said.

"Well he's talking to the right people," Carlo replied.

Almost immediately Carlo's phone rang again.

"Kevin, you're alive," Carlo cheered.

"Of course I'm alive and Casper is dead."

"Did you kill him? I heard you had an old sword." Carlo explained.

"I killed Casper's spirit when I killed Satan's plans. It was God who actually killed Casper," Kevin replied.

"God killed him? How?" Carlo asked

"In his all-consuming fire," Kevin replied. "I'll be back in a couple of days and we'll wrap this case up."

"A couple of days?" Carlo whined.

"It's a mess down here. It'll take that long until the streets are clear enough to drive on," Kevin explained.

"As long as you're safe I guess I can live with another two days," Carlo replied. "See you then."

Kevin needed at least two more days to continue searching the debris in the Lower Ninth Ward. He was hoping to find some sign of the burnt Casper, the cleaved chalice, or the crucifix with the bloodied pulp of Bartholomew nailed to it before some local media outlet came upon it.

On his second day of looking, with the help of the local Archdiocese and one of the local New Orleans FBI field agents, he found all three under the collapsed wall of Bartholomew's house. It was almost five blocks away from where it originally had stood, but it was all there lying beneath the flayed skin still crucified to the wall.

He arranged to have it boxed and shipped back to Birmingham before the media was allowed into the area.

EPILOGUE

"Bad news *Jefe*," Meathook said to the cartel boss Juan Diego Vasquez.

"I've got enough bad news with the Sinaloa Cartel muscling in," Vasquez replied.

"That *pendejo* Samuelson got himself and five of our best men killed trying to kill Caressa and Bridges," Meathook reported.

"Did he hit either of them?"

"No, our source says both agents are fine," Meathook replied. "You want me to take care of it?"

"No, forget about the agents. Cancel the damn hit. It's already cost me too much money. We got too many other problems that we need to take care of."

Meathook knew that wasn't Vasquez talking. Vasquez was too vengeful of a man. He was like a bulldog that never let go once it got its mouth on you. If Vasquez made up his mind to kill someone he never rested till they were dead. No, someone somewhere had told Vasquez to back off. The rules of the game were changing and this made Meathook nervous.

"So by destroying the chalice made from Bartholomew's skull you ruined Satan's plans that he had devised over fifty years ago?" Paige said.

"Satan needed chalices from all the apostles he had created to participate in the rape of Emily Sue Whitman. By destroying one, the set couldn't be completed. He would have to begin again," Kevin explained.

"There's a great story for you, Paige," Carlo said.

"Like anybody will believe that," Paige replied.

"It is the truth," Carlo replied.

"Since when did the truth start making headlines?" Paige snapped back.

Kevin smiled at their exchange. They had obviously been together too long.

"How did Simon Caldwell fit into his plan?" Carlo asked.

"Simon was never meant to be one of the Apostle Serial Killer's victims," Kevin said. "It was just by chance that his name matched the name of one of Christ's Apostles and he happened to get assigned to the investigation and then caught."

"Why didn't Casper just kill him?" Paige asked.

"I think Casper was a lonely person and enjoyed the company, as strange as that may seem," Kevin replied. "I also believe he needed someone to share in his accomplishments. Someone he could gloat to."

"I do have some bad news," Carlo said. "The other six chalices have disappeared."

"Disappeared! How did that happen?" Kevin asked.

"The expert sent from Washington was a fake. He picked the safe, removed the chalices and a lot of cash and disappeared," Carlo said

"What'd he look like?" Kevin asked.

Paige and Carlo looked at each other.

"Of the seven people who actually saw him we got seven completely different physical descriptions that nowhere near describe the same person," Carlo explained.

"Woland!" All three of them said at once.

"The chalices will do him no good now that the cycle is broken. I'm sure of that," Kevin repeated.

"The DNA came back as a positive on Casper so I guess the Apostle Serial Killer case is officially closed," Carlo said.

"It will be when Supervising Agent Billings does the press conference in a couple of hours," Kevin replied.

"You know he wants us both at that conference," Carlo said.

"He can just continue to want, because I'm not going," Kevin declared.

"I don't think that's a smart career move, Buddy," Carlo replied.

"I'm not sure the FBI is the career I want to be in anymore," Kevin reflected. "I might just explore some other options."

"Other options! You're talking crazy. You're made for this stuff," Carlo replied.

"I don't know. I think God may have a different path in mind for me," Kevin said.

"This wouldn't have anything to do with a phone call from the Vatican would it?" Carlo asked.

"Possibly," Kevin said with a smile. "I've always wanted to see the world."

"Exactly what did the Vatican offer you?" Carlo asked.

"They didn't offer me anything. At least not yet. They just asked me a question." Kevin explained.

"And what was that question," Carlo asked.

"Do you believe in miracles?"

www.ingramcontent.com/pod-product-compliance
Lightning Source LLC
Chambersburg PA
CBHW030105100526
44591CB00009B/281